SECOND EDITION

Mindful Leadership

SECOND EDITION

Mindful Leadership

A Brain-Based Framework

Michael H. Dickmann
Nancy Stanford-Blair

CORWIN PRESS
A SAGE Company

For information:

Corwin Press
A SAGE Publications Company
2455 Teller Road
Thousand Oaks, California 91320
www.corwinpress.com

SAGE Publications India Pvt. Ltd.
B 1/I 1 Mohan Cooperative
    Industrial Area
Mathura Road, New Delhi
India 110 044

SAGE Publications Ltd.
1 Oliver's Yard
55 City Road
London EC1Y 1SP
United Kingdom

SAGE Publications Asia-Pacific Pte. Ltd.
33 Pekin Street #02-01
Far East Square
Singapore 048763

Printed in the United States of America.

Library of Congress Cataloging-in-Publication Data

Dickmann, Michael Haley.
Mindful leadership : a brain-based framework/Michael H. Dickmann,
Nancy Stanford-Blair.—2nd ed.
    p. cm.
Rev. ed. of: Connecting leadership to the brain.
Includes bibliographical references and index.
ISBN 978-1-4129-6409-8 (cloth)
ISBN 978-1-4129-6410-4 (pbk.)

  1. Leadership. 2. Intellect. I. Stanford-Blair, Nancy. II. Dickmann, Michael Haley.
Connecting leadership to the brain. III. Title.

HM1261.D53 2009
303.3'4—dc22   2008022893

This book is printed on acid-free paper.

08 09 10 11 12 10 9 8 7 6 5 4 3 2 1

Acquisitions Editor:	Debra Stollenwerk
Associate Editor:	Megan Bedell
Editorial Assistant:	Allison Scott
Production Editor:	Jane Haenel
Copy Editor:	Carol Anne Peschke
Typesetter:	C&M Digitals (P) Ltd.
Proofreader:	Caryne Brown
Indexer:	Molly Hall
Cover Designer:	Michael Dubowe
Graphic Designer:	Brian Bello

Contents

Preface to the Second Edition: A Refined Framework

To strip any idea down to its core, we must be masters of exclusion.

—Heath and Heath (2007, p. 16)

With the benefit of feedback from many audiences, this second edition presents an updated framework for connecting leadership to the headwaters of human capacity. Like the first edition, this edition bridges emerging knowledge about brain-enabled intelligence to more effective leadership practice. To that end, the reader engages a framework that supports the *mindful leader,* a leader who is attentive to the nature and nurture of intelligence in the process of influencing others toward the achievement of goals. Notably, it is a framework that informs organizational leadership across a broad audience, including leaders at all levels of education, business, not-for-profit organizations, health care, protective services, and government.

This revised volume retains core features of the original edition, including

- A practical framework for tightening leadership connections to human capacity for achieving goals
- Description of current scientific understanding of six dimensions of brain-enabled intelligence (i.e., physiological, social, emotional, constructive, and dispositional)
- Specific examples of *mindful leadership* practices that nurture the nature of intelligence
- Structured reflection exercises that connect *mindful leadership* purpose and principles to the reader's experience and context
- Graphic illustrations that visually support narrative content

Major changes between the first edition and this second effort include significant revisions in the organization and illustration of updated content. That editing includes the judicious exclusion of content deemed less essential to core concepts. This second edition also incorporates an expanded chapter format to facilitate reader engagement of more focused and concise segments of information. Specifically, second-edition content is reorganized from 7 to 12 chapters within three major parts.

- Part I examines the implications of breakthroughs in knowledge about brain-enabled intelligence for forming deeper understanding of human nature and leadership. It also introduces a practical framework for the *mindful* processing of knowledge about the nature of intelligence toward leadership advantage.
- Part II engages mindful *attention* to current knowledge about prominent dimensions of intelligence (i.e., physiological, social, emotional, constructive, and dispositional). It also models mindful *articulation* (i.e., connection) of essential knowledge about the nature of intelligence to compatible leadership behavior.
- Part III examines defining attributes of *mindful leaders* and models the mindful *application* and *adjustment* of knowledge about the nature of intelligence to standard and prescribed leadership practice. This concluding segment also engages summary reflection about proactive mind shifts and personal next steps.

Ultimately, this revised edition remains true to the intent of the first edition: to help readers further "grasp the essence of leadership that is relevant to the modern age" and to elevate leadership from being "one of the most observed and least understood phenomena on earth" (Burns, 1978, pp. 1–2). The related goal for this updating and further sculpting of content is the expectation one would reasonably hold for a second edition: a better book.

Acknowledgments

We appreciate having a second opportunity to communicate with readers about *mindful leadership* attention to the nature and nurture of intelligence. We are personally mindful that this is an opportunity that would not be possible if not for the support of family members who encourage our commitment to the project. In that same vein, we continue to be inspired and supported by our creative colleagues in the School of Leadership and the College of Education and Leadership at Cardinal Stritch University. Beyond the support of immediate colleagues, we acknowledge the greater community of scholars that collectively contributes to the rich knowledge base we reference in this work.

Acknowledgment is also due the reviewers of our prior work who offered specific and practical counsel about how to improve the product. Finally, the writing of this book would not have happened without the support and guidance of the editorial and production staff at Corwin Press.

PUBLISHER'S ACKNOWLEDGMENTS

Corwin Press gratefully acknowledges the contributions of the following reviewers:

John Brummel
Principal
Mililani High School
Mililani, HI

Jeffrey Loftus
History Teacher and History Department Chair
Cedar Park Middle School
Portland, OR

than enthusiastic response from her graduate adviser, as demonstrated by his comment, "What makes you think that there is a connection between leadership and the brain?"

A Reasonable Question

The adviser's question may have been Socratic, sarcastic, or cynical in intent. Perhaps it was merely an attempt at humor, an observation that the collective behavior of people in positions of authority implies a brainless nature. Whatever its intent, the question is both legitimate and revealing. It is legitimate because it is human nature (i.e., the nature of the human brain) to question the what, why, how, when, and where of things, including the relationship between leadership and the brain. It is a revealing question because it suggests that the relationship between leadership and the brain has not been adequately investigated, much less understood or appreciated.

An Underlying Question

The question lurking beneath the adviser's inquiry is not whether leadership is connected to the brain. The answer to that question is obvious, given the brain's physiological presence and mediating role in all human activity—that is, the brain is always at the party and leadership always dances to the tune of the brain. However, this natural connection may be at risk if not well understood and nurtured. Accordingly, the more important connection question is not whether but *how* the brain is accessible to leaders who seek to influence others toward the achievement of goals.

A Question to Be Refined

It might also be anticipated that the adviser, in the responsible manner of an academic mentor guiding proposed scholarship, would have further questions for his graduate student. One such question would surely be, "How are you interpreting the term *brain*?" Again, this is a reasonable question. If one is going to explore the connection of leadership to something, it is best to know what the interpretation of that something is— and here arises a bit of a problem.

The good news is that the beginning of the twenty-first century is witnessing a convergence of information from investigations in diverse fields of study (neurophysiology, neuropsychology, cognitive psychology, developmental psychology, evolutionary psychology, evolutionary biology, primatology, ethology, linguistics, psychophysics, mathematics, philosophy, anthropology, archaeology, and computer science—to name a few) that sheds new light on qualities of the human brain. The downside of this expanding knowledge is that it is generating as many questions as it does answers. The result is ongoing interpretation of brain physiology and processes, particularly the relationship of the brain to conceptualizations of human mind and intelligence.

This text embraces a broad interpretation of the human brain as a collection of physiological structures that support electrochemical communications within neural networks that enable, among other things, consciousness and intelligence. This orientation is both compelling and useful for the exploration of leadership–brain connections. Moreover, it is an interpretation that is in alignment with interpretations rendered by investigators across diverse fields:

- The hypothesis of physiologist Francis Crick (1994) that our brains are responsible for our mental lives through "the behavior of a vast assembly of nerve cells and their associated molecules" (p. 41)
- The theoretical perspective of neurophysiologist William Calvin (1996) that intelligence is "the high-end scenery of neurophysiology— the outcome of many aspects of an individual's brain organization that bear on doing something that one has never done before" (p. 11)
- The thesis of philosopher John Searle (Searle, Dennett, & Chalmers, 1997) that brain processes cause consciousness, but "consciousness itself is a feature of the brain" (p. 8)
- The neuropsychological view of Michael Gazzaniga (1998) that "how the brain enables mind is the question to be answered in the 21st century" (p. xii)
- The neurological description by Marian Diamond (Diamond & Hopson, 1998) of the multiple lobes of the brain neocortex "that collectively interpret our sensations, initiate our movements, and enable us to think, speak, write, calculate, plan, create, organize, and do all the other things that make us human" (p. 41)
- The perspective of brain combinatorial capacity offered by psychologist Steven Pinker (2002): "The ability to conceive an unlimited number of new combinations of ideas is the powerhouse of human intelligence and the key to our success as a species" (p. 236)
- The neurobiological conclusion of Gerald Edelman (2004) that "the process of consciousness is a dynamic accomplishment of the distributed activities of populations of neurons in many different areas of the brain" (pp. 6–7)

Chapter 1, "A Louis Moment," portrays the current opening of the black box of intelligence as a *Louis moment* (i.e., comparable to Louis Pasteur's historic discovery), one in which significant new information influences shifts in perception and behavior. *Main idea:* Informed by a convergence of scientific breakthroughs in knowledge about the nature of intelligence, leaders are presented with an extraordinary opportunity to better inform their perception of leadership purpose and behavior.

Chapter 2, "A New Sense of Nature," reviews evolving knowledge about intelligence as a brain-enabled capacity for processing information to survival advantage. As technology-assisted science reveals brain architecture and processes, the nature of intelligence is less mysterious to us—but nonetheless intriguing. We now have a better sense of the multidimensional nature of the phenomenon as operated by the collective attributes of the brain toward the acquisition and application of knowledge. At the same time we are pressed to know and achieve more by its exercise—to cultivate a better sense of capacity in self and others. *Main idea:* The brain has everything to do with who we are and what we do. Leadership is all about influencing who we are and what we do. As science better informs us about how the brain enables intelligence, there is an implicit opportunity for anyone to better understand and engage that capacity, including leaders.

Chapter 3, "A New Sense of Leadership," examines leadership as a valued phenomenon, with particular attention to the influence of context. *Main idea:* Leadership, whether exercised by presidents or parents, is always a process of influencing others toward the achievement of a goal. However, how the process is nuanced is always subject to the influence of environmental context. Emerging knowledge about the nature of intelligence in the context of the early twenty-first century offers momentous opportunity for leaders to cultivate a more informed understanding of their influence on the human systems they lead. It is an opportunity to evolve as a *mindful leader,* one who is attentive to the nature and nurture of intelligence in the process of influencing others toward the achievement of goals.

Chapter 4, "A Mindful Framework," presents a framework for aligning leadership behavior to the human capacity for achieving purpose. The framework design both mirrors and accesses the natural processes of the brain. Specifically, it structures mindful engagement of four components:

- *Attend* to information about the nature of intelligence.
- *Articulate* perception of the nature and nurture of intelligence.
- *Apply* perception of the nature and nurture of intelligence to compatible behavior.
- *Adjust* information, perception, and behavior from application experience.

Main idea: Given that most leaders are not and will never be neuroscientists or cognitive psychologists, the technical and rapidly evolving knowledge base about the brain and human intelligence must be organized and applied to leadership behavior in a purposeful and practical manner. A framework that structures attentive articulation of knowledge toward practical applications and adjustments in behavior (as both standard and prescribed practice) is useful to that end.

Part II: Minding Revelation

Part II models the first two components of the framework introduced in Chapter 4. That is, the reader will mindfully *attend* to information about brain-enabled intelligence to *articulate* perception of the essential nature and nurture of human capacity.

Chapters 5–10 engage the reader in processing information about the *physiological, social, emotional, constructive, reflective,* and *dispositional* dimensions of intelligence. Each chapter is organized to describe the following:

- The *gist* of the targeted dimension of intelligence (i.e., a foundation of information that is useful in forming a general sense of the phenomenon)
- The *essence* of the dimension (i.e., a discernment of essential qualities)
- The *implications* of the dimension for practice (i.e., compatible behavior)

This format both models and facilitates the distillation of essential knowledge about the nature of intelligence from a large and expanding information base. Each chapter visits one of six dimensions of intelligence (think of this as visiting six windows or elevations, each offering a particular view of intelligence). Across the six chapters, you will observe brain-enabled intelligence to be a multidimensional and integrated phenomenon. You will also construct a knowledge base that supports subsequent articulation of the nature and nurture of intelligence. For example, you will discern that

- The *physiological nature* of intelligence is big, mind–body connected, high maintenance, and malleable.
- The *social nature* of intelligence is expectant, dependent, extended, and virtuous.
- The *emotional nature* of intelligence is attentive, judgmental, motivating, and managed after the fact.
- The *constructive nature* of intelligence is sensory, social, emotional, reflective, and susceptible to a double bind.

- The *reflective nature* of intelligence is manipulative, executive, unifying, and promising.
- The *dispositional nature* of intelligence is macro, mandatory, malleable, and either maximizing or minimizing.

After the construction of personal understanding about the *essence* of intelligence (e.g., essential qualities of *physiological, social, emotional, constructive, reflective,* and *dispositional* dimensions), each chapter models the articulation of relationships between the essential nature of intelligence and compatible nurturing behavior. That articulation of perception process is structured by the following format:

The nature of intelligence is ___ } **If–then** { Compatible behavior is ___.

Part III: Following Through

Part III brings the framework introduced in preceding chapters into sharper focus by examining *mindful leadership attributes* and further modeling the final two components: how to *apply* articulated perceptions about the nature of intelligence to compatible behavior and *adjust* perception and behavior from application experience. This concluding part also engages summary reflection about proactive next steps.

Chapter 11, "Mindful Leadership," is a putting-it-all-together chapter. It begins by examining adherence to mindful purpose and principles within the framework introduced in Chapter 4. The ultimate purpose of mindful leadership, it is proposed, is a mindful organizational culture that collectively attends to the nature and nurture of intelligence, a culture in which the cultivation of capacity is a goal in itself. The principles of mindful leadership are the components of the mindful framework (i.e., attend to information, articulate perception of nature and nurture, apply perception of nature and nurture to behavior, and adjust perception and behavior from application experience). Those components are revisited and fleshed out with specific examples and active referencing to reader context. Within the principle of applying perception to behavior, six *standard applications* are described:

- *Support the physiological platform that enables intelligence* (e.g., attend to brain fitness, stimulate neural development).
- *Promote social relationships* (e.g., facilitate meeting of minds, cultivate common purpose, extend the mind's reach).

- *Harness the power of emotion* (e.g., ease, excite, and evaluate states of mind).
- *Expedite the construction of knowledge* (e.g., justify construction, facilitate construction, extend construction).
- *Build a culture of reflection* (e.g., structure thinking, challenge thinking).
- *Cultivate productive dispositions* (e.g., cultivate broad habits, target specific habits).

Chapter content also models *prescribed applications* of knowledge about the nature of intelligence to leadership practice. Within that content, the reader will experience a four-step prescriptive practice process:

1. Clarification of *need* (i.e., a specific purpose or goal)

2. Assessment of the *nature* of intelligence required for achieving the need

3. Assessment of options for providing supportive *nurture* for the required intelligence

4. Composition of a *narrative* plan of action that will nurture the nature of required intelligence toward the achievement of the need

Chapter content concludes with an examination of individual and coached practice as means of *adjusting* behavior from application experience. *Main idea:* A mindful leader is attentive to the nature and nurture of intelligence in the process of influencing others toward the achievement of goals. Such attention entails adherence to mindful purpose and principles of behavior within a supportive framework that structures attention, articulation, application, and adjustment.

Chapter 12, "Mindful Shift," observes that we humans are creatures of habit, but we are also able and willing to make adjustments in light of new experience and knowledge. In our better moments, we consciously engage this ability to learn and adjust. Thus might leaders proactively engage emerging knowledge about the nature of intelligence to better inform leadership behavior. To that end, this final chapter invites the reader to confront, push, and step beyond established perceptions of leadership. Chapter content also structures summary interpretation of the implications of mindful leadership in personal context. *Main idea:* The convergence of new discoveries about the brain and the intelligence it enables, coupled with the challenges confronting humankind at the threshold of this millennium, both accommodates and compels proactive reflection about leadership purpose and practice.

YOUR ROLE

You are your brain. If you want to understand why you feel the way you do, how you perceive the world, why you make mistakes, how you are able to be creative, why music and art are inspiring, indeed what it is to be human, then you need to understand the brain.

—Hawkins (2004, pp. 1–2)

A Shared Journey

Leadership is a natural and broadly practiced phenomenon. Accordingly, a broad view of leadership is in order as one proceeds through this book. If it is important for leadership perception to be informed about the nature of the brain and its capacity for intelligence, such information is valuable to both formal and informal leaders, whether they be politicians, CEOs, administrators, officials, directors, teachers, coaches, parents, or anyone else in a position to influence others toward the achievement of a goal. This book guides an investigation of leadership connections to the essential nature of human capacity, as that nature is currently being revealed. It is an opportunity to think about and see leadership from a different vantage point. It is a journey that invites the companionship of all who seek to better understand and practice leadership.

A Tollway

This journey requires the exercise of the very intelligence attended to by mindful leaders. Specifically, participants must engage physiological, social, emotional, constructive, reflective, and dispositional dimensions of intelligence (at the executive bidding of the prefrontal lobes of the cerebral cortex) to think their way to a refined understanding of leadership. In mindful recognition of that natural process, chapter narratives will often speak directly to you and otherwise invite your active participation.

Part I

Breaking Through

Emerging insight about brain-enabled intelligence prompts reflection about how leaders engage the potential of self and others. We are witnessing the unfolding of momentous breakthroughs in knowledge about what makes us tick. It is an opportune moment for cultivating a more informed sense of the nature of intelligence in individuals and organizations—and how leaders might best nurture that capacity toward the achievement of purpose.

Chapters 1–3 examine how a breakthrough moment in knowledge is enabling a new sense of human nature and leadership. Chapter 4 introduces a practical framework for seizing the moment.

1

A Louis Moment

We take great pleasure in "getting it." We love to see patterns emerging from seeming chaos, whether in doing a crossword puzzle or doing science.

—Calvin (2004, p. 93)

Similar to the import of Louis Pasteur's historic revelation about the nature of contagious disease, current revelations about the nature of the brain represent a momentous breakthrough in knowledge. As observed by Restak (2001, p. xvi), "only recently—with the development of powerful technologies—have we been successful in delving into the secrets of the Brain." The opening of the black box of brain-enabled intelligence further qualifies as a *Louis moment* of discovery because as the nature of this defining capacity is better understood, aligned shifts in behavior will evolve across human affairs.

LOUIS'S MOMENT

In 1857, Louis M. Pasteur and his associates were investigating the problem of wine spoilage and related food preservation and health issues. In conducting his inquiry, Pasteur devised a simple experiment that proved the biogenesis of life (i.e., life comes from life), thereby establishing an empirical base for the theory of the spread of contagious disease by microorganisms. That scientific insight was a dramatic revelation of how a previously unknown universe acted on the human condition. Moreover, the ultimate impact of the breakthrough in knowledge was subsequently

Figure 1.1   The Dynamic of Influence Between Information, Perception, and Behavior

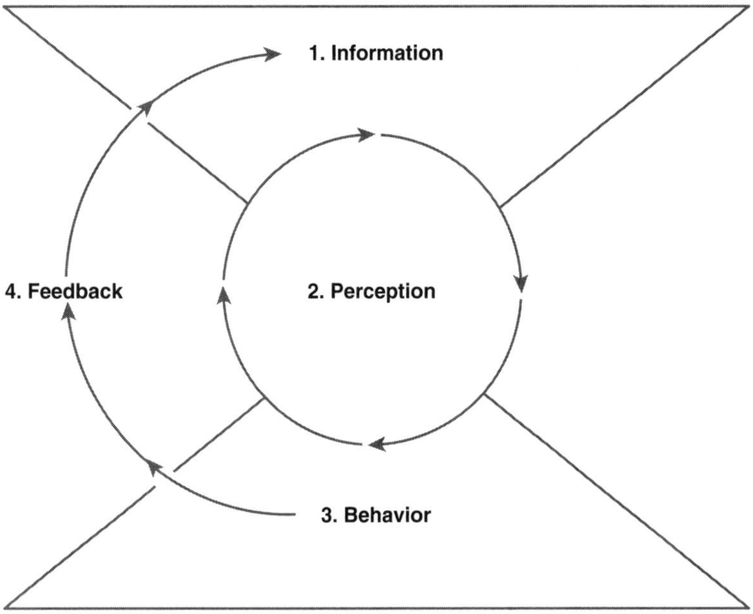

1. Information

4. Feedback   2. Perception

3. Behavior

1. A body of information within a field of knowledge is engaged and processed by the brain.

2. The processing of information influences the formation of perception (i.e., essential understanding).

3. Perception influences choice of behavior within all possible options.

4. Behavior experience provides feedback that influences (i.e., further expands) information that influences perception.

research and development it spurred, ultimately resulted in enhanced health and life expectancy for much of humankind—an extraordinary return from rather simple experiments that empirically proved the biogenesis of disease-bearing microorganisms.

In recognizing his scientific contributions, however, we also necessarily note that most people alive today do not possess much knowledge of Louis Pasteur or his work unless they have a personal or professional interest in the history of biological science. It might be that most adults are able to retrieve some textbook memory of Monsieur Pasteur, a French scientist associated in some manner with an important scientific discovery. But if they were to be completely honest, they would also admit that they survive rather well with limited knowledge of Louis Pasteur himself. However, it would be difficult to locate anyone, from young children on, who do not have a grasp of the essential knowledge derived from Pasteur's experiment and did not act in accordance with that understanding. Thus we have an example of people distilling the *gist* (i.e., the essential points or general sense) of an important body of knowledge. They have distilled essential knowledge—what is important to know in a fundamental fashion—from a quantity of available knowledge. They have grasped the *big idea*.

A MINDFUL MOMENT

A Breakthrough in Knowledge

In terms of quantity, degree, and speed of change, it is not unreasonable to judge the early twenty-first century as rivaling any prior time period. An informed resident of the planet today could hardly be unaware of the current unfolding of seismic movements in social, economic, political, environmental, scientific, and technological realms.

Of course, it is easier to recognize a convergence of significant developments from a historic distance. For example, it is easy to observe the convergence of a wide range of advances in technology and humanistic thinking during the Renaissance. It is more difficult to fully appreciate the uniqueness or magnitude of meaningful developments occurring in the present. Preoccupied with the demands of the moment, we must make a conscious effort to perceive the collective effect and direction of change that is happening concurrently—that is, to see the forest for the trees. However, the difficulty one might experience in appreciating significant events in the moment does not relieve one of the need to see and understand their import.

A particularly momentous development within the big picture of contemporary events is recent breakthroughs in knowledge in neuro-science and related fields of brain research and theory. This surge in understanding about the human brain and the intelligence it enables is comparable to Louis Pasteur's dramatic breakthrough in understanding of microorganic contagion in the nineteenth century. Contemporary scientific progress in revealing the nature of intelligence is a *Louis moment* of discovery—discovery that is facilitated by converging advancements in technology and diverse scientific inquiries at the dawn of the twenty-first century. Furthermore, similar to the impact of Louis's revelations about the nature of disease, as the black box of intelligence is opened and its nature revealed, there can be no going back to less informed and aligned behavior in the conduct of human affairs.

An Opportunity for Shift

Breakthrough advances in knowledge about the fundamental nature of brain-enabled intelligence encourages reflection about many aspects of human behavior, including leadership. Leaders are well advised to explore the headwaters of intelligence: the 3-pound physiological mass cradled in the cranium. The leadership connection to the brain is always assumed, given the brain's mediating role in all interactions between people. However, emerging knowledge about the nature of intelligence presents an opportunity to better understand and tighten the connection—an opportunity for leaders to become more mindful of how they engage the intelligence of self and others.

It is also important to recognize that breakthroughs in understanding and thinking of the magnitude that we are talking about here happen, but they seldom just happen. They usually evolve at the prodding of proactive and persistent inquiry. Perkins (2000) speaks to this in his description of a fivefold structure that characterizes the process of breakthrough thinking.

- Breakthrough thinking characteristically entails a long period of searching.
- A typical breakthrough arrives after little or no apparent progress.
- The typical breakthrough begins with a precipitating event.
- When a breakthrough happens, it happens as a cognitive snap: Things fall into place rapidly, with not much time separating the precipitating event from the solution.
- The breakthrough transforms one's mental or physical world in a generative way, changing both thinking and action.

Perkins's characterization of the process of breakthrough thinking is helpful in interpreting the opportunity at hand for a better understanding of leadership. Humankind highly values leadership and has consciously sought to understand its critical attributes for many centuries (i.e., a breakthrough characteristically entails a long period of searching). But although many models and theories of leadership have evolved from this long search, it is fair to say that common perception and unifying theory remain elusive (i.e., a typical breakthrough arrives after little or no apparent progress). However, the current convergence of extensive and diverse scientific inquiry with applications of advanced microtechnologies has generated a surge of new knowledge about the nature of brain-enabled intelligence (i.e., the typical breakthrough begins with a precipitating event). Given the breakthrough in knowledge about brain-enabled intelligence, a transformation in leadership understanding of the nature of human capacity may be at hand (i.e., when a breakthrough happens, it happens with a cognitive snap, and things fall into place). Subsequently, a breakthrough in understanding about the nature of capacity encourages a breakthrough in leadership thinking about compatible behavior that nurtures that capacity, both in self and in others (i.e., breakthroughs transform in a generative way, changing both thinking and action).

In short, current breakthroughs in understanding about what underlies human capacity for learning and achievement present a critical opportunity for a parallel breakthrough in understanding of the nature of leadership.

A Necessary Shift

Reflection about the nature of leadership is an ongoing need, given that leadership is contextually influenced. The magnitude of interwoven social, economic, political, environmental, and technical challenges facing humankind at the beginning of the twenty-first century certainly argues for reflection about how leadership might be rendered more effective. Developments transpiring during your time on the planet raise daunting problems to be resolved in the areas of computer technology, genetic engineering, civil rights, democratic government, sustainable environments, space exploration, and social and economic globalization. It is indeed an interesting time to be alive and part of such a dramatic convergence of change and challenge. Moreover, it is a time in history that places a high premium on engaging human capacity to solve problems—"to figure it out."

The good news is that breakthroughs in knowledge about human capacity both press for and enable a breakthrough in understanding of effective leadership. Emerging knowledge about how people learn and achieve as individuals and in groups can no more be ignored than knowledge about the sun as the center of the solar system or germs as agents of contagion. Unprecedented insight about the *physiological, social, emotional, constructive, reflective,* and *dispositional* dimensions of intelligence (as examined in Chapters 5–11) presents an extraordinary opportunity to construct a more informed sense of human nature. It is also an opportunity for leaders to construct a more informed sense of their influence on the collective capacity of a group toward achievement of purpose.

SUMMARY OBSERVATIONS

- It is human nature to ask questions and strive mightily to figure things out.
- Periodically, human inquiry strikes a vein of significant new knowledge.

- Breakthroughs in knowledge influence perceptual shifts that, in turn, influence change in behavior; that is, significant new knowledge provokes change in how people understand their world and, subsequently, how they behave in it.
- You need not know everything for change in your perception and behavior to happen; essential understanding is the key.
- Current breakthroughs in knowledge about the human brain and the intelligence it enables are converging with other advances in knowledge and technology at the beginning of the twenty-first century.
- Leadership attention to breakthrough knowledge about brain-enabled intelligence is opportune and necessary. To better understand and engage intelligence in self and others is to more effectively influence responses to twenty-first-century challenges.
- Breakthroughs in knowledge about brain-enabled intelligence hold promise for aligned breakthroughs in leadership theory and practice.

READER REFLECTION

- How does information influence perception?
- How does perception influence behavior?
- What would be another example (other than that of Louis Pasteur) of a breakthrough in knowledge leading to a significant shift in human understanding and behavior?
- Can you recall an instance in which new information led to a significant shift in your perception and behavior?
- Why might a leader be interested in learning more about brain-enabled intelligence?

2 A New Sense of Nature

We may not be able to explain intelligence in all its glory, but we now know some of the elements of an explanation.

—Calvin (1996, p. 11)

As technology-assisted science reveals brain architecture and processes, the nature of intelligence becomes less mysterious to us— but nonetheless intriguing. We now have a better sense of the phenomenon. At the same time we are pressed to know and achieve more by its exercise—to cultivate a better sense of capacity in self and others.

WHAT'S A BRAIN FOR?

The Basic Business

Gazzaniga (1998) observes that evolutionary biologists are guided in their efforts to understand the brain by an essential question posed in the investigation of any biological organ or system: What is this for, and why does it do what it does? In the case of the brain, he observes that the flippant answer to the question is sex. The more complete explanation is that the brain's purpose—its primary business, if you will—is to make decisions that ultimately serve the reproductive success of its host body. This purpose is a legacy spawned in the primordial soup that supported the first life forms on the planet, a genetically programmed directive to survive and reproduce. Such a blunt, no-frills description of brain purpose may appear unappreciative of the complex and refined operations of the brain. Nevertheless, understanding the nature of human intelligence requires this perspective of original and prevailing brain purpose.

It is also important to acknowledge that brains did not exist until they were needed. Early life forms on the planet were brainless—as well as heartless, breathless, sightless, and, in many other ways, less. Over the vast span of evolutionary time, however, the biological process of natural selection favored mutations that produced more complex life forms. The more sophisticated organisms realized survival advantages in cardiovascular, respiratory, and visual systems. This evolution of specialized subsystems in complex organisms valued adaptations that led to the development of brain structures. In effect, as life on the planet progressed from simple storefront operations to complex, multidimensional enterprises, centralized management systems were in demand. The brain thus emerged as a biological adaptation in concert with other adaptations such as the heart, lungs, and eyes. It evolved from progressive mutations to centralize management of the integrated elements of organisms and processing of environmental information.

The business of the brain, then, is the monitoring and adjustment of the internal elements of an organism in concert with monitoring and processing of information about the organism's external environment. A brain performs this integrated internal–external information processing function to enhance the survival of its host body system. This is the basic business conducted by all brains in all animals, be they reptiles or primates. Millions of years of performing these basic responsibilities under diverse environmental conditions inevitably produced a brain that became extraordinarily good at the survival business—so good, in fact, that it began to refine and expand its basic business.

The Business of Intelligence

Absent disease or other conditions of dysfunction, your brain admirably attends to the basic survival business of managing internal elements of its host physiological system. This aspect of what the brain does is so fundamental and established that it operates mostly beyond your conscious awareness or control. Moreover, this survival service does not distinguish a human brain from the brains of other animals, particularly other primates. The human brain's adeptness in the survival business of acquiring and processing environmental information is a different story, however—a story that differentiates human development, experience, and potential. As Pinker (1997) observes, it was the refinement of a capacity to process information that helped our ancestors resolve problems associated with a foraging way of life, "in particular, understanding and outmaneuvering objects, animals, plants and other people" (p. 21).

The survival business of the brain has been refined and expanded in humans to a highly evolved capacity for interpreting, organizing, and applying information—the business of intelligence. This capacity for processing and applying information is represented physiologically in the uniqueness of our brain structure and size. It is a capacity that is demonstrated in analysis, conjecture, and imagination. It is compounded in applications to problem solving and creativity. We survive and thrive by this capacity for acquiring and applying knowledge, particularly in the context of new challenges. Simply put—with reference to the old James Bond theme song—nobody does it better.

AN INTRIGUING MATTER

Human intelligence is irrepressibly intrigued with itself. This is not a matter of vanity or self-indulgence; it is simply the nature of the phenomenon. The more it knows about its nature, the more it wants to know.

Self-Aware

Upon evolving to a point of conscious self-awareness, human intelligence inevitably understands its value to human welfare and wants to know more about its nature and potential. You can test this assessment yourself by answering two simple questions:

- Given the option, is it generally to the advantage of an individual or a group to have more or less capacity for intelligence in any given situation?
- If new information becomes available about how human intelligence works and can be used or improved to greater advantage, do you want to know about it?

The fact that you are reading this book pretty well anticipates your response to the second question. Your response to the first question (despite the disposition of your intelligence capacity for considering alternatives) is also predictable if you are being honest about what you would want for yourself and those whom you care most about. Furthermore, your responses to both questions probably are executed without any deep conceptual reflection about what intelligence is; you have an immediate, innate sense of its importance. After all, you know intelligence is a determining force in the quality of human existence because you observe its imprint everywhere you look.

In Your Face

The imprint of human intelligence surrounds you. You need only to look out from your vantage point of the moment to observe evidence of humankind's extraordinary capacity for acquiring and applying knowledge—a capacity that defines and sets the species apart. Looking up from this text in any building interior, for example, you will immediately observe products such as furnishings, art works, printed material, appliances, communication technologies, and energy systems. Note that the most rudimentary artifact, a pencil or coffee mug, is the product of complex knowledge. Every human product that meets your eye represents integrated applications of accumulated knowledge in natural, physical, and social domains. Such representations are everywhere.

If a window view is available to you, your gaze will predictably fall on architectural structures, transportation modes, and alterations of landscape. With the advantage of a high-rise location, your view might observe human engineering involving the infrastructure of manufacturing, commercial, recreation, energy, and transportation systems. In a more rural environment, you would probably observe land clearings, irrigation systems, buildings, and managed plant growth and animal husbandry. And if by chance you look up from this narrative while traveling in a human intelligence–produced car, boat, train, or plane, your observation of the products of species capacity for acquiring and applying knowledge will be further magnified.

You need not look up from this page to appreciate the evolved status of intelligence. You are reading an arrangement of symbols that comply with evolved rules for language, printed on material produced by evolved knowledge of science and distributed in accordance with evolved economic principles. Better yet, you can simply close your eyes and reflect on any exemplary social, political, economic, technological, or artistic product of human intelligence that comes to mind, and your intelligent mind generates the picture.

The artifacts of intelligence surround us. We can see, hear, smell, taste, and feel it. We are well advised to periodically pause and appreciate the imprint of intelligence—tracks leading from handheld tools and primitive communal shelters to technologies that harness the power of atoms and support complex social structures. Tracking such products of intelligent minds tells us where we have been in our long evolutionary story. It also provides clues about paths to the future and the requisite intelligence for moving forward.

Begging to Know More

Experiencing the products of intelligence certifies its presence, but it does not explain the phenomenon itself. Nor does it address fundamental questions about where it comes from and how it works—questions heretofore difficult, if not impossible, to answer. As a matter of fact, humans developed and exercised extraordinary intelligence long before they knew what they were working with, much less had a word to describe it. Inevitably, however, human intelligence became aware of itself. And we, as its current hosts, are engaged in a vigorous campaign to further understand its nature. This is a natural progression in the evolution of intelligence. Awareness of this extraordinary ability to process information has fueled intrigue about its potential. There is a sense that there is more to know—that one might go to a next level and do better yet by this talent.

A DEFINITION IN PROGRESS

The challenge of definitively understanding the highly evolved and complex nature of human intelligence is not to be underestimated. The apparent paradox is that if our brain were so simple that we could understand it, we would be so simple that we couldn't.

Common Understanding

It is highly improbable that a reader of this book would not have a basic conceptualization of what intelligence is. You have encountered interpretations of intelligence through a variety of media over your lifetime, and it is likely that you have engaged in some direct study of the topic in your formal educational experience. It is also safe to assume that you are provoked on many occasions (perhaps while at work or listening to the evening news) to reflect, discuss, or even write about intelligence as it relates to qualities present or lacking in human behavior. To demonstrate to yourself the understanding your brain has constructed about intelligence, we suggest that you take a minute (literally) to complete the following sentence stem:

Intelligence is _____.

Invariably, this prompt produces a wide range of responses about what individuals understand intelligence to be. However, there are general themes that you can compare with your attempt at definition. For example, does your definition in some way describe intelligence as the ability to learn, think, organize information, solve problems, respond to novel situations, imagine, create, or make judgments or decisions?

and the neuroscience interpretations put forward by Barlow (1987) and Gould and Gould (1994). It is also a general definitional perspective that accommodates current theory about the multiple and malleable nature of intelligence as described by Gardner (1983, 1999), Perkins (1995), Sternberg (1996), and others. And when the dust clears at the end of the definitional debates, fairly simple language about the capacity of the human brain to figure things out emerges, language that is consistent with a straightforward dictionary definition of intelligence: "the capacity to acquire and apply knowledge" (*American Heritage Dictionary*, 2000, p. 910). Thus from myriad definitional explorations, a serviceable conceptualization of intelligence emerges.

> *Intelligence*: The collective attributes of the brain that enable capacity for acquiring and applying knowledge in diverse and novel situations.

A REVEALING MOMENT

A Time of Enlightenment

Humankind has long been intrigued with and invested in developing a better understanding of the nature of intelligence. That persistence is producing spectacular results as new light is being cast in dramatic fashion on the nature of the phenomenon. Technology-assisted investigations into physiological architecture and processes have been particularly effective in prying the lid off the mysterious black box of the brain. Magnetic resonance imaging provides cross-sectional images of the soft tissues of the living brain. Functional magnetic resonance imaging has evolved to observation of real-time cognitive activity in the brain. The positron emission tomography imaging process tracks the consumption of radiolabeled glucose in the brain to map mental activity. Electroencephalographic and magnetoencephalographic mappings read faint electrical outputs and magnetic fields generated by the brain's neural networks, thereby measuring brain wave patterns and activity during specific events. The technology of spectrometers adds further insight into the workings of the brain by measuring the status of essential brain chemicals (i.e., neurotransmitters) during different brain states and activities.

Integrated with investigations across many fields of inquiry in the past several decades—including evolutionary biology, animal research, and clinical studies of human subjects—microtechnology-aided science has generated an almost surreal increase in information about the inner workings of the brain. The information thus revealed sheds light on the essence of humankind, illuminating how we think, feel, learn, and act. We cannot help but be attracted to this dawning of new knowledge. It is a real-time revelation about what makes us us. What has been hidden and mysterious is being revealed: how the brain processes sensory information, constructs meaning and memory, engages emotion, and reflectively applies prior knowledge. Furthermore, what had been suspected or assumed is either verified or challenged by the unfolding science.

For example, the intuitive speculation that the mind, once stretched, never returns to its original shape is now verifiable through technologies that observe the environmentally stimulated construction of dendrite and axon connections between neural cells. The physical stretching of the brain's neural network can now be physically observed. The significance of this confirmation of the plasticity of neural networking cannot be over-estimated, given that it repudiates the once common perception that human intelligence is fixed by nature and unalterable by nurture.

A More Informed Sense of Nature

Given the current convergence of scientific discovery, there is momentous opportunity for cultivating deeper understanding of the underpinnings of human nature. We are positioned to construct a more informed sense of what empowers all learning and achievement and subsequently nurture what is now known about nature.

Notably, perspective adjusts to the quality of information sources. This is not unlike an adjustment in an eyeglass prescription. In that instance, the introduction of new lenses in appropriately prescribed configurations results in enhanced eyesight. The analogy can be made for the introduction of new information about the nature of intelligence. Emerging knowledge about brain-enabled intelligence, in effect, provides new lenses through which we can better observe human nature (Figure 2.1). Thus enlightened, we can bring into focus a more informed understanding of our natural capacity for learning and achievement. For example (as will be addressed in greater detail in Chapters 5–10) we are able to observe that the multidimensional nature of intelligence involves the following:

• *A physiological dimension:* The capacity to learn and achieve operates on a biological platform of cells, circuits, and chemicals in the brain. It is a platform that is *big, mind–body connected, high maintenance,* and *malleable.* Virtually unlimited in its capacity for processing information, the brain is the body and the body is the brain. What affects one affects the other. To do its work well, the brain demands both quantity and quality in nutritional care and environmental experience. Most important, the brain's

Figure 2.1　Lenses of Insight About the Multidimensional Nature of Intelligence

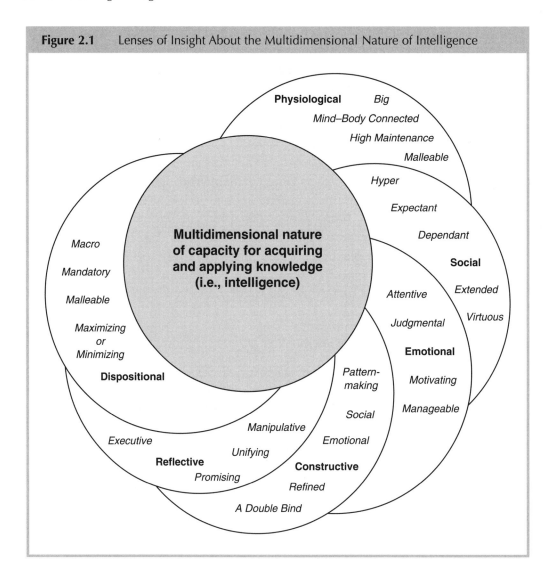

neural networks are modified by experience. Neural plasticity in learning continues throughout the lifespan. Thus, the nature of brain capacity for acquiring and applying knowledge (i.e., intelligence) is not fixed but malleable by environmental nurture.

• *A social dimension:* Born of rich social experience over millions of years, the brain is endowed with *hypersocial instincts:* natural and powerful abilities for memory, language, empathy, sympathy, collaboration, and reasoning. Indeed, the brain's social bias is socially *expectant, dependent, extended,* and *oriented to virtue.* The unfolding of brain capacity for learning and achievement is expectant of the same social experience that constructed it. Moreover, social experience is the great provocateur of the quality of thinking and learning that the brain depends on to realize its potential. To satisfy this overarching need and disposition for interaction in a society of mind, the brain invents media that extend social interaction beyond face-to-face encounters (e.g., art, writing, print, telephone, radio, film, television, Internet). The brain also has an instinctive social sense of virtue, as demonstrated by its moral orientation to prosocial behavior.

• *An emotional dimension:* Emotion moves the brain to *attention, judgment, motivation,* and reasoned *management* of mind–body states. It involves neural and glandular systems that trigger changes in mind and body in response to evaluation of external and internal information, reflexive changes that arouse brain attention to what is important. Examples of emotion-triggered mind–body states are fear, anger, joy, sorrow, surprise, and disgust. The reflexive arousal systems associated with emotion initiate immediate and automatic responses (i.e., fight or flight) to environmental stimulation. Subsequently, emotional centers interact with rational reasoning systems in the brain to judge the merits of events and available options. Emotion also plays a role in motivation by arousing and sustaining passion about things that matter. Furthermore, emotion represents a brain–body function that is manageable, but only after the fact. This brain ability to recognize and mediate emotional responses after they occur is known as emotional intelligence.

• *A constructive dimension:* The fundamental genius of the human brain is its capacity for interpreting useful information patterns. It is an ability that is *pattern making, sensory, social, emotional,* and *refined*—but also susceptible to *a double bind.* The brain is a lean, mean pattern-making machine, a biological platform of extraordinary capacity for constructing meaning and memory from diverse information sources. It constructs knowledge of the world from sensory input stimulated by environmental experience, and direct, rich experience influences the quality of such construction. Social interaction is a primary source for rich environmental experiences, but emotion also plays an important role in the construction of what the brain understands and remembers. The brain is aroused and sustained in its attention to knowledge constructions that are emotionally judged to be worthy of the time and effort. The construction of meaning and memory is further facilitated by rich emotional contexts that reference the organization of important information patterns. Moreover, what is constructed and remembered is continually refined and reconstructed by the brain through ongoing examination of relationships to new information. Nevertheless, the brain has to be wary of a double bind because

3 A New Sense of Leadership

Organizations that have learned how to think together and that know themselves are filled with intelligent action. People are constantly taking initiative and making changes, often without asking or telling.

—Wheatley (2005, p. 70)

Leadership, whether exercised by presidents or parents, is always a process of influencing others toward the achievement of a goal. The process stays the same as goals change. However, context directs the game. That is, *how* leaders influence others adapts to the environment in which leadership is attempted. For example, in a context of rich revelation about the nature of intelligence, leaders have reason to reconsider their understanding of effective leadership practice. There is momentous opportunity for cultivating a deeper sense of leadership—a perspective of the phenomenon that is aware of the past, informed by the present, and more responsive to the future.

OF ASSUMED VALUE

An Observed Phenomenon

A popular human pastime is the observation and analysis of leadership. Leadership naturally intrigues people, capturing their attention and finding its way into all manner of conversation and discourse. Leadership is there—at the center or hanging around the edges—in discussions about business, education, government, sports, religion, science, history, environment, family, or any current problem or crisis. Whatever the topic, there is inevitable observation, insinuation, and assumption related to what someone did, should have done, is doing, or will do about something that needs doing—be it the boss, a presidential candidate, or a Little League coach. Such proclivity for the analysis of leadership is universally exercised across every form of human endeavor. It is born of intuitive intrigue and valuation that play out in countless conversations at dinner tables, water coolers, and corner pubs. As confirmation, you need only to reflect on the content of recent conversations you have engaged in. Was there reference to the behavior of a director, administrator, conductor, chairperson, manager, coordinator, or coach—possibly with some negative or positive judgments cast on that leader's performance?

The value and expectation people hold for leadership cannot be overestimated. There is an assumed connection between leadership and the success of any organization or initiative. This association is so strong that calls to sack the coach, CEO, superintendent, or government official quickly follow perceptions of organizational failure. As stocks rise or fall, the season is won or lost, or productivity increases or decreases, the leader's behavior is inevitably analyzed, and leadership tenure is secured or jeopardized accordingly. Leaders are associated with the fulfillment of organizational purpose, be it winning a game, selling a product, or any other achievement goal.

By all appearances, then, we humans are of the mind that leadership makes a difference. Assuming that this assessment is accurate, it is nevertheless reasonable to question as to why it is so and what leaders do to make the assumed difference. To answer those questions and, in the process, further construct a sense of leadership, we will next examine conceptualizations of leadership, the biological and social roots of leadership, the influence of context on leadership, and the evolution of leadership theory.

A Natural Occurrence

There is an innate striving in all forms of matter to organize into relationships. There is a great seeking for connections, a desire to organize into more complex systems that include more relationships, more variety. This desire is evident everywhere in the cosmos, at all levels of scale.

—Wheatley and Kellner-Rogers (1996, p. 30)

Nature's propensity for organizing complex and evolving systems will be commented on further in later chapters. However, it is noted here that the organization of anything has basic requirements. For example, an initial action, a first step, a lead event of some sort is a necessary attribute in the organization of systems large and small, simple and complex. The organization and transformation of systems also require progressive encouragement and support. Accordingly, in nature we observe initial bonding, divisions, and transitions that cue, guide, and otherwise influence the behavior of other elements in an environment. In the biological world this is a matter of survival. Survival requires organization, and organization requires initiation and facilitation. Something or someone must take the lead in getting things rolling, showing the way, setting the pace, sustaining momentum—making things happen. Organic relationships don't just happen; they follow a lead, and one thing leads to another. Thus prompted by the genetic code and encouraged by environmental experience, organisms construct and operate themselves through cellular interactions that influence the organization of cellular relationships.

Leadership is a natural phenomenon that is observable in the survival behavior of life forms throughout the biological world, from simple cellular structures to complex organisms. Illustrations of such behavior include the lead shoot of a tree or shrub that establishes a path for plant development (similar to the pioneer axon fibers that establish pathways for other axons to follow in the neural network development of a brain), the foraging ant scout that leads the colony to a food source, the alpha wolf that sets the pace for the hunt, and the matriarch elephant that guides the migration of the herd. The process of individual biological elements influencing other biological elements in the achievement of a common survival goal is sometimes subtle, sometimes obvious, but always a fundamental and pervasive exercise by which nature conducts its business.

A Social Construction

Nature's affinity for organizing systems became manifest in human development. As will be described in Chapter 6, the social experience of early humans provided ample opportunity to observe the behavior of others and to look to others for help, guidance, and example. From millions of years of social intimacy, the human brain evolved a refined conscious awareness of self in relation to others. This evolutionary breakthrough enabled reflection about probabilities and options. It is at this point that the natural phenomena of system organization and leadership entered a new arena: that of a brain that was capable of conscious reflection about systems (e.g., social hierarchies and coalitions) and how individuals influence each other in systems. Thus human awareness of self in relation to others was accompanied by awareness of the potential of self and others to influence those relationships—a primal sense of leadership.

FAMILIAR BUT ELUSIVE

Of all the hazy and confounding areas in social psychology, leadership theory undoubtedly contends for top nomination.

—Bennis (1959, p. 259)

Although the study of leadership has continued to expand in the decades since Bennis's lament, agreement about the nature of leadership remains an elusive goal. We may readily observe leadership to be a natural phenomenon that is socially valued and pervasively practiced, yet we find it difficult to get a definitive grip on it. This is not unexpected in fields of behavioral science, where disagreement and lack of consensus among scholars are common. After all, as Rost (1991) observes, leadership is a socially constructed reality that cannot be seen or touched but only inferred through observation. And the observation of human behavior, in many social contexts by many scholars, has inevitably generated many interpretations about leadership. The product of this ongoing inquiry is a deepening and broadening of insight about the complex nature of leadership. Definitive clarity about what leadership is, unfortunately, is not a reasonable expectation. To paraphrase Stogdill (1974), it is more reasonable to expect the creation of as many definitions of leadership as there are people who attempt to define it.

Leadership, similar to the phenomenon of intelligence examined in Chapter 2, is an open concept that probably will never be conclusively defined. Yet everyone has a personal understanding, derived from life experience, of what leadership means to them. To demonstrate the meaning your brain has constructed for the phenomenon of leadership, we ask that you pause to complete the following sentence stem:

Leadership is _____.

Chances are that your personal interpretation of what leadership is will differ in some manner from that of any other person. However, it is as likely that your informal definition will generally correspond to statements people commonly make when asked to complete the same sentence stem, for example, statements that suggest leadership is

Taking charge

Helping others achieve goals

Problem solving

Directing resources to a purpose

Showing the way

Facilitating the actions of a group

Exercising power and influence

Making things happen

Coordinating a collective effort

Informal descriptions such as these generally reflect dictionary definitions that frame leadership in terms of a capacity to command, direct, or guide the actions of others. Such description takes on further meaning when interpreted in context, such as conducting a musical performance, directing a play, or heading a political party. Prevalent perceptions of leadership are also discernible in scholarship that refines common interpretations to deeper understanding. Consider Burns's (1978) observation:

> Leadership is the reciprocal process of mobilizing by persons with certain motives and values, various economic, political and other resources; in a context of competition and conflict, in order to realize goals independently or mutually held by both leaders and followers. (p. 425)

Burns stresses the leadership dimensions of reciprocity and goal orientation, that is, leadership as an interactive process between people that is engaged to reach a singular or mutually held goal. More recently, Gardner (1995) offered another perspective in his analysis of the qualities of exemplary leaders, describing them as "persons who, by word and/or personal example, markedly influence the behaviors, thoughts and/or feelings of a significant number of their fellow human beings" (pp. 8–9). By attending to the act of influence on behavior, thoughts, and feelings, Gardner acknowledges that leaders sway, inspire, and otherwise modify the thinking and behavior of others.

Coupled with scholarly interpretations by experts, common definitions of leadership generally describe a phenomenon that engages, influences, and makes things happen.

BASIC IN NATURE

Scholars will continue to investigate leadership, construct leadership models and theories, and analyze leadership issues. Such inquiry generates contextual insight and nuanced understanding of the phenomenon. But while scholars ponder, practitioners must perform. Accordingly, from a multitude of scholarly efforts, it is important to capture the basic attributes of leadership, thereby providing a fundamental orientation for practitioners. Northouse (2003, p. 3) demonstrates the construction of such an interpretation through his identification of several central components of the phenomenon of leadership:

- Leadership is a *process* between a leader and followers.
- Leadership involves *influence* that affects followers.
- Leadership occurs in the context of *groups*.
- Leadership involves the attainment of *goals*.

Northouse uses these four components as the basis for his definition of leadership as "the process whereby an individual influences a group of individuals to achieve a common goal" (2003, p. 3). Reduced even further, with the acknowledgment that leadership may be exercised by more than one person in interactions between individuals in a group, a serviceable definition emerges:

Leadership is a process of influencing others toward the achievement of a goal.

This is a definition that draws from the body of research and theory to render a fundamental interpretation of the essential components of leadership (Figure 3.1). As such, it is the definition used in the examination of leadership connections to intelligence that follows in this chapter and the remainder of the book.

INFLUENCED BY CONTEXT

Behavior Adapts to Environment

The fundamental nature of leadership remains constant over time and context. Leadership is always a process of influencing others toward the achievement of a goal. But all human behavior, leadership included, evolves in an environmental context. Established behaviors persist until environmental challenges prompt adaptation or alternative practice. As the Durants (1968) observed in *The Lessons of History*, human culture evolves under the influence of experience and context. Through examination of economic history across hunter–gatherer, agricultural, and industrial stages of development, for example, they observed that the behavioral

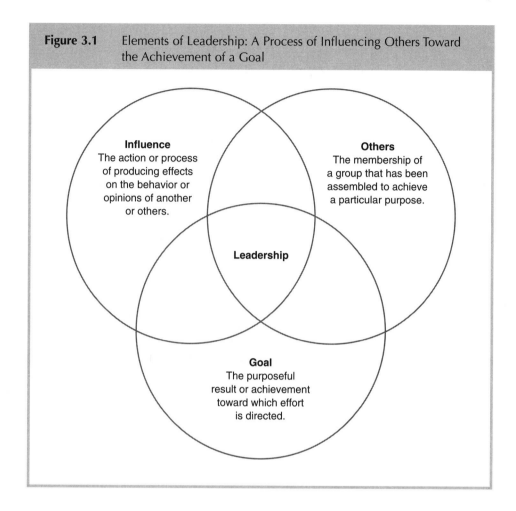

Figure 3.1 Elements of Leadership: A Process of Influencing Others Toward the Achievement of a Goal

Influence
The action or process of producing effects on the behavior or opinions of another or others.

Others
The membership of a group that has been assembled to achieve a particular purpose.

Leadership

Goal
The purposeful result or achievement toward which effort is directed.

code of one stage was changed by the next. Leadership is not exempt from such contextual influence.

The exercise of leadership in human culture responds to different contexts by making adjustments in the leadership behaviors engaged in to influence others toward goal achievement. Specifically, adjustments are made in how the leader and followers interact and, subsequently, how the leader exerts influence on group achievement. Those adjustments reflect changes in environmental conditions and human needs that inform the leader—and the subsequent shifts in perceptions of appropriate behavior that emerge.

From Club to Computer

Men, women, and children have been exercising leadership behavior for as long as human beings have banded together and cooperated to survive (Pellicer, 1999). Therefore, it is possible to examine different incarnations of leadership as it evolved in changing social, economic, and technological contexts. Such examination is a way to understand how leadership has been contextually practiced as a mirror of the times.

To make this point before proceeding further, you are invited to actively assess the influence of context on leadership. For example, how did the contexts of prehistoric times, the agrarian age, the rise of world religions and military empires, feudal society, the industrial age, and the computer revolution inform human perceptions about how to behave as leaders? The following directions will assist your reflection about this question:

1. Select one of the historical time periods just referenced (e.g., prehistoric times).

2. Envision yourself as a leader in that time and space.

3. Identify a goal that you are trying to help others achieve in that context.

4. Reflect on what would *inform* your leadership practice in that context (i.e., What would assail your senses and enter your mind; what would you see and hear?).

5. Describe your *perception* of the role of a leader in that context.

6. Describe specific leadership *behavior* that you might engage in to influence the group in the achievement of the identified goal.

With reference to this reflection, consider further the various influences on leadership behavior in the following contexts.

Leadership in Prehistoric Times. Driven by the need to gather food and other resources and somehow survive with limited defenses against powerful adversaries, prehistoric leadership might have perceived value for influencing unquestioning compliance in others through fierce demonstrations of strength. Such perception would perhaps be informed by basic survival instincts and the example of elders. That perception, in turn, would favor leadership behavior that ruled by physical strength and unilateral decisions to ensure swift actions in dangerous environments.

Leadership in the Agrarian Age. Perhaps informed by the need for more complex cooperation in the conduct of agricultural activity, a agrarian age leader might be more disposed to influence through bargaining and trading of goods and services. The environment was more stable, and goals were more long-term in nature, as represented by the time and patience needed for crop production. Leadership behavior was further informed by a greater sense of community and interdependence. The resulting leadership perceptions probably favored behaviors that influenced achievement through communication skills, coalition building, and patience.

Leadership in an Age of Industrialization. Informed by new technologies and increased competition in the marketplace and by the goals of high productivity and profitability, an industrial age leader might have perceived value for fast-paced, hard-driven decisions with an eye on the bottom line. Further informed by the emergence of efficiency studies and scientific management, the prevailing leadership perception probably favored decision-making behavior aligned to data and quotas.

Leadership in an Age of Computers. Informed by global systems, rapidly expanding knowledge bases, and ever-evolving technologies, a computer age leader would reasonably perceive value for flexible networking within and beyond the membership of the organization. Given the challenge of pervasive and fast-paced change, a leader would also be disposed to broadly cultivate talents and distribute leadership responsibilities across the organization.

From your own reflection and the contextual scenarios described here, it should be clear that context is the environmental medium by which leadership behavior is informed. Thus informed, a leader inevitably forms perceptions of leadership behavior deemed appropriate to environmental conditions and goals. In this manner, leadership perception of an advantageous behavioral mode of influence adapts to context.

THEORIZED IN CONTEXT

The quest to understand what causes leaders to lead and followers to follow has prompted much pondering about attributes of effective leadership. From great man theory (leaders are born, not made) to system theory (leaders are made, not born), the quest has explored many paths in many contexts. A brief review of selected leadership theories that emerged in the past hundred years illustrates this point.

Trait Theory and the Measurement Movement

The twentieth century heralded systematic study of leadership. The leader was perceived to be the one unquestionably in charge. The effective leader could get results and loyal followers at the same time through some endowment of certain personality traits, such as intelligence, birth order, socioeconomic status, and childhood experience. This theory coincided with the development of measurement in the field of psychology, providing the impetus for measuring traits through checklists, tests, rating scales, and interviews. Unfortunately (and somewhat predictably), no definitive characteristic or combination emerged. Yet the basic tenet of command and authority suited an industrial age. Although trait theory is still alive and well in some attempts to benchmark leadership, it is often criticized as an input model lacking consideration of outcomes.

Behaviorist Theory and Leadership Style

Henry Ford and other Detroit automakers exemplified leadership at the beginning of the twentieth century. Driven by the goal to maximize profit through use of new technologies, this era of leadership valued efficiency, productivity, and scientific process. Associated goals were to minimize waste, streamline industry, and gain wealth through competition. Frederick Taylor and other proponents of scientific management informed leadership behavior. The perception was that leadership was to manage the worker by the maxim of "don't think, just do" in a humdrum existence of work driven by mechanical technology (Rost, 1991). The belief that what leaders do matters most became a far more significant orientation than that of leadership traits, thus drawing attention to leadership style.

Bureaucratic Control

Big government characterized leadership by the mid-twentieth century. Driven by the perceived need for control in an era marked by depression and nationalism, a command mentality took over. This era of leadership valued rank and prestige, rules and regulations, and restrictive boundaries to control information flow. The goal was management of large systems with clear boundaries and direction from the top. Theorists such as Elton Mayo and theories of structural and bureaucratic control informed leadership behavior. The perception of a leader was that of a bureaucrat who functioned within the structural frame of policy and procedure.

Situational Leadership

By the late 1960s and early 1970s, leadership was examined in the context of distinctive characteristics of the setting to which the leader's success could be attributed (Hoy & Miskel, 1987). In the rebellious 1960s, a more egalitarian view of society informed leadership, professing that a person could be a follower or a leader depending on the circumstances. Concerned with both the goal and the needs of relationships with others, leadership theory was beginning to recognize the complexity of leadership. Ultimately, situational leadership was found to be lacking because the theory could not predict leadership skills that would be more effective in particular situations. However, the theory did advance leadership perception by highlighting the readiness and capacity of members in an organization to share in leadership influence and responsibilities.

Transformational Leadership

By the 1980s, nonleader leadership, or the concept of many leaders, was proposed as a basic tenet of effectiveness. Barnes and Kriger (1986) suggested that previous theories of leadership were insufficient because they presumed a single leader with multiple followers. For the first time, leadership was examined as a characteristic of the entire organization, in which roles overlap and complement one another. The needs and goals of the organization were seen as shared commodities. Murphy (1988) and others rejected the "hero-leader" framework and helped conceptualize the capacity of leadership that runs throughout an organization. Informed by a rising sense of motivation and morality, empowerment and idealism became popularized as appropriate leadership characteristics. However, critics soon appeared on the scene with questions about pragmatism and results. How would a leader go about achieving true transformation?

Systemic Leadership

Recent theories of leadership have been characterized by the examination of entrepreneurial information systems. Driven by the free flow of information, the 1980s and 1990s valued teaming, strategic planning, and a combination of bottom-up and top-down decision making. The goal was instant communication to meet the pressing need to succeed in a competitive global marketplace. Management gurus such as Deming (Deming & Walton, 1988), Juran (1988), and Senge (1990) offered theories of systems thinking to inform leadership behavior. The perception of leadership that emerged was that of a proactive system thinker who cultivated systemic capacity for strategic change.

PRIMED TO EVOLVE

"Seeing" the alternative form can be difficult when your culture guides you to seeing the usual explanation.

—Calvin (2002, p. 23)

Leaders in the twenty-first century need to challenge old assumptions and examine ingrained habits of behavior. In *Mindfulness,* Langer (1989) suggests that intelligent behavior has three characteristics: creating new categories of thinking, openness to differing viewpoints and new sources of information, and flexibility and adaptability in resultant actions. In contrast, mindlessness is characterized by an entrapment in old categories, by automatic behavior that precludes attending to new signals, and by action that operates from a single perspective (p. 4). Attempts to further advance theoretical and practical understanding of effective leadership will advisedly embrace this issue of mindfulness. It is particularly important to do so, Zohar (1997) would advise, given the need to cultivate a perception of leadership that rejects the certainty of Newtonian organizations and eschews predictability, a theory of leadership that thrives on uncertainty, that can deal with creativity and rapid change, and that can release the restraints on the potential of human beings who work in organizations.

Primed by Sense of Context

In this first decade of a new millennium, humanity can look back at a century that witnessed catastrophic wars, the dawn of atomic energy, exploration of the solar system, civil rights movements, genetic engineering, microcomputer technology, globalization of economic and communication systems, the rise and fall of totalitarian governments, genocides, the growth of political terrorism, and tenuous expansion of democratic forms of government. And, while still adjusting to events of past decades, we are engaging a new century that promises to be as eventful and challenging, particularly in respect to prevailing issues of equity, justice, and quality of natural environment. A thoughtful assessment of the challenge and change ahead would necessarily conclude that humankind must become ever more adept and disposed in the exercise of intelligent leadership behavior.

Primed by Sense of Capacity

How we see and do leadership must adapt to the circumstances of the twenty-first century. The times call for a conscious adjustment in our mental model of the phenomenon. Senge (1990) describes the construction of mental models as an ongoing process of clarifying and refining the assumptions, generalizations, and images that influence understanding and action. As projected across our earlier consideration of how leadership behavior is informed by context, the current environment advises that there is both need and opportunity for more effective alignment of leadership behavior to the nature of capacity in the process of influencing the achievement of compelling goals. The assumptions underlying this premise are as follows:

- Human capacity for acquiring and applying knowledge (i.e., intelligence) represents the essential asset in any organization, an asset that is distributed throughout the membership, not just in the "head of the head."
- Leadership influences the extent to which an environment is intelligence friendly and organizational intelligence is productively engaged.
- In an era of breakthroughs in knowledge about human capacity, leaders are obliged to access that knowledge to better inform their influence on organizational purpose.

Simply put, the construction of a mental model of leadership that is appropriate to the twenty-first century hinges on how leaders see the others they aspire to influence toward the achievement of whatever goals. Given scientific revelations about the nature of human capacity, leaders must move beyond a superficial sense of what members of a particular group are able to do and how they might best do it. A leader in an intelligence-enlightened era must cultivate essential understanding of what people bring to the table by virtue of their species. An enlightened leader will understand leadership as a process of influencing *the capacity that lies within others* toward the achievement of a goal (Figure 3.2).

Primed by Sense of Alignment

In constructing a mental model of leadership that is appropriate to current context, a leader will rely less on intuition or insight gained from trial and error in attempting to influence others. Scientific revelation about the brain-enabled elements of capacity that leaders aspire to influence makes it possible (and advisable) for leaders to attend to those in the process of marshaling human resources toward the achievement of results. It is an extraordinary opportunity for consciously aligning leadership behavior to the intelligence capacity that underlies all human achievement. It is an opportunity that both envisions and enables capacity-connected leaders, leaders who are more aligned in perception and practice to how people best exercise capacity in achieving goals (Figure 3.3).

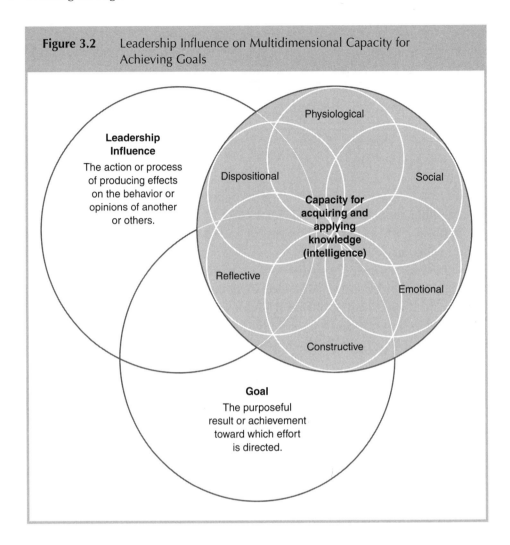

Figure 3.2 Leadership Influence on Multidimensional Capacity for Achieving Goals

Primed by Sense of Advantage

What advantage does enlightenment about the nature of intelligence have to offer leadership influence on the achievement of goals? After all, leadership that is uninformed about the nature of intelligence remains naturally aligned to a perceived need to achieve a particular goal through influence on others. However, a leader in this circumstance (the circumstance of most leaders?) is dependent on intuition and feedback from trial-and-error initiatives to influence others in the achievement quest. This is not to say that leaders in such circumstances are not or have not been effective in their leadership influence. Examples of people who were or are uninformed about the nature of intelligence yet perform effectively as leaders are abundant in historic and current context. Nevertheless, such leaders are necessarily working in the dark. They benefit from astute

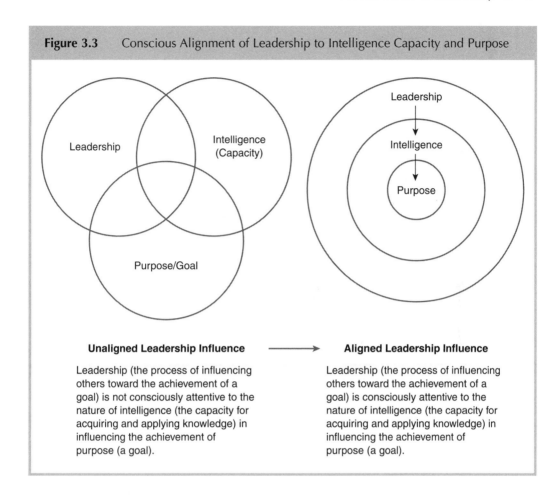

Figure 3.3   Conscious Alignment of Leadership to Intelligence Capacity and Purpose

Leadership

Intelligence (Capacity)

Purpose/Goal

Leadership

Intelligence

Purpose

Unaligned Leadership Influence ⟶ **Aligned Leadership Influence**

Leadership (the process of influencing others toward the achievement of a goal) is not consciously attentive to the nature of intelligence (the capacity for acquiring and applying knowledge) in influencing the achievement of purpose (a goal).

Leadership (the process of influencing others toward the achievement of a goal) is consciously attentive to the nature of intelligence (the capacity for acquiring and applying knowledge) in influencing the achievement of purpose (a goal).

observations of what does and doesn't work in helping people success-fully achieve a specific purpose, but the bottom line is that many leader-ship initiatives miss the mark or are deflected (you might reflect about your own leadership experience in relation to this observation). Leadership that is informed about the nature and nurture of intelligence, on the other hand, anticipates advantage from knowing more about what makes people tick (Figure 3.4).

SUMMARY OBSERVATIONS

- Leadership is a natural and socially valued phenomenon.
- Leadership is the process of influencing others toward the achieve-ment of a goal.
- The basic process of leadership remains constant, but how influence is exercised within the process is informed by the specific context in which it occurs.

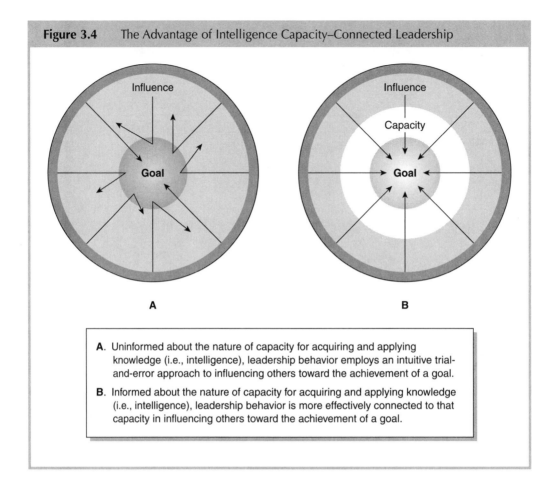

Figure 3.4   The Advantage of Intelligence Capacity–Connected Leadership

A. Uninformed about the nature of capacity for acquiring and applying knowledge (i.e., intelligence), leadership behavior employs an intuitive trial-and-error approach to influencing others toward the achievement of a goal.

B. Informed about the nature of capacity for acquiring and applying knowledge (i.e., intelligence), leadership behavior is more effectively connected to that capacity in influencing others toward the achievement of a goal.

- Emerging knowledge about the nature of intelligence makes it possible to observe leadership from a more informed perspective of capacity for achieving purpose.
- Twenty-first-century context enables conscious alignment of leadership behavior to the nature of intelligence in influencing others toward the achievement of goals.

READER REFLECTION

- How would you explain the nature of leadership to a colleague?
- How does context influence leadership practice?
- What contemporary events or developments are influencing leadership practice?
- How should leadership practice evolve in the twenty-first century?

4 A Mindful Framework

Our understanding of the nature and processes of leadership is most likely to be enhanced as we come to understand better the arena in which leadership necessarily occurs—namely, the human mind. Perhaps this characterization should be pluralized as human minds, since I am concerned equally with the mind of the leader and the minds of the followers.

—Gardner (1995, p. 25)

Emerging knowledge about the nature of intelligence offers implicit opportunity for better understanding of how to nurture that capacity in self and others. For leaders, it represents a momentous opportunity for cultivating a more informed understanding of their influence on the human systems they lead. It is an opportunity, no less, to envision the *mindful leader*—a leader who is consciously attentive to the nature of intelligence in the process of influencing others toward the achievement of goals.

THE MINDFUL CONNECTION

The needs and opportunities of our time call for leaders who are conscious stewards of organizational intelligence. However, there are no sure formulas or lists prescribing how to best respond to the circumstance. Rather, leaders must engage their brains in proactive reflection about how to best connect to the brains of others to get things done. In doing so, they will necessarily assess the merits and means of mindful leadership.

Beyond the Obvious

What is beyond question is that leadership is connected to the brain. Given the brain's commanding role in the mediation of all human behavior, this connection is not optional. Whether we are dancing, playing cards, or selling real estate, the what, why, and how of human behavior are all directly connected to the physiological mass that occupies body space between your ears: the brain. The question is not *whether* leadership is connected to the brain, but *what* is being connected to and *how* that connection might be optimized.

It should also be clear that leadership necessarily interacts in some manner with nearly every aspect of brain function and activity. This comprehensive relationship is ultimately defined by a connection between leadership and the intelligence the brain enables. That is, a leader is more concerned with what the brain does than the brain itself. Intelligence, then, is *the* leadership–brain connection for a leader to be mindful of.

The bottom line is that brain-enabled intelligence is the immediate force behind who we are and what we do, and leadership is about influencing who we are and what we do. Leaders necessarily influence others through neural pathways because that is the medium that enables the multidimensional capacities that leaders connect to in self and others. There is no choice in this matter. Such connection inevitably occurs, whether intuitively or consciously, disastrously or productively, because qualities of intelligence are the means by which the brain creates mind and connects to other brains.

A Fundamental Problem

Bateson (1979) suggests that the fundamental source of most, if not all, significant problems confronting humankind is a pervasive and problematic gap between the way humans think and the way nature works. That is, we need to apply our minds toward cultivating a deeper understanding of and appreciation for how nature conducts its business.

Bateson's admonition is worth bearing in mind in a twenty-first-century context that both requires and accommodates a closing of the gap between how we think about leadership and how nature works. There is need and opportunity for cultivating more conscious perspective on behaviors that nurture the nature of intelligence in the process of influencing others. Escalating challenges to the quality of human existence necessitate such perspective. Emerging knowledge about our capacity for acquiring and applying knowledge accommodates a shift in view. Thus informed about the nature of intelligence, leaders are positioned to become more natural and effective in leadership behavior and are encouraged to do so by being more mindful of the capacity they hope to influence.

THE MEANING OF MINDFUL

The learning process, by which patterns are sorted out so that increasingly more sense is made of a complex world, goes on incessantly, and each individual, in a purely individual way, gathers features and clues that gradually mount. Progressively, the pattern is grasped more sharply and greater discrimination becomes possible.

—Hart (1983, p. 77)

To be mindful is simply a matter of being thoughtful or attentive. Given a context that is generating new knowledge about the multidimensional nature of human capacity, a twenty-first-century leader has much to be mindful about. The breakthrough in knowledge enables more informed leadership influence on others toward goal achievement—a more mindful approach to how to best nurture the nature of capacity toward the achievement of a need. This mindful alignment of nurture to nature and need reflects the wrinkle new knowledge about intelligence brings to a classic reflection. Traditionally, leaders identified a goal (i.e., a need) and then contemplated what might be done to influence (i.e., nurture) others toward achievement of that purpose. The informed refinement in that reflection process (made possible by breakthroughs in knowledge about intelligence) is as follows:

1. What is the *need* (i.e., the goal to be achieved or problem to be resolved)?

2. What dimensions of the *nature* of human intelligence are important to achieving the need (e.g., physiological fitness, social interaction, emotional commitment, knowledge construction, reflective reasoning, collaborative disposition)?

3. How might I best *nurture* the dimensions of intelligence that are important to achieving the need?

Such adjustment in the reflective narrative that necessarily occurs in a leader's mind is not inconsequential. It is reflection that is consciously mindful of aligning nurturing leadership behavior to the nurture of capacity for achieving a need (Figure 4.1).

Figure 4.1   Mindful Leadership Alignment of Nurture, Nature, and Need

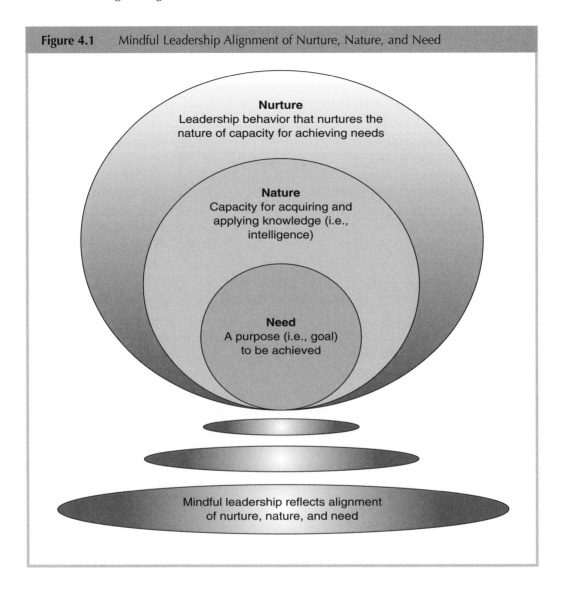

THE MEANS TO BE MINDFUL

Neural networking within and between the brains of leaders and followers always has been and will be the medium for conducting leadership. It is the same medium at work in all human interactions, including parenting, teaching, or conducting commerce. Currently, we are witnessing breakthroughs in knowledge about the nature of intelligence at work in neural networking. How soon and to what degree this new knowledge will favorably influence leadership practice is a matter of how mindful leaders are in proactively engaging the evolving knowledge base.

In Lieu of a Miracle

Architects have an expression for describing the relationship between vision and achievement: "First you see it, then you build it." A cautionary addendum to this maxim would be that just because you see it does not mean it is going to happen. A comic interpretation of this point is a variation of a cartoon portraying the dilemma of good ideas coming to naught for lack of action.

> A group of executives are standing in front of a large flowchart depicting a complex project. The chart includes extensive description of mission, goals, line and staff relationships, communication routes, and the like. One of the executives points to the spot where the flowchart narrows to an empty box and asks, "And what happens here?" Another group member responds, "Then a miracle occurs."

The implied message is that meaningful change or progress occurs only when what is envisioned is translated into specific action. That is, an insight or idea is not truly potent until acted on—because it is only action that produces tangible results. This is a message that merits the attention of leaders who aspire to better align their behavior to emerging knowledge about the nature of human intelligence. Simply put, reflection about the import of evolving knowledge does not advance beyond the status of an intellectual exercise if compatible behavior is not determined and enacted as a result. Thus, although it is important to first see the nature of brain-enabled intelligence, the ultimate task is to consciously build nurturing connections to that nature within leadership's influence on the achievement of needs. To do this, there is need for a framework that will facilitate leadership alignment of nurture, nature, and need—a framework that forgoes reliance on a miracle in favor of structured support for the human capacity to figure things out and get things done.

The Power of a Framework

> *Framework: A structure for supporting or enclosing something else, especially a skeletal support used as the basis for something being constructed; a set of assumptions, concepts, values, and practices that constitutes a way of viewing reality.*
>
> —*American Heritage Dictionary* (2000, p. 697)

It is not difficult to make a case for the contributions of frameworks in human affairs. The words in the definition cited here (e.g., *structure, support*) imply the practical value of a framework. Furthermore, examples of the importance of frameworks abound. It would not be possible to build a house or any other structure without first *framing* it, both mentally and physically. The founders of the United States of America *framed* a national constitution that accommodates amendment. The details of treaties and other formal agreements emerge from preliminary *frameworks* for deliberations.

The power of a framework lies in its facilitation of physical and mental endeavors to construct, compose, or adjust something that is important to accomplish. A framework is a means by which to focus and organize resources toward a desired effect.

The Most Powerful Framework on Earth

As noted in Chapter 2, the business of the brain is survival. To that end, it assembles neural networks that organize information to useful purposes. This physical construction of neural networks is perpetuated throughout the human lifespan as connections are continually refined by ongoing discernment of useful patterns within the richness of available information. Thus a brain continually constructs its understanding of the world and directs behavior accordingly.

The human brain is extraordinarily good at the business of interpreting and organizing information patterns. The key to this is the brain's adeptness at using established patterns to frame the organization and refinement of new patterns. In this fashion, the value of an initial information pattern is compounded; it becomes a framework that provides structure for further interpretation of information. It is this capacity for continually framing and reframing the construction of knowledge that qualifies the human brain as the most powerful framework on Earth—an unparalleled source of structure and support for the endless formulation of knowledge and aligned action.

Thinking Frameworks

Ultimately, the brain has evolved to conscious appreciation for frameworks that facilitate its information processing needs. It demonstrates this value by creating frameworks to serve its interests in many contexts. Formal information processing structures, such as scientific methods, system analysis, and lateral thinking, are examples. The brain also designs frameworks to support thinking about specific subjects. Examples relevant to leadership include Covey's (1989) framework for exploring the habits of highly effective people, Deming and Walton's (1988) 14-point structure for organizing ideas about total quality management, and Senge's (1990) framing of learning organizations through five learning disciplines. Similarly, Gardner's (1983) frames-of-mind orientation to multiple intelligences and Sternberg's (1985) depiction of a triarchic intelligence represent frameworks intended to facilitate reflection about human intelligence.

A Mindful Framework

In the presence of emerging revelations from brain science, leaders have the option, if not the obligation, to proactively seek out and act on this knowledge. The opportunity before them is to consciously construct personal understanding of brain-compatible leadership behavior that advances the capacity of individuals and organizations toward achievement of common purpose. A framework is useful to that end.

From a perspective of the value of frameworks in general and the human brain's affinity for frameworks in particular, this chapter presents a framework for structuring mindful reflection about leadership connections to the nature of intelligence. The framework design respects natural brain capacity for organizing information to useful purpose. Specifically, it structures the mindful organization of knowledge about the nature of intelligence toward the interpretation of compatible leadership behavior. The framework assembly supports that process through four components.

- *Attend* to emerging information about the nature of intelligence.
- *Articulate* perception of the nature and nurture of intelligence.
- *Apply* perception of the nature and nurture of intelligence to compatible behavior.
- *Adjust* information, perception, and behavior from application experience. (See Figure 4.2.)

ATTENTION TO INFORMATION

Make the Commitment

The initial stage in this mindful framework for connecting leadership to the brain is the engagement of the powerful operating system between your ears to access and assess the potential of intelligence-aware leadership. This begins with accessing information that speaks to the merits of the issue, such as the content of the first three chapters of this book. Further commitment must be secured through engagement of information sources that serve up the meat of emerging knowledge about the nature of human capacity. Given encounters with credible information, your brain will be encouraged to engage subsequent framework components.

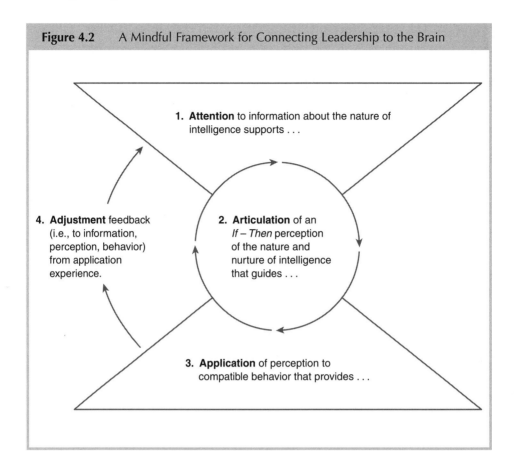

Figure 4.2 A Mindful Framework for Connecting Leadership to the Brain

1. **Attention** to information about the nature of intelligence supports . . .

4. **Adjustment** feedback (i.e., to information, perception, behavior) from application experience.

2. **Articulation** of an *If – Then* perception of the nature and nurture of intelligence that guides . . .

3. **Application** of perception to compatible behavior that provides . . .

The good news is that your brain is interested in knowing about itself. Furthermore, information processing is the brain's business, a business continuously conducted from womb to tomb. In this case, it is conscious processing of information to construct understanding about the nature of intelligence and the leadership implications thereof.

Be Realistic

Without a provisional framework, we would be simply swamped with data, knowing neither what we should be looking for nor what it might mean.

—Mithen (1996, p. 62)

Consider the standard joke heard at professional gatherings that focus on brain research and theory: "You are going to be introduced to a lot of new information about the brain at this conference, some of which is undoubtedly true." The attempt at humor makes the point that knowledge about the nature of the brain is vast, complex, and constantly adjusting to new revelations from ongoing investigation. What we know today may be significantly altered or even debunked by tomorrow's discovery. Despite the emergent nature of the knowledge base, we are compelled to examine the implications of what we know at the moment. Furthermore, if this evolving reservoir of knowledge is to productively inform human behavior, it must be engaged in a practical fashion.

Consider further that we all benefit from a more informed sense of the nature of intelligence, but few are inclined to pursue a parallel career in neuroscience. Accordingly, a practical approach to constructing understanding about brain-enabled intelligence for most is to judiciously mine essential information from rich sources. Specifically, the advisable approach is to capture the gist (i.e., general sense) and essence (i.e., essential qualities) of available information. This cultivation of heart-of-the-matter knowledge from credible sources is consistent with what Gazzaniga (1998) tells us is the brain's natural affinity for acquiring the gist of things rather than attending to details. Such an approach does not unrealistically aspire to the knowledge level of an expert in the field, but it does recognize a need to construct essential understanding.

Get a Grip

Brains make sense of the world by selectively processing information and constructing useful mental patterns and models. The brain is subject to this behavior in all circumstances, including an investigation of itself. Accordingly, anyone who aspires to understand the nature of the human brain and the intelligence it enables must embrace two realities:

- Your brain cannot construct useful patterns (i.e., understanding) without first accessing and processing relevant information. That is, if you have a thirst for knowledge, you have to go to the river and draw water. In this particular instance, the source to be tapped is the reservoir of information about the brain.
- Your brain need not engage all available information to construct useful patterns. A river of knowledge contains more than what can be productively consumed. Consequently, you need to be selective about where and what to draw from the reservoir of information about the human brain.

With these admonitions in mind, what might a leader do to organize the torrent of emerging knowledge about the brain? A necessary first step is to engage credible sources of interpretive and summary information through literature, video, the Internet, seminars, or other media (Chapters 5–10 provide a start). A leader is also advised, as a practical consideration for anyone not versed in cognitive and neuroscience, to attend to established investigation sites.

Such discrimination is similar to that practiced by paleontologists, anthropologists, and archaeologists in the selection of dig sites. Those scientists do not excavate at random across every possible site in their pursuit of discovery about the geological and historical past. Rather, they carefully judge the merits of candidate investigation sites by evidence of prior and potential finds. Thus we observe the focusing of investigations in potent areas such as the Black Hills of North America, the Olduvai Gorge of Africa, and river and coastal sites across the Middle East. In like manner, we will advisedly use a discriminating approach to the vast knowledge base about the brain and the intelligence it enables. Specifically, we are advised to investigate dimensions of the knowledge base that have been investigated productively and hold promise for further revelations.

The dimensions of intelligence reviewed in this text (i.e., the physiological, social, emotional, constructive, reflective, and dispositional dimensions introduced in Chapters 1–4 and further examined in Chapters 5–10) provide handles by which your brain can get a grip on an intimidating knowledge base. They are not *the* dimensions of human intelligence. Rather, they represent rich, credible investigation sites—fertile ground on which to construct personal understanding about the intelligence end of the brain's business. Furthermore, each of the six dimensions meets three criteria:

- It represents a productive area of scientific investigation that draws on the research and theory of substantial and authoritative sources.
- Its absence would render human intelligence either inoperative or dysfunctional.
- It is functionally applicable to the leadership framework described in this chapter.

The salient point is, process information about the brain as you will, but process it you must if said information is to productively inform behavior. And assuming that commitment of effort, you would seek to make sense of all that is known about the nature of intelligence by distilling the essence of what is important to know.

Process Gist for Essence and Implications

The examination of intelligence organized across Chapters 5–10 models how a leader might productively attend to emerging information toward the articulation of informed perceptions that guide applications to compatible behavior. The six chapters present summary information about the physiological, social, emotional, constructive, reflective, and dispositional dimensions of intelligence. Each chapter is organized to describe the following:

- The *gist* of the targeted dimension of intelligence (i.e., a foundation of basic information that is useful toward forming a general sense of the phenomenon)
- The *essence* of the dimension (i.e., a summation of essential nature, qualities)
- The *implications* of the dimension for practice (i.e., compatible behavior)

The intent of this format is to facilitate the distillation of essential knowledge about the nature of human intelligence (Figure 4.3). In engaging this attending process in Chapters 5–10, you will visit six dimensions of intelligence. You might think of this as visiting six rooms, each offering a particular view of intelligence. Across those views, you will observe that brain-enabled intelligence is a multidimensional phenomenon. You will also construct a knowledge base that supports subsequent articulation of the nature and nurture of intelligence. For example, you will discern that

- The *physiological nature* of intelligence is big, mind–body connected, high maintenance, and malleable.
- The *social nature* of intelligence is expectant, dependent, extended, and virtuous.
- The *emotional nature* of intelligence is attentive, judgmental, motivating, and managed after the fact.
- The *constructive nature* of intelligence is sensory, social, emotional, reflective, and susceptible to a double bind.
- The *reflective nature* of intelligence is manipulative, executive, unifying, and promising.
- The *dispositional nature* of intelligence is macro, mandatory, malleable, and either maximizing or minimizing.

ARTICULATION OF PERCEPTION

To articulate, as the term is used in this framework, means to reveal or make something clear and distinct in relation to other parts. It is a matter of putting things together in such a way that there are clearly understood terms of agreement. A brief exercise in logic would reveal the importance

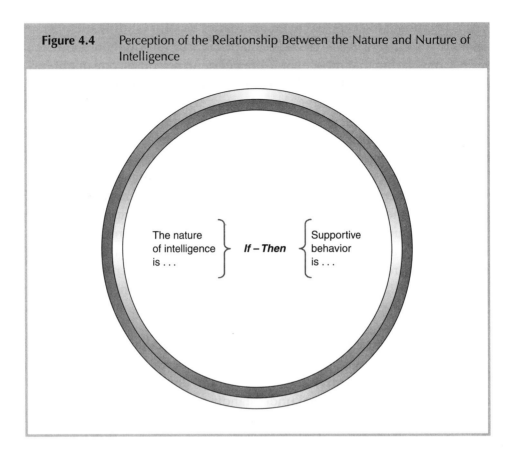

Figure 4.4   Perception of the Relationship Between the Nature and Nurture of Intelligence

provide experience with this articulation process, and the process is modeled further in Chapter 11. Following conscious articulation of nature and nurture, the framework applies that connection to practice.

APPLICATION TO PRACTICE

The natural business of the brain is to attend to information that matters, process useful patterns from the information attended to, and then apply the acquired patterns to informed behavior. This framework mirrors that natural brain activity. The first component structures brain attention to substantive information sources. The second component consciously applies the information processing operations of the brain to the articulation of personal perception of the essential nature of human intelligence and the implied relationships therein to compatible leadership behavior. The third component is where the action is. It is where knowledge about the nature and nurture of intelligence is applied to leadership practice as either standard practice or prescribed practice. Both applications are further described in Chapter 11. Because application is the third component of the framework,

Table 4.1   Articulating Perception of the Nature and Nurture of Intelligence
Relationships

Nature of Intelligence	Perception of Nature & Nurture	Nurturing Behavior
The *social nature* of intelligence is expectant, dependent, extended, and virtuous. The brain is endowed with hyper social instincts—powerful abilities for memory, language, empathy, reasoning, and collaboration. The brain's natural bias is socially expectant, dependent, extended, and oriented to virtue. The unfolding of brain capacity is expectant of the same social experience that formed it over evolutionary time. Social experience provokes the thinking and learning that the brain depends on to realize its potential. To satisfy this dependency on other minds, the brain invents mediums that extend social interaction beyond face-to-face encounters (art, writing, print, film, Internet). The brain also has an instinctive sense of moral virtue orientated to pro-social behavior.	←——— *If–then* ———→	Facilitate meetings of minds • Cohorts • Work teams • Task groups • Support groups • Alternate groups • Group processing • Mentoring • Coaching Cultivate common purpose • Mission orientation • Needs assessment • Visioning • Consensus building • Goal setting • Action planning • Problem solving • Progress assessment Extend the mind's reach • Conferencing • Advanced training • Book groups • Professional affiliation

it will connect better to your brain after you have experienced the attending and articulation components laid out in Chapters 5–10. A bit of a preview is in order here, however, as provided in following sections.

Application to Standard Practice

Assuming attentive articulation of substantive knowledge of intelligence, the ultimate goal would be to apply that understanding of nature and nurture to compatible leadership behavior. This application orientation aspires to translate internalized knowledge to standard operating procedure—the way you do leadership. In effect, it applies *if–then* articulation of the nature and nurture of intelligence to natural, everyday practice. This assumes an investment in attending to and articulating essential understanding of intelligence. Given that investment, applications to standard practice might play out somewhat like the following in an intelligence-savvy leader's brain.

- Given my understanding that intelligence operates on a biological platform of cells, circuits, and chemicals, my standard practice is to nurture brain fitness through actions that promote movement, nutrition, humor, and novelty.
- Given my understanding that social experience is the great provocateur of thinking and learning, my standard practice is to facilitate social interaction through actions that promote thinking in pairs, triads, groups, and alliances.
- Given my understanding that emotion is the means by which the brain attends, judges, and is motivated, my standard practice is to harness the power of emotion through actions that promote norms, affirmation, mission, and conflict resolution.
- Given my understanding that the brain is a lean, mean pattern-making machine, my standard practice is to facilitate the construction of meaning through actions that promote assessment, sensory engagement, questioning, and coaching.
- Given my understanding that the brain reflectively manipulates information and options before action, my standard practice is to structure thinking through actions that promote brainstorming, debating, analyzing, solving, and creating.
- Given my understanding that dispositions maximize the exercise of intelligence, my standard practice is to target productive thinking habits through actions that promote accuracy, listening, open-mindedness, persistence, and collaboration.

Application to Prescribed Practice

In addition to application of internalized knowledge about intelligence to standard practices, there is need for mindful application of knowledge in a prescribed manner. This prescriptive approach involves the conscious laying out of a course of action to be followed in given context. That context might affect self, a specific system, a particular situation, or a combination thereof. This prescriptive application approach does not replace application of knowledge to standard practice. That application approach aspires to internalize and translate knowledge about intelligence to everyday behavior. Prescribed practice complements and extends application to standard practice as a more formal reflection about what should be done. It is a staged reflection process for prescribing specific leadership behavior in specific context (Figure 4.5).

1. Clarification of *need:* What is the goal or purpose to be achieved?

2. Assessment of the *nature* of intelligence required for achieving the need: What dimensions of intelligence will influence the achievement of the goal?

3. Assessment of options that might *nurture* the required intelligence: What behaviors will support the intelligence required for the achievement of the goal?

4. Composition of a *narrative* plan of action: What strategic or collective actions will be conducted to nurture the nature of targeted dimensions of intelligence toward achieving the need?

ADJUSTMENT FROM EXPERIENCE

The process by which information influences perceptions that direct behavior is dynamic rather than linear (refer back to Figure 4.2). Application experience thus provides important adjustment feedback to information sources that warrant ongoing attention and articulation to guide behavior. This, then, is the focus of the fourth and final component of the framework: the progressive adjustment of informed leadership connections to intelligence.

It is only natural that perception and behavior realize upgrade benefits from the processing of application experiences. This is simply the same process that is at work when we get feedback about how to better ride a bike from the experience of riding a bike. The adjustment component of the framework is not onerous in any case, as you discover in your further engagement of this component in Chapters 11 and 12. The following strategies forecast that content in the final chapters.

Practice

We are always well advised to engage the time-honored means for mastering any skill or disposition: practice. Mindful leadership evolves in understanding of the nature and nurture of intelligence from application

Figure 4.5   Prescriptive Application of Knowledge About Intelligence to Practice

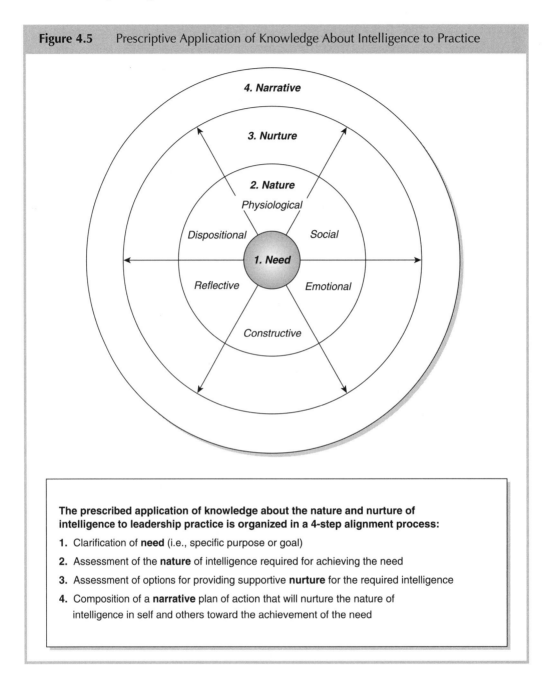

The prescribed application of knowledge about the nature and nurture of intelligence to leadership practice is organized in a 4-step alignment process:

1. Clarification of **need** (i.e., specific purpose or goal)

2. Assessment of the **nature** of intelligence required for achieving the need

3. Assessment of options for providing supportive **nurture** for the required intelligence

4. Composition of a **narrative** plan of action that will nurture the nature of intelligence in self and others toward the achievement of the need

to standard practice and prescribed application to self, systems, and situations. A leader must consciously apply well-informed knowledge until it becomes second nature—a natural and effective means for attending to the nature of intelligence in the process of influencing others toward the achievement of goals.

Coach

A leader is further advised to engage in collaborative inquiry with colleagues when exploring leadership connections to the brain and making mindful adjustments to leadership practice. As described in Chapter 6, social engagement is essential to the productive exercise of constructive and reflective dimensions of intelligence. Collegial coaching of the nature and nurture of intelligence also promotes mindful leadership throughout an organization, as will be observed in Chapter 11.

SUMMARY OBSERVATIONS

- A *mindful leader* is consciously attentive to the nature of intelligence in the process of influencing others toward the achievement of goals.
- A mindful leader is interested in understanding and nurturing the nature of intelligence that the brain enables, as opposed to just knowing about the brain itself.
- A proposed framework for structuring the mindful organization of knowledge about the nature of intelligence toward the interpretation of compatible leadership behavior incorporates four major components:

  Attend to credible information about the nature of intelligence.

  Articulate perception of the nature and nurture of intelligence.

  Apply perception of nature and nurture to compatible behavior.

  Adjust information, perception, and behavior from application experience.

READER REFLECTION

- How would you describe the purpose of the framework described in this chapter to someone else?
- How would you describe the purpose and process of each framework component?

Part II

Minding
Revelation

Multiple dimensions of human intelligence operate as an integrated whole within the brain–body system. A dimensional organization of information about the nature of intelligence is useful to your brain's construction of understanding about a complex phenomenon. It is a practical means for processing scientific revelations about what makes people tick and what might be done to favorably influence the powerful nature of that neural ticking.

Chapters 5–10 engage the first two components of the framework introduced in Chapter 4 by *attending* to and *articulating* current knowledge about the nature and nurture of intelligence.

5 Physiological Nature

And here we are, sitting in a hut in the woods, looking back on a process that has taken three or four billion years. And in us, this long process has finally become aware of itself.

—Gaarder (1996, p. 426)

THE PHYSIOLOGICAL BASE

Gaarder's (1996) Darwinian analysis concludes that life evolved to awareness of self several billion years after its inception in the primal seas of the young planet Earth. That is, in humans, evolution created a life form that is capable of consciously contemplating its relationship to the grand scheme of nature. As you are engaging that capacity in a conscious reflection about itself, you might appreciate the magnitude of its evolution. You will further observe that it is effortless for you to do so, given that the physiological nature of your brain is big, mind–body connected, high maintenance, and malleable—qualities that are examined in this chapter (Figure 5.1).

THE GIST OF IT

Getting to Know You

The physiological architecture of the human brain is the platform on which human intelligence performs its extraordinary feats of conscious thought. It is also the biological bridge to an extended physiology of subconscious intelligence. Accordingly, construction of personal understanding about the nature of intelligence is served by visiting its physiological

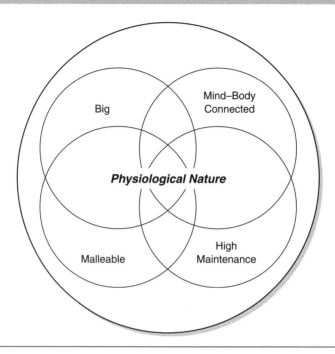

Figure 5.1 The Physiological Nature of Intelligence

The **physiological nature** of intelligence is

Big: *Human intelligence is physiologically enabled. It operates on a biological platform of cells, circuits, and chemicals that is virtually unlimited in its capacity for processing information.*

Mind–Body Connected: *The brain is the body and the body is the brain, and what affects one affects the other.*

High Maintenance: *To do its work well, the brain demands both quantity and quality in nutritional care and environmental experience.*

Malleable: *Neural networks in the brain are modified by experience, and plasticity in learning continues throughout the lifespan. Intelligence capacity is not fixed but malleable by the quality and quantity of environmental experience encountered.*

underpinnings—a peek under the hood. A brain-friendly way to initiate this examination is to access what your brain knows about itself. To that end, take a moment to locate a pen or pencil and write down

- three or four things you know about the nature of your brain, and
- one or two questions you want answered about the nature of your brain.

~Reflection Time~

Whatever your response to this reflection exercise, it demonstrates a natural interest in the workings of the brain. You know something about it and probably want to know the answers to a few things you don't know. What you specifically know or want to know is not that important. What matters is that you are a member of a species that is motivated and able to accumulate such knowledge.

First Impressions

Picture yourself lifting the top of your skull, removing your brain, and holding it in your hands (we know you can do this because of your brain's capacity for imagination). You will note that it weighs approximately 3 pounds and is comparable in size to a large grapefruit or two fists held together palm to palm. This soft biological mass is composed primarily of water (78%), fat, and protein. It is slippery from the protective fluid and thin membrane that buffer it within the hard shell of the cranial skull. There in your hands is the major component of the human central nervous system. Neurally and chemically connected to the entire human physiology, it simultaneously monitors and regulates other body organs and systems, operates movement and communication, and centrally processes environmental information. You are contemplating the collection of biological structures that enables conscious contemplation. With brain in hand, you are gazing on and thinking about that with which you think.

On this initial observation, the human brain thus exposed may appear somewhat inadequate for the important and complex tasks attributed to it. Therefore, to understand how the brain performs its myriad responsibilities, you will find it useful to examine the components of this special parcel of anatomical real estate. To that end, neuroscientists map the geography of the human brain in a variety of ways to organize relationships between its physical components and perceived functions. Such mapping describes the physiological terrain of the brain by regions, structures, hemispheres, lobes, areas, cells, and circuits. New technology has recently enhanced such territorial investigation, progressively revealing the operational secrets of specific locations within the brain. Understanding of the holistic operations of this integrated collection of biological structures remains a more difficult puzzle to solve, however. Nevertheless, mapping the territory is a necessary and valuable approach to composing the big picture of the inner workings of your brain. Your exploration thus proceeds to the examination of exterior regions.

Surface Features

Scanning the exterior of your brain, you will observe first and foremost the *cerebrum,* the large forebrain component of the central nervous system that almost completely enfolds other brain structures. A lateral view of this structure is perhaps the most common visual image people have of their brain (Figure 5.2). The surface of the cerebrum is dominated by the convolutions of its mantle area called the *cerebral cortex.* This outer, gray-matter region of the cerebrum is about as thick as a grapefruit peel (*cortex* is from Latin for "bark or rind"). A rich vertical and horizontal network of neural cells dominates it. The horizontal organization is marked by a six-layer lamination of cells, and the vertical organization features a multitude of columnar structures. It is deeply folded as an evolutionary means to provide maximum surface space, increasing the number of brain cells that can be accommodated by the restricted space in the skull. John Dowling (1998) captures the significance of this physiological feature in his observation that the human brain is qualitatively similar to the brains of other animals but quantitatively different. That is, a more highly developed cerebral cortex is the physiological base from which the higher neural functions of humans evolve, such as language, logic, and creativity. If you were to compare the cortex of your brain with that of other highly evolved animals, particularly your primate relatives, you would quickly discern the advantage in size and density of the cortical area of the human brain. Indeed, the cortex is the crowning glory of human brain mass. Most significant, the majority of the neurons housed in your cortex are undedicated, meaning they are not committed to specific survival tasks. Rather, they are abundantly available on demand to be applied to any thinking task that arises (i.e., the reason why, as examined in Chapters 9 and 10, this is prime brain territory for developing productive leadership connections).

Hemispheres

As you further observe the surface of your brain, you will notice deep furrows or fissures in the folds of the cortex. Most noticeable is the prominent enfolding called the medial sulcus, which divides the cerebrum from front to back into two hemispheres (see top view of brain presented in Figure 5.2). The motor areas of the right hemisphere are responsible for movement on the left side of the body, and the left hemisphere is responsible for movement on the right side of the body. The two hemispheres are connected by a thick concentration of neural communication fibers known as the *corpus callosum.* The significance of this connection is that your brain has each hemisphere assume different information processing responsibilities while maintaining a communication bridge that informs and coordinates

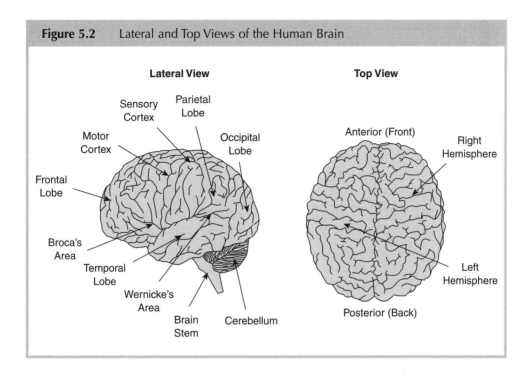

Figure 5.2 Lateral and Top Views of the Human Brain

Lateral View

Sensory Cortex
Parietal Lobe
Motor Cortex
Occipital Lobe
Frontal Lobe
Broca's Area
Temporal Lobe
Wernicke's Area
Brain Stem
Cerebellum

Top View

Anterior (Front)
Right Hemisphere
Left Hemisphere
Posterior (Back)

the activities of one with the other. This is an evolutionary strategy that seeks to maximize the efficiency of available brain resources. While one hemisphere is processing information in parts and sequence, controlling fine motor skills, and recognizing positive emotional states, the other is seeing the larger picture, controlling gross motor skills, and responding to negative emotional states. In effect, your brain determines which hemisphere will do what but insists that the two keep in touch with each other about what they are doing.

Lobes, Strips, and Areas

Neuroscientists divide each cortical hemisphere of the brain into four lobes (again, see Figure 5.2). Rotating your brain in your hands, you can locate the area that aligns with your forehead. This area of each hemisphere is called the *frontal lobe*. The foremost portion of this area is the prefrontal lobe, which is associated with critical thinking, problem solving, creativity, and planning—the complex reasoning processes that most distinguish the mental abilities of humankind. Reflective mediation of emotional responses is attributed to an interior region of this area called the orbitofrontal cortex. To the lower rear of the frontal lobe in the left hemisphere (reversed to the right hemisphere in 5% of the population) is a portion of cerebral landscape called *Broca's area*. Located in proximity to the primary motor area associated with face, tongue, and jaw movements, this area is concerned with the production of language—another distinguishing human capacity. Immediately behind the frontal lobe in each hemisphere is a strip called the *motor cortex*, which controls voluntary movement in the opposite side of the body.

Rotating your brain 180 degrees, you will observe the back area of each hemisphere, called the *occipital lobe*. This area has primary responsibility for processing visual information. The area of the brain above the occipital lobe in each hemisphere is called the *parietal lobe*. Its primary functions involve the processing of sensory information from the opposite side of the body. In relation to that function, the parietal lobe interacts with other brain areas to recognize threats and opportunities. A strip at the front portion of the parietal lobe adjacent to the motor cortex is the called the *somatosensory cortex*, the area where your brain receives feedback about pain, pressure, temperature, and touch.

With a quarter turn of your brain to either side, you will locate the *temporal lobe* above and around the ear area in each hemisphere. This area assumes primary responsibility for hearing and a role in memory and learning. A particular area at the junction of the left temporal, occipital, and parietal lobes (again, reversed to the right hemisphere in 5% of the population) has been identified as *Wernicke's area*. This site is located between the primary auditory and visual areas of the cortex and is concerned primarily with comprehension of speech and the organization of words in speaking, reading, and writing.

Below the Surface

It is helpful at this point in your examination of your brain's physiology to bisect the entire mass front to back along the deep fold of the medial sulcus. This division of your brain into two halves provides what is known as a medial view of the brain, a view that reveals features and structures that are partially or completely hidden beneath the mantle of the cerebral cortex. You now have access to a mapping scheme that organizes the physiological terrain of your brain by regions of the hindbrain, midbrain, and forebrain (Figure 5.3).

The *hindbrain* emerges from the *spinal cord* (the portion of the central nervous system that is not in the head but, in effect, is an extension of the brain) and is composed of the medulla, pons, and cerebellum. These combined structures are commonly called the *brain stem* and, with the cerebellum, represent older architecture in the evolutionary development of your brain. The brain stem is a communication corridor for ascending sensory and descending neural information between brain and spinal cord

Figure 5.3   Medial View of Human Brain

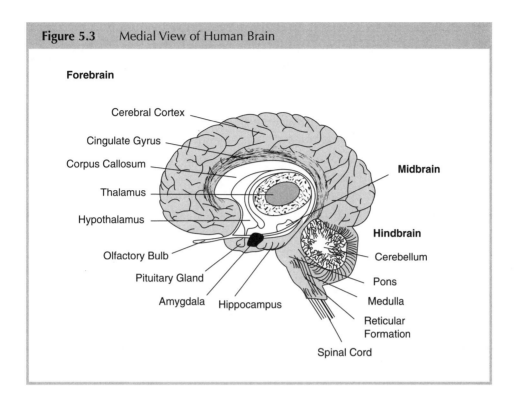

connections to the rest of the body. A network of *nuclei* (i.e., clusters of brain cells called neurons) in this stem section form the *reticular formation* to regulate involuntary body motor activity such as heart rate, respiration, blood pressure, and gastrointestinal function in relation to what is happening in and around the body. This regulation operates subconsciously in the brain stem, thus relieving your conscious brain of constant attention to basic life support system management. The reticular formation further extends its connections in the brain to form the *reticular activating system*, which regulates levels of arousal and consciousness in relation to changing conditions in the environment. The reticular activating system performs this function by focusing on relevant stimuli and filtering out trivial sensory information. Nuclei in the brain stem also play a critical role in the production of chemical agents that assume cellular communication and maintenance roles throughout the brain. The *cerebellum* (Latin for "little brain") is attached to the brain stem below the occipital lobes of the cerebral cortex at the back of the skull. It is associated with movement, balance, and memory of how-to procedures and processes that become automatic, such as riding a bike or learning multiplication tables. Communication between the cerebellum and cerebral cortex about body movement is mediated by neurons in the brain stem. A relationship is also suspected between the cerebellum and the cognitive activity that occurs in the frontal cortex when movement facilitates thinking and learning—as when you move to write, draw, act out, or verbally express what is in your head.

The *midbrain* is a small area located at the top of the brain stem. This section is also called the midbrain and tectum structure. Its responsibilities are to mediate visual reflexes and to coordinate head and eye movements. In the distant evolutionary past, the midbrain had more extensive responsibility for integrating sensory inputs and controlling motor outputs. As the mammalian brain evolved, however, much of this function was transferred to the cerebral cortex of the forebrain.

You have already observed the exterior of your *forebrain*. It rests on top of the hindbrain and midbrain and is composed of structures that mediate sensation, movement, memory, thinking, and consciousness. However, the longitudinal view before you provides an interior perspective of the dominating proportion of the forebrain allocated to the folded cerebral cortex. You are also able to observe the arch of hundreds of millions of neural fibers in the corpus callosum that forms a communication bridge between the two cerebral hemispheres. Other structures in the forebrain are also observable.

The *thalamus* (from Greek for "chamber" or "inner room") is a walnut-size structure at the bottom of the forebrain in an area called the diencephalon (i.e., area around the thalamus, hypothalamus, and pineal gland) just above the brain stem. It functions as a receiving and distribution center that relays incoming sensory and motor information to appropriate areas of the cerebral cortex for further processing, thus informing the brain about what is happening outside of the body and what the body is doing. All sensory information (with the exception of information from the olfactory system, which is directly networked to the cortex) is received and directed to other processing sites by the thalamus.

Below the thalamus in the diencephalon is the thumbnail-size *hypothalamus,* which relays information about what is happening in the body to other areas of the brain. In interpreting and communicating such information, the hypothalamus serves a primary role in regulating basic drives and body states, such as temperature, sexual activity, and appetite. It also interacts with the pituitary gland, to regulate body state, and the medulla area of the brain stem, to control autonomic (subconscious) nervous system regulation of internal organs such as the heart, lungs, and bladder.

The *pituitary gland* rests beneath the hypothalamus and is regulated by hypothalamic neurons that promote or inhibit the release of pituitary hormones into the bloodstream. Pituitary gland secretions, in turn, engage the endocrine system in the release of other hormones into the bloodstream to adjust body chemistry in a manner dictated by the hypothalamus.

The *hippocampus* is not actually observable in a medial view of your brain. If you peel back some layers of the temporal lobe area of the cerebral cortex, however, you will see a crescent formation that is shaped a bit like a seahorse. This structure is associated with indexing of information throughout the brain, thereby enabling learning and the formation of memory.

The *amygdala* is an almond-size structure that sits at the tip of the hippocampus. It is an area that processes sensory information in a manner that integrates emotion with memory. The amygdala thereby plays a role in initiating reflexive emotional behavior. It also prompts reflective reasoning about appropriate modulation of emotional responses.

Another Way to See It

A medial view of your brain also provides a general perspective of its stem-to-cortex evolutionary progression. This view of the organization of brain structures is particularly helpful in examinations of how and why the brain exercises emotion and reason (as examined in Chapters 7 and 9).

The structures of your brain stem and cerebellum represent features of a brain system that evolved approximately 500 million years ago. These elements of a more primitive central nervous system were all that was required of life forms—such as reptiles—that featured highly programmed regulation of body systems and responses to the environment. If your life experience consists of fixed patterns of feeding, fighting, fleeing, and reproducing, you really do not need much more than a brain stem and a cerebellum. Modern-day reptiles provide ample evidence of the adequacy of such a brain for managing the basics of movement, respiration, and digestion.

The next major stage in brain evolution occurred in mammals that developed new structures around the top of the brain stem—including the thalamus, hippocampus, and amygdala—that enabled more sophisticated processing of information patterns. The development of these mammalian brain structures, commonly called the limbic system (from the Latin *limbus*, meaning "ring"), maintained the services of the reptilian brain structures while adding refined capacity for learning, memory, and emotional response. This brain structure also featured the early development of a primitive cortex that is suspected to have evolved from the information processing functions of the olfactory lobe.

As the survival needs of some mammals evolved to incorporate more elaborate multisensory information processing, your brain moved on to the next major stage of evolutionary development, leaving other mammals (e.g., rats, cats, dogs, and pigs) far behind in the qualities of complexity and capacity. The major feature of this stage is observed in the development of a large cerebrum covered by a folded and multilayered cortex, a development that was notable in primates and most dramatic in humans. This modern structure represents approximately 80% of your brain and contains the massive concentration of intricately connected nerve cells that enable conscious reasoning. It is thoroughly integrated with the structures and operations of the stem and limbic areas. Your brain is the product of progressive evolutionary developments, but you have one brain that incorporates the advantages of all its evolutionary stages.

Going Micro: Cells, Circuits, and Chemicals

Your exploration of brain features has been very basic to this point. Indeed, your examination has been very similar to that conducted by anyone across history (e.g., a warrior, artist, or surgeon) who has had the opportunity and disposition to dismantle a human brain. This general orientation to the physiology of the brain is certainly a necessary and helpful beginning to understanding the physiological platform that enables intelligence. Left at this stage, however, your investigation is comparable to observing the features of the earth from the vantage point of the moon. You have engaged the big geographic picture of brain structures, functions, and relationships. Now you are invited to move in for a closer look at the landscape. Using the power of advanced microtechnologies, you will bring into focus the cellular and chemical foundations of human intelligence.

To begin, we suggest that you place the two halves of your brain back together and rotate it 90 degrees. Now slice it vertically from top to bottom into an anterior (front) section and a posterior (rear) section. Putting the anterior section aside, you now have a vertical cross-sectional view of the central posterior brain (Figure 5.4) to orient your examination of neurons, glial cells, dendrites, axons, myelination, synapses, and neurotransmitters.

Matter Gray and White

Your first observational experience with the microstructure of your brain will note that which is visible to the naked eye. However you slice it, a cross-section of the brain immediately reveals a coloration difference between dark and pale areas. The darker areas are commonly called the *gray matter*, and the lighter areas are called the *white matter*. Gray matter areas get their dark hue from the concentration of brain cells known as neurons in the compact six layers of the cerebral cortex and in concentrated clusters called nuclei in the thalamus, hypothalamus, basal ganglia, brain stem, and other areas of the brain. White matter areas draw color from the fatty white substance called *myelin* that coats fibers known as axons, which extend from *neurons* as communication channels to other neurons in the brain, both near and far. Given this visual image and basic background of information, you can see that your brain's cellular

Figure 5.4   Vertical Cross-Sectional View of the Central Posterior Human Brain

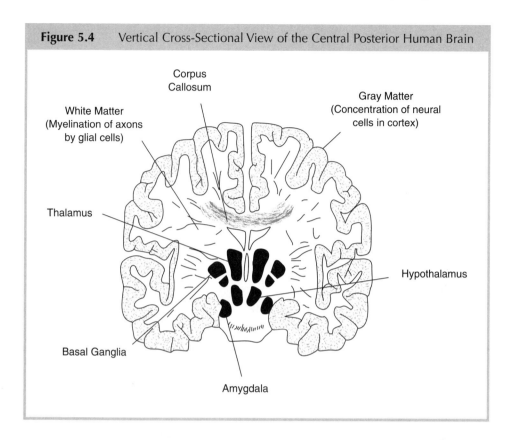

organization concentrates neurons in specific sectors (e.g., the cerebral cortex) and then connects those sectors through axonal networks (e.g., the corpus callosum). An impression emerges of a system of interconnected systems. Different sectors have specialized capacities, but these sectors are intricately coordinated in communication and function.

The Neural Landscape

Your investigation of your brain must now rely on technological revelations about cellular structure and activity beyond the view of the human eye. It is this microscopic examination of gray and white matter that explains how your larger brain structures perform their magic.

The neuron is the principal cellular unit of the central nervous system (i.e., the brain). These cells are the units that receive, integrate, and transmit electrochemical signals in neural networks that produce body movement and mental activity. Indeed, all human behavior is the result of communication between neural cells. The three main components of a neural cell that collectively serve this information processing responsibility are the *cell body,* an output fiber called the *axon,* and multiple input fibers called *dendrites* (Figure 5.5). This communication process works as follows:

1. Dendrite input fibers receive *neurotransmitter* (i.e., chemical) information from other neurons.

2. The information received triggers electric energy in the dendrite that is then interpreted by the cell body to be either inhibitory or excitatory.
   - Inhibitory input causes the cell to rest.
   - Excitatory input drives the cell body to generate an action potential (i.e., an electrical impulse that results from the interaction of positively and negatively charged ions of sodium, potassium, calcium, and chloride across the cell membrane).

3. The axon conducts the electrical impulse as a stimulant to the release of neurotransmitters stored in vesicle sacs in its terminal ports.

4. The neurotransmitters float into a *synapse*, a small space between the axon and a dendrite extension from another neuron (see Figure 5.5).

5. Receptors on a dendrite receive the neurotransmitters, and the process is thus initiated in another neuron.

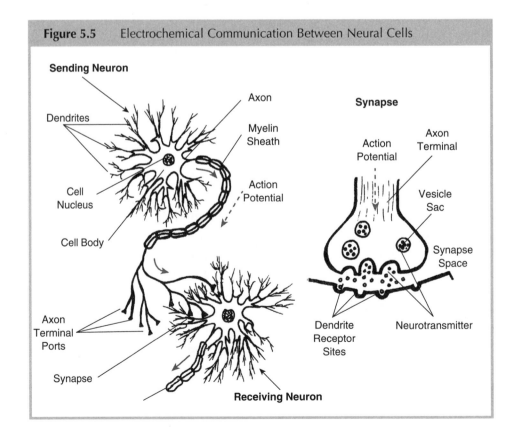

Figure 5.5   Electrochemical Communication Between Neural Cells

Simply stated, neurons are your brain's communication agents. They talk to one another through exchanges of electrochemical codes. You can visualize the process by looking at your right hand and arm. The palm of your hand represents the cell body of a neuron. Your fingers and thumb represent the dendrite extensions. When the dendrites receive a chemically coded message from a synapse interaction with another neuron (wiggle your fingers), that code may generate the firing of an electrical impulse (arch the palm of your hand), which is then conducted by the axon to its terminal ports (follow the movement of the impulse from the palm of your hand to the tip of your elbow), where the stimulation causes the release of select chemicals into a synapse space between the axon terminal and a dendrite of another neuron (wiggle the fingers of your left hand next to your right elbow). Thus the conversation moves from neuron to neuron.

Although this process can be visualized simply, it is much more difficult to comprehend in its full complexity and capacity. The human brain has a communication community of an estimated 100 billion neurons, which are concentrated in layers in the cerebral cortex and nuclei clusters in other brain structures, such as the thalamus, hypothalamus, hippocampus, amygdala, and brain stem. These neurons use nerve fibers and additional neurons in the spinal cord and hormone transmissions in the bloodstream to communicate with and manage the entire body system. Consider further that approximately 30,000 neurons can fit on the head of a pin and that a single neuron may use hundreds of dendritic branches to communicate with tens of thousands of other neurons (picture yourself having an ongoing conference call conversation with as many people!), each of which is linked to a like number of other neurons within a collective network that approximates a quadrillion (that's right, a million billion) neural connections. And all of this action takes place at a very fast pace, with action impulses traveling down axons at speeds of up to 220 miles per hour—which may not seem extraordinarily fast until the distance covered is considered. With that perspective, the word *instantaneous* may come to mind (just as these words come to mind the instant you read them). If you put this statistical information together with reference to the complex body management and thinking tasks performed by the neural community within a human skull, a picture should begin to emerge of the awesome power of the neural engine that drives human intelligence.

The Supporting Cellular Cast

The work of neurons is supported by an estimated 1 trillion *glial cells*. More formally called interneurons or neuroglia, glial (from Greek for "glue") cells provide the physical structure for the movement and organization of neurons in your brain. They also deliver nutrition and other maintenance services to neurons and form insulating *myelin* shields (i.e., white matter) around the axons of neurons. The myelination process is particularly important because the production of this fatty coating both protects and increases the efficiency of communication signals between neurons throughout your brain. A useful mental picture, then, is that of a 10:1 ratio between the supporting cast of glial cells and the starring neural cells that produce mental activity and body movement. Glial cells provide the support that enables neural networks to perform dazzling feats of information processing.

Messengers

Neurons are the communication agents of the brain, but neurotransmitters are the chemical messengers used to do the actual communication footwork. Many different chemicals are at work in and around the cellular structures of your brain, perhaps as many as 100 different compounds. The word *neurotransmitter* is itself a general term that describes an array of chemicals that carry information in your brain. Neurotransmitters are generated and stored in neurons and, in response to excitatory stimulation, are released to be received by other neurons. It is by interpreting these chemically coded transmissions of information that neurons "talk" to each other and collectively monitor functions and direct behavior.

The major types of neurotransmitters are *amino acids*, derivatives of amino acids called *amines*, and constructions of amino acids called *neuropeptides*. Amino acid neurotransmitters such as *glutamate, glycine, aspartate*, and *gamma-aminobutyric acid* directly carry rapid inhibitory and excitatory messages between neurons, thus performing essential on–off roles in neural communication. Amines are often called *neuromodulators* because they generally act at the synapse to modulate the reception of the amino acid neurotransmitters at the target neuron. Common amine neurotransmitters include the following:

- *Epinephrine.* Also known as adrenaline, epinephrine is produced and active in your brain and as a hormone in the adrenal glands above the kidneys (a hormone is a chemical, usually a peptide or steroid, that is generated and released into the bloodstream from one part of the body to influence a physiological effect in other parts of the body). In both its neurotransmitter and hormone roles, epinephrine functions as a messenger that engages your brain in the communication of a stress response throughout the body.
- *Norepinephrine.* Also known as noradrenaline, norepinephrine is similar in composition and function to epinephrine. It is also produced as a hormone in the adrenal glands. Norepinephrine is the

neurotransmitter most involved in the arousal of alertness and the fight-or-flight response that stimulates the eyes, heart, lungs, and muscles while inhibiting the activity of the digestive and reproduction systems.

- *Dopamine.* Dopamine is involved in the communication of body movement and positive moods or pleasure; imbalances of dopamine are associated with Parkinson's disease and schizophrenia.
- *Serotonin.* Serotonin is associated with relaxation and the regulation of mood and sleep; depletion of serotonin has been linked to depression. Antidepressant drugs are designed to reduce the absorption and prolong the activity of serotonin in synapses.
- *Acetylcholine.* Although it is not truly an amine, acetylcholine is often associated with that group of neurotransmitters because of its capacity to modulate and directly excite or inhibit neural communications. It is associated primarily with muscular movement and memory formation.

Neuropeptides are neurotransmitters composed of chains of amino acids that are produced and active in your brain, primarily as neuromodulators. Peptides are also produced elsewhere in your body, where they perform a hormonal role, particularly in the stomach as a part of the biological mechanism of "gut instinct." Representative neuropeptide neurotransmitters are *endorphins* (your brain's natural opiates), which are associated with pain reduction and feelings of pleasure and euphoria.

A Work in Progress

A mind once stretched never returns to its original shape.

—Anonymous

Your examination of microlevel brain architecture and activity reveals the physiological foundation of intelligence. It is at this level that the communication of electrochemically encoded information within an integrated community of many billions of neurons is observed. This is the process that manages and directs all human activity. It is a phenomenon that probably challenges your conscious brain's comprehension of its own complexity and potential. You may be understandably impressed by the information processing marvel in your hand, a biological mass that makes the most sophisticated computer technology look primitive in comparison. But that is as it must be, given that the information processing capacity of the human brain conceives and creates the information processing capacity of computer technology.

The news about human information-processing capacity gets even better if you observe brain cellular activity over time. Such observation reveals an extended development schedule, one that is literally lifelong. To observe the developmental experience of the human brain, you will once again use the visual enhancement advantages of microtechnology. This time, however, you will reference time-lapsed video footage of the biological history of your brain's development.

Your historical investigation begins with the observation of your *neurogenesis* (i.e., development of your nervous system) in your mother's womb. About 3 weeks after your conception, mesoderm cells formed a flat structure called the *neural plate* on the backside of your embryo formation. In the following week, this plate folded inward to seal at the top and ends, forming a *neural tube*. The neural tube then became the structure that developed into your central nervous system. The anterior region evolved into your forebrain, midbrain, and hindbrain, and the posterior region became your spinal cord.

Viewing the film record of your prenatal brain development, you will be impressed with both the quantity and quality of construction activity. You observe brain cells being generated at a rate of hundreds of thousands per minute during the remainder of your gestation period, producing an abundance of neurons that exceeds your eventual needs. These neurons then migrate to organized layers and clusters of the interconnected structures of your brain according to the genetic blueprint of the human genome you inherited from your parents. This migration is facilitated by *radial glia* (a type of glial cell) that provide scaffolding systems by which neurons find their way to the layers of the cortex and other predetermined locations. As your neurons collect at their designated stations, they begin to form synaptic connections and test initial communication networks by spontaneously firing electrical impulses. During this process your developing brain generates many more neurons and connections than will survive to the time of your birth. The apparent reason for this prolific production and networking of cells is to ensure the eventual success of neural communication systems. Accordingly, neurons that fail to migrate to the right location or establish proficient synaptic connections are pruned away to make way for the cellular networks that prove to be most advantageous to your brain's survival mission.

As you follow your brain's progress into the seventh month of development, you will note that the generation of neurons is complete and that neural pruning is under way long before you are born. You will also observe the development of convolutions in the cortical region as your brain begins to engage the structures and networks associated with sensory organs and the processing of environmental information. This brain development is what prepared you to come into the world hardwired to recognize sounds, shapes, and other sensory patterns. As a matter of fact, you began to use this cortical region to organize and distinguish patterns of sensory information (the initiation of your human capacity to learn) while still in the womb. Accordingly, you were familiar with various environmental patterns—such as your mother's voice—on your arrival into the world.

Now, to realize and appreciate a defining characteristic of brain development, fast-forward the video record of your brain's cellular activity from birth to adolescence. What you will observe from this quick graphic survey of the youth of your brain is that it continually engages in the generation, restructuring, and pruning of neural networks. Your brain does this as a result of genetic directions for the timely construction of communication channels that serve developmental events in your life, such as mastery of visual and auditory acuity, bipedal mobility, and language. However, there is also a determining element of environmental influence in this precocious networking activity. The basic rule at work here is that networks that are stimulated and productive are networks that are promoted and supported. A neuron will initially commit to associations with other neurons if there is either genetic direction or environmental stimulation to do so. Lacking sufficient exercise of electrochemical interaction, however, a neuron will either seek other neural relationships or simply die. Thus, neural networks associated with your ability to move, see, hear, talk, read, write, and solve problems are genetically installed in your brain and then refined or diminished by environmental experience.

As you continue your video review, you will observe surges of neural network expansion, restructuring, and pruning during strategic periods of your childhood and adolescent development. These surges mirror progressive developmental stages, such as mastery of motor skills, language, and abstract thinking. An important point to make, however, is that modification of neural networking is always occurring in your brain, to a greater or lesser extent, throughout its development to a mature brain at about 16 years of age. Referencing time-sequenced atomic microscope imaging, you will notice the collective product of genetically induced and environmentally nurtured development. Specifically, you will see extensive bifurcation (branching) of dendrites and myelination of axons extending from the neurons that originated in the womb many years earlier. This growth of bushy dendrites increases the mass of gray matter, and the myelinated sheathing of axons increases the mass of white matter. Together, the addition of gray and white matter contributes to the significant weight increase that occurs in a human brain between birth (approximately 1 pound) and maturity (approximately 3 pounds).

This brain maturation process is exceedingly long in humans, reflecting biological commitment and adaptation to the qualities of the adult product. Simply put, by allowing progressive and ongoing modification of neural networking over a prolonged period of time, nature produces an extraordinary physiological capacity for information processing. And here is the kicker—the really good news and a salient reference point about adult brains—this trait of neural modifiability, often called *plasticity*, will continue throughout your lifetime.

In effect, the human brain is never complete. Studies conducted by Diamond, Krech, and Rosenzweig (1964), Greenough and Black (1992), and others have firmly established the positive effect of environmental enrichment on dendritic branching, synapse formation, and axon myelination in animals of all ages. Investigations of the effects of aging on the mental acuity of human subjects by Schaie and Willis (1986) and Snowdon (2001) are representative studies that draw the same conclusion: Capacity to learn and thereby maintain and reconfigure neural networks throughout the lifespan is strongly correlated with the richness of environmental experience. Specific enrichment factors for humans include level of education, physical activity that enhances blood flow and oxygenation, professional and cultural activities that introduce novelty and challenge, perception of accomplishment and making a difference, and hanging out with smart people. Thus the physiological base of human intelligence is factory installed, but it is a base that is perpetually under construction.

All in all, it is a pretty good deal. You are given a genetic endowment of more neurons than you need and the capacity to continually capitalize on and refine what you are given. It is a good deal if you take advantage of it. You need to apply environmental stimulation to that end because it is not only a matter of using it or losing it; it is a matter of using and continually adjusting your neural architecture to ongoing advantage.

Maintaining the System

The relationship between food, physical activity, and learning is hardwired into the brain's circuitry.

—Ratey and Hagerman (2008, p. 3)

Stepping back from your technologically enhanced review of the cellular nature of your brain, you are once again observing a 3-pound biological mass resting in the palm of your hand. As you move to replace it in its cranial nest, however, you might engage in one more reflections about its physiological circumstance, the quite obvious observation that your brain is connected to your body. A more specific observation is that your brain has a reciprocal arrangement with your body. The brain's business is the survival and welfare of its host body, and the brain is in turn dependent on the body for its own welfare. But ultimately, it is your brain that has the responsibility to make conscious decisions about these mutual welfare issues, and a wise brain takes good care of that which cares for it.

Your brain consumes approximately 20% of your body's supply of energy (mostly in the form of glucose) in the process of operating and maintaining its neural networks. This is a high energy demand for a biological system that represents only 2% of your body weight. This energy is obtained primarily from the flow of blood through the carotid artery, which supplies the brain with high levels of oxygen and nutrients such as glucose, protein, and trace elements. Because of its high water composition, your brain also needs extensive and regular hydration. Other physiological welfare needs include regular exposure to light (preferably natural) and opportunities to rest.

Your body serves the multiple welfare needs of your brain. The body provides nutrients and environmental activities that affect the brain, either directly or indirectly. So what should your brain communicate to its body about its welfare needs? Well, that topic can be exhaustively pursued through a review of related literature about diet, exercise, mental health, and the like. But a quick and serviceable response to the question is that Mom was right. That is, common cultural knowledge about healthy living practices—as traditionally communicated by mothers to children—is very much attuned to optimizing the brain–body relationship. Specific examples are the following:

- Eat balanced meals of fruits, vegetables (particularly leafy greens, broccoli, beans), fish (a good source of omega-3 fatty acid), lean meats, whole grains, nuts, eggs, and dairy products that provide the proteins, unsaturated fats, minerals, and complex carbohydrates that nurture brain health and operation.
- Drink plenty of water, 8 to 12 glasses per day.
- Exercise and change body position often to enhance blood oxygenation and flow.
- Get a good night's sleep, and try to take brief naps during the day.
- Get out into the fresh air and natural light as much as possible.
- Breathe deeply and laugh often.
- Minimize sugar, alcohol, caffeine, fast food, artificial flavorings, and additives.
- Tobacco and other drugs? What would Mom say?

Commonsense care of your body has probably always been a matter of concern to you. As you replace the top of your skull and put your brain back into normal operation, however, you might now have a more refined perspective of what is at stake. Attention to your physical welfare is not only a matter of a healthy body; it is very much a matter of a healthy mind.

ESSENCE

No technology has received more attention from natural selection, more refinement via natural selection, than intelligence. Everywhere around us is evidence of the tendency of intelligence to grow through evolution. The most spectacular example, with all due modesty, is us.

—Wright (2000, p. 280)

The very brain that ponders the wonders of the universe has reason to stand in awe of itself as "the most complex structure, natural or artificial, on earth" (Green, Neinemann, & Gusella, 1998, p. 427). Whether you find the information in this chapter about brain physiology to be interesting or a bit tedious, it is important to understand and appreciate what the brain enables. The physiology of your brain provides a biological platform of enormous capacity for operating all other dimensions of intelligence. The relationship is more than that, however, in that the physical capacity that supports the social, emotional, constructive, reflective, and dispositional dimensions of intelligence is itself a product and a beneficiary of those same capacities. The exercise of that which physiological capacity enables in turn nurtures greater physiological capacity.

One might necessarily conclude that nature has composed the most complex and productive creation in the universe within your head. Your brain is a 3-pound collection of physiological structures that inter-actively regulate and operate all human behavior. Moreover, if not maintained and operated as nature intends, that creation will not realize its potential.

Is it advisable for a leader to dismiss the physiological underpinnings of intelligence? If not, what is most important to know about the physio-logical brain? The answer to those questions must ultimately be con-structed in the leader's brain, but from the information presented in this chapter, one might reasonably surmise that it is important to understand how the physiological brain is big, mind–body connected, high mainte-nance, and malleable.

Big

Human intelligence is physiologically enabled. It operates on a biological platform of cells, circuits, and chemicals that is virtually unlimited in its capacity for processing information. The physical capacity of your brain for productively acquiring and applying knowledge exceeds what might be commonly appreciated. Look at it this way: The danger is not that your brain will be required to process more than it can handle. Rather, the real jeopardy is that it will be underused.

Mind–Body Connected

The brain is connected to the entire physiology of the human body. It is a system of physiological systems within a physiological system. The brain is the body and the body is the brain, and what affects one affects the other. The body is a highly integrated extension of the brain. The entire physiology—hands, heart, stomach, and everything else—is intimately engaged in the work of the brain. Information processing is not limited to the body region between the ears and behind the eyes. The brain is in an information processing partnership with the body.

High Maintenance

Brain capacity for intelligence is affected by the care and nurture of its host system. To do its work well, the brain demands both quantity and quality in nutritional care and environmental experience. The advantages of the most complex brain on the planet come at a price. The brain's neural business requires high maintenance (e.g., hydration, nutrition, rest). Fitness of the body directly influences how the brain is supported and sustained in conducting its business.

Malleable

Every human brain, absent significant developmental miscues or physical trauma, is a powerful physiological system for processing information. However, each individual brain is rendered unique by its particular life experience.

Neural networks in the brain are modified by experience, and plasticity in learning continues throughout the lifespan. Intelligence capacity is not fixed but malleable by quality and quantity of environmental experience. Your brain is a work in progress. Dendrites will branch and axons will strengthen by virtue of experience.

Some neural networks in the brain are genetically dedicated to regulatory operations (e.g., respiration, body temperature) and, once established, do not change over the lifespan. Other networks are genetically generated and environmentally reinforced for the operation of specific functions such as vision, movement, and language. The defining characteristic of the human brain, however, is the extensive expanse of neural circuitry that is undedicated and environmentally responsive. Concentrated in the cerebral cortex gray matter of the brain, these neural networks exercise a capacity for plasticity over the lifespan. They are responsive to novel situations and therefore continually construct networks that accommodate new understanding and skills. They also enable the sophisticated mental activities of projection, creativity, and problem solving. Most important, this capacity for generating environmentally stimulated neural networks establishes the physiological base of intelligence modifiability. Human intelligence continually evolves from environmental experience.

IMPLICATIONS

The more you work your heart and lungs, the more efficient they become at delivering oxygen to your body and brain. With the increased blood flow, of course, comes the chemical cascades that produce serotonin, brain-derived neurotrophic factor (BDNF), and other nourishing molecules.

—Ratey and Hagerman (2008, p. 251)

Describing a physiologically big, connected, demanding, and malleable brain sets the stage for contemplating what might be done to nurture what nature provides. It seems reasonable that one would attend to the care of the organ that underlies every quality of what it means to be human. To that end, for example, one would seek to support the physiological platform that enables intelligence by attending to brain fitness and stimulating neural networks (Figure 5.6).

Attend to Brain Fitness

The information processing capacity of the brain is enabled by a biological platform of cells, circuits, and chemicals that is dependent on care from its host body. Everything the brain experiences through its sensory mechanisms and body connections affects its performance. Accordingly, a leader will attend to brain fitness through practices that promote movement, exercise, nutrition, and stress management.

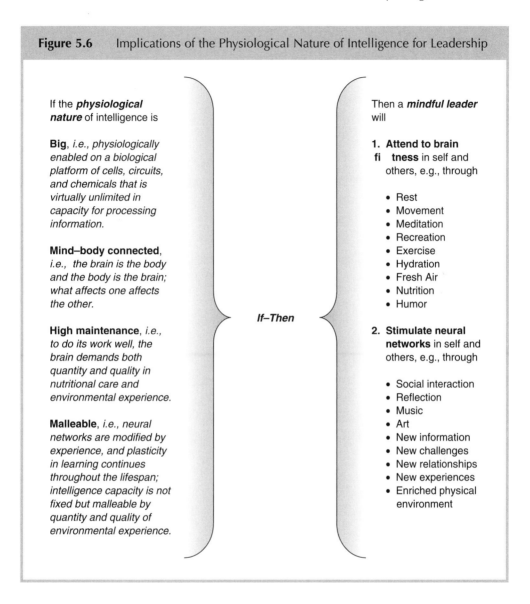

Figure 5.6 Implications of the Physiological Nature of Intelligence for Leadership

If the *physiological nature* of intelligence is

Big, *i.e., physiologically enabled on a biological platform of cells, circuits, and chemicals that is virtually unlimited in capacity for processing information.*

Mind–body connected, *i.e., the brain is the body and the body is the brain; what affects one affects the other.*

High maintenance, *i.e., to do its work well, the brain demands both quantity and quality in nutritional care and environmental experience.*

Malleable, *i.e., neural networks are modified by experience, and plasticity in learning continues throughout the lifespan; intelligence capacity is not fixed but malleable by quantity and quality of environmental experience.*

If–Then

Then a *mindful leader* will

1. **Attend to brain fitness** in self and others, e.g., through

   - Rest
   - Movement
   - Meditation
   - Recreation
   - Exercise
   - Hydration
   - Fresh Air
   - Nutrition
   - Humor

2. **Stimulate neural networks** in self and others, e.g., through

   - Social interaction
   - Reflection
   - Music
   - Art
   - New information
   - New challenges
   - New relationships
   - New experiences
   - Enriched physical environment

Stimulate Neural Networks

Neural networks continue to develop throughout the lifespan according to the quality and quantity of environmental experience. Accordingly, a leader will engineer experiences involving social interaction, meaningful challenge, novelty, and rich sensory stimulation.

READER REFLECTION

- What is essential to know and do about the physiological nature of intelligence?

6 Social Nature

In humans, our need to engage in social reasoning—particularly coordination and cooperation as well as competition—drove the evolution of our larger brain size and of intelligence generally.

—Goleman (2006, p. 329)

GETTING TO KNOW YOU AND ME AND WE

Our brains evolved from a rich history of social experience. Qualities of brain size, architecture, consciousness, and capacity for language and cognition are all traced to social roots. The physiological structure of the brain is the platform on which intelligence performs, but social experience is an influential architect and operator of the platform. Understanding why and how your brain is social, therefore, is important to understanding the intelligent mind the brain enables. To that end, this chapter examines the socially hyper, expectant, dependent, extended, and virtuous nature of the brain (Figure 6.1).

THE GIST OF IT

Social disposition is something that most of us intuitively understand and appreciate. Kipling captured the concept in a classic observation.

> *Now this is the Law of the Jungle—*
>
> *As old and true as the sky;*
>
> *And the Wolf that shall keep it may prosper,*

But the Wolf that shall break it must die.

As the creeper that girdles the tree trunk,

The law runneth forward and back—

For the strength of the Pack is the Wolf,

And the strength of the Wolf is the Pack.

—Kipling

Figure 6.1   The Social Nature of Intelligence

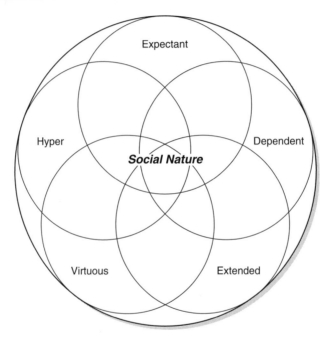

The **social nature** of intelligence is

Hyper: *Born of rich social experience over millions of years, the human brain is endowed with hyper social instincts: natural and powerful abilities for memory, language, empathy, sympathy, collaboration, and reasoning.*

Expectant: *The unfolding of brain capacity to think, learn, and achieve is expectant of the same social experience that constructed it.*

Dependent: *Social experience is the great provocateur of thinking and learning.*

Extended: *To satisfy its overarching need and disposition to interact in a society of mind, the human brain has invented a variety of media that extend social interaction beyond face-to-face encounters.*

Virtuous: *The brain has an instinctive moral orientation to prosocial behavior.*

Nature's Way

To understand why your brain is social, you need to start at the beginning, with the subatomic particles spawned at the origin of the universe that organized into atomic structures, which in turn organized as the basic molecules present in the gas cloud of the protoearth. These basic molecules organized into more complex chemical compositions as the earth formed its solid mass and cooled to a temperature that supported liquid water. Taking advantage of this condition approximately 3.5 million years ago, webs of interacting molecules complex enough to exhibit qualities associated with life (i.e., the ability to metabolize, reproduce, and evolve) organized into cellular life forms. Nature thus demonstrated from the very beginning a dispositional pattern of organizing simple structures into complex and evolving systems. This pattern prevailed in creating a "world of stunning complexity where molecules join in a metabolic dance to form cells, cells interact with cells to form organisms, and organisms interact with organisms to form ecosystems, economies and societies" (Kauffman, 1995, p. vii). Thus the human brain is first and foremost the product of nature's propensity to organize parts into systems, be they atoms or galaxies. Your brain exhibits this character as the most complex cellular and molecular system on Earth. Furthermore, it is a system that is disposed to interact with like brain systems to organize and interact in a vast array of social systems, ranging from families and teams to governments and religions.

Selfish gene theory provides further interpretation as to why the human brain is, in its biological essence, social. This theory proposes that individual life forms consistently do things that promote the survival of their genes. From the very beginning of life on Earth individual cells and organisms engaged in altruistic and cooperative behavior as the means to improve the chances that their common genetic code would survive, replicate, and participate in natural selection. Thus genes direct host cells in the organization of host organisms that range from simple bacteria to the mass and complexity of whales. Repetition of this pattern is observed as organisms formed by societies of cells in turn organize societies of like organisms. Exemplars of such cooperative societies include ants, termites, bees, wolves, dolphins, and, of course, humans and their primate relatives.

Behind the biological development and operation of complex systems, then, is the principle that genes are selfish and cooperation works. Genes form chromosomes, chromosomes form genomes, genomes form cells, cells form complex cells, complex cells form bodies, and bodies form colonies (Ridley, 1996). From this theoretical perspective, the human brain is both produced and directed by societies of genes dedicated to the construction of social systems that serve their purposes of replication and participation in natural selection. This phenomenon becomes most interesting when genes evolve to a point where they create a host organism (i.e., a human) that is aware of the process and in possession of advanced capacities for learning and surviving in unpredictable environments. At this stage, the organism's capacity for processing information, assessing alternatives, and predicting outcomes culminates in consciousness. It is at this point in a long evolutionary journey that humans realize the power to rebel against the dictates of their genes (Dawkins, 1991).

Three and a half billion years is a long time. Nevertheless, it is just a long preface to the story of the social nature of human intelligence. If cooperation is woven into the genetic structure of all living things, what is special about the social nature of humans? The pace of the story picks up as we fast-forward to mere millions of years ago, when our ancestors began to realize the benefits of living in social relationships with like organisms, and one thing led to another.

The Experience

I sense that stepping into the light is also a powerful metaphor for consciousness, for the birth of the knowing mind, for the simple and yet momentous coming of the sense of self in the world of the mental.

—Damasio (1999, p. 3)

More than 50 million years ago our primate ancestors generated a large brain size through a propensity for good cost–benefit calculations and associative learning in pursuit of food sources (Mithen, 1996). Individuals also benefited from living in social colonies, which offered extended vigilance and protection from enemies, including the calculated probability that predators would harvest members of the group who were slower and more accessible than themselves. Greater numbers of eyes, ears, noses, and limbs enhanced the scavenging and foraging of food. Variables of group size and proximity favored mating opportunities. All of these circumstances enhanced prospects for survival, reproduction, and the natural selection of advantageous physiological adaptations.

Beyond the immediate advantages of cooperative group living was the pervasive and determining effect of social interaction on the nature of the brain. In effect, the context of social existence became the cauldron in which human intelligence coalesced. You can best understand this by using that very intelligence to reflect on what your ancestors' social existence would provide, need, and reward.

Specifically, it was important to be attuned to the other members of the group if one were to take advantage of early warnings or communication of other important information. This need encouraged the development of refined sensory processing of visual and auditory information aligned to the body and vocal signals of associates. The name of the game was (and still is) that those who could best discern from verbal or nonverbal information what other members were doing, or were likely to do, had a survival edge. This skill in interpreting communication cues became an important means for establishing relationships and hierarchies among members of a group, resulting in enhanced collaboration in surveillance, food gathering, and problem solving. It also promoted capacity for memory of individuals, events, relationships, geography, and food sources. Ultimately, it placed a high premium on being attuned to the emotional status of others as a variable in anticipating behavior and opportunities.

The acquisition of emotional acuity was a pivotal development in the evolution of primates. It emerged from the refinement of social observation skills over millions of years to produce a sense of empathy and sympathy for the experiences of others. It was a development that encouraged acuity in recognizing and communicating a wide range of emotional experiences. It also laid the emotional groundwork for moral and artistic reflection. The neural ability to perceive what another was experiencing encouraged the reasoning operations involved in calculation, imagination, and moral judgment.

Siegel (1999) proposed that having this ability to "mind read" enabled rapid detection of the emotional state of another. In essence, our ancestors developed the neural ability to perceive and then feel what another member of the group was experiencing; they could get into the head of another and calculate options of reciprocity, cooperation, alliances, and deception. Most important, in the process of developing this capacity, they became aware of self as separate from the other. The operative term here is *aware*, as in consciousness. Social experience thereby moved beyond building brain capacity for organizing and processing environmental information to building a brain that was aware of its awareness. Thus informed, the selective pressure for what Humphrey (1976) called social intelligence was refined in the brains of advanced primates and early humans through hypothesis building and testing about the behaviors of others. By the time our modern human ancestors arrived on the scene approximately 100,000 years ago, this neural ability to infer, predict, and plan had become a defining species quality.

If the circumstance of social existence promoted mental capacity to anticipate behaviors and events, the infinite observation of what the other guy was doing also encouraged mimicking of behavior and associative learning. Most notably, approximately 2.5 million years ago, a human ancestor put together the neural patterns needed for tool making. This entry into tool technology was subsequently observed, mimicked, and refined through the advantage of social proximity. The social opportunity to observe a particular tool application (e.g., the breaking of animal bones with a stone hand axe) also promoted associative adaptations of that technology (e.g., the projection of a stone missile in the direction of an enemy or food source). Similarly, social observation and interaction facilitated brain organization of information about the natural environment, such as geographic markers and distribution of resources, habits of animals, and rhythms of seasons and plant growth.

This social aspect of learning is a constant in human experience and clearly evident in every instance of significant achievement. Advances in art, science, and technology are never the products of lone genius. The contributions of individuals are to be noted and respected, but no individual mind is unaffected by the minds of others. The landing of a vehicle on the moon, discovery of a cure for disease, or production of a work of art is always the accomplishment of a society of mind. Direct contributors to a specific technological, scientific, or cultural product deserve credit for their interpretation or refinement of information gleaned from other minds. But where is the mind that could or would profess an absence of neural bridging to the ideas and experiences of others?

Leading minds in contemporary fields, such as computer technology and medical research, are engaging in the same social learning practices as those used by early ancestors investigating hand tools and food sources; they observe what others are doing and then mimic and adapt what they observe. A discriminating advantage in contemporary social learning is the benefit of access to a greater range of other minds through multiple language communication vehicles.

Language itself is a product (many would say *the* product) of our ancestors' social experience. Dunbar (1993) proposes that this capacity first emerged as a social language within the intimacy of communal life. You can imagine the composition of meaningful sound patterns over millions of years that communicated information in the social proximity of grooming (e.g., "That feels good!"), tool making (e.g., "No! Hold it this way!"), and foraging (e.g., "This is a good place to search"). Progressively, repetitive vocal signaling patterns associated with specific activities promoted neural networks that were adept at recognizing and producing arrangements of sounds (e.g., Broca's area and Wernicke's area). Strings of sounds formed words, strings of words formed sentences, and syntax enabled infinite sentence constructions. Thus the neurological way was paved for the expeditious communication of information and ideas between brains—and the capacity for a brain to talk reflectively to itself.

The Picture in the Pieces

For as long as we have been around as humans, as wandering bands of nomads or cave dwellers, we have sat together and shared experiences. We have painted images on rock walls, recounted dreams and visions, told stories of the day, and generally felt comforted to be in the world together. When the world became fearsome, we came together. When the world called us to explore its edges, we journeyed together. Whatever we did, we did it together.

—Wheatley (2002, p. 4)

A picture emerges of a social shaping of the modern human brain that was prolonged and profound. This shaping experience was linear in the general terms of social acuity, leading to a level of consciousness that facilitated mental capacity for technology, reasoning, and language, but there was also a nonlinear aspect. It was not simply a matter of one thing leading to another; rather, it was a matter of many developments influencing one another at the prodding of a social existence. For example, among the many collateral developments during this long history of social experience, our ancestors were enticed by food sources to spend less time in trees and to master bipedalism. This evolutionary event encouraged brain growth of the neural circuitry needed for two-footed balance and sophisticated hand dexterity (e.g., as in the use of tools). Adaptation to upright posture also provided an elevated perspective for visual scanning of the landscape and reduced body exposure to the sun. Both of these effects enhanced scavenging opportunities for food, notably meat, in environments in which four-legged competitors were disadvantaged. Scavenging, in turn, further promoted social communication to coordinate division of labor in hunter–gatherer groups. Success in the acquisition of meat provided the clothing and shelter needed to survive in temperate climates and the rich protein diet needed for growing brain size and complexity. It also accommodated a longer lifespan and prolonged child development—and the further social learning and development opportunities thereof.

The evidence about the human brain's long history of social experience is abundant but also incomplete and yet to be definitively assembled. Archaeologist Steven Mithen (1996) surmised a sequential and modular development of social, technical, natural history, and language intelligence. These specialized intelligences eventually coalesced in a cognitive fluidity that integrated the contributions of each module. He proposed that this transition from a "Swiss army knife" modularity to a harmonization of mental abilities was provoked by language and facilitated by consciousness. In effect, the advancement of language ability allowed the conscious brain to share with itself and others what the various modules knew and were able to do. This breaking down of mental modular walls, Mithen (1996, pp. 194–195) concluded, enabled the imagination and creativity associated with the origin of art and religion during a cultural explosion in human development 60,000–30,000 years ago.

Neurologist Antonio Damasio (1999) reinforced the perspective that conscious awareness of self and surroundings was a critical turning point that opened human evolution to the creation of technology, science, art, conscience, religion, and social and political organization. The emergence of high consciousness in humans heralds the dawn of individual forethought, of minded organisms capable of shaping their environmental responses through mental awareness and concern for self. Damasio further observed that the neural underpinnings of consciousness enabled knowledge of emotional states such as sorrow or joy, suffering or pleasure, embarrassment or pride. He concluded that the emergence of high consciousness provided the key to a life examined, a learner's permit for knowing about and acting on the biological urge for self-preservation—an awareness that, at its most complex level, leads to concern for other selves and improvement of the art of life.

Theoretical neurophysiologist William Calvin (1996) arranged the pieces of the puzzle in somewhat similar fashion in his conjecture of a quantum leap in cleverness during human evolution. He acknowledged many contributing variables in a social context, including opportunities to observe and mimic, respond to novel situations, and develop sensory templates appropriate to a versatile diet. However, Calvin speculated that intelligence received a critical boost from the refinement of a core brain specialization, such as that associated with language. Specifically, the human brain developed a facility and passion for stringing things together. In the case of language it was sounds to words to sentences. But, as Calvin pointed out, improvement of multifunctional brain mechanisms that serve one critical function (i.e., language) might have had the effect of aiding other functions. Thus the neural mechanisms associated with the who, what, where, when, why, and how rules of language syntax might have been borrowed for other uses, such as the stringing of pieces and patterns of information together in analytic and creative processes before committing to an action.

This big picture of human social experience will continue to come into focus through ongoing investigation and debate by scholars in many fields of study. And although many important details are yet to be resolved, the prominent influence of social experience on the nature of human intelligence is beyond dispute. The neural networks forged by that evolutionary experience speak for themselves.

The Result

> *Relationship experiences have a dominant influence on the brain because the circuits responsible for social perception are the same as, or tightly linked to, those that integrate the important functions controlling the creation of meaning, the regulation of body states, the modulation of emotion, the organization of memory, and the capacity for interpersonal communication. Interpersonal experience thus plays a special organizing role in determining the development of brain structure early in life and the ongoing emergence of brain function throughout the life span.*
>
> —Siegel (1999, p. 21)

The social heritage of your brain's evolutionary experience is displayed in its physiological size and organization, emotional acuity, capacity to create and manipulate mental templates, and disposition to "figure things out." It is a dynamic society of cells and molecules, a biological system both formed by and open to environmental influence. As a result, we observe that social heritage in the brain as follows.

The brain is endowed with highly evolved mechanisms for social interaction. As Ridley (1996, p. 6) observed, "One of the things that marks humanity out from other species, and accounts for our ecological success, is our collection of hyper-social instincts." Capacity for semantic and syntactic language communication is an obvious and significant example of evolved neural mechanisms for social interaction. But the human brain has refined acuity for other communication vehicles as well, such as voice inflection and body language. For example, humans and other primates are the only animals that have muscle endings in their facial skin. This quality is connected to neural networks that direct and interpret an extensive repertoire of facial expressions. Accordingly, your brain is always qualifying the verbal messages directed by or to you by accompanying visual and auditory information about the face and tone that delivers it. Refined social instincts are also facilitated by your sensory capacities for smell, taste, and touch. Much of this sensory processing of social information occurs at a subconscious level, but you become consciously aware of it as you revel in the aroma, feel the tension, taste the fear, read between the lines, and experience gut feelings in your interactions with other people.

The evolution of consciousness generated neural networking that accommodates meaning, memory, emotion, and reflection. An enriched social existence in diverse habitats valued the construction of mental templates that organized useful environmental information from extensive sensory stimuli. It was important to be able to store and retrieve who, what, where, when, why, and how information. Most notably, cerebral space expanded to serve the reflective manipulation of information involved in calculation, planning, and imagination. These neural networks in the frontal lobes and other cortical and subcortical areas also evolved to mediate the awareness and management of emotions. Collectively, a community of neural networks emerged—a system of socially inspired communication channels that shared information and expertise for survival purposes. Thus your brain is wired with a highly integrated capacity to learn, remember, reason, and manage emotions to good effect—a capacity that is most effectively actualized in a context similar to the social environment that engineered it.

The social nature of the brain requires social unfolding of its potential. The idea that ontogeny (the developmental stages of an individual organism) recapitulates phylogeny (the evolutionary stages of a species) is a concept that is often used—and debated—in biological inquiry. In general application, it is a concept that is useful to the understanding of the social nature of human intelligence. Specifically, you know from prior examination of brain physiology that the fundamental work of the human brain occurs through the flow of electrochemically encoded information at the neural cell level. You also know that the formation and growth of neural networks is both genetically and environmentally directed. In the case of the evolutionary development of your human brain (its phylogeny), the social experience of your ancestors over time favored the development of specific neural networks. These networks progressively influenced the genetic adaptations that recently served as the blueprint for the construction and operation of your individual brain. But the developmental experience of your brain during your lifetime (its ontogeny) requires relationships with its environment, particularly interpersonal relationships, to realize its potential. The unfolding of your brain's genetic program depends on social experience. In effect, "human connections shape the neural connections from which the mind emerges" (Siegel, 1999, p. 2).

The brain is experience expectant and experience dependent. The experience expectations of the human brain are most readily observed in the genetically generated excess of neural networks that occur at various times in development from birth through adolescence. It is as if nature constructs networks with the expectation that they will eventually have something to do (much like a communication company constructing a cable grid in anticipation of future subscribers). And that is indeed what nature is doing. Neurons are created in abundance and placed in prescribed locations, with dendritic and axonal extensions at the ready.

Some of these networks are engaged and dedicated to subconscious regulation of body systems (e.g., cardiovascular) by a genetic program that remains constant throughout the lifespan. However, other networks expect stimulation as cues for their engagement and refinement of operation. Experiencing such stimulation, these preliminary networks are extended, reinforced, and pruned to greater efficiency. Early childhood examples of this process are the requirements for environmental stimulation of networks that are ready and willing to do sight, hearing, language, and various motor skills. These are critical use-it-or-lose-it requirements that are commonly met in normal human environments.

Greenough, Black, and Wallace (1987) proposed that the experience-expectant mechanisms of the human brain represent an aspect of plasticity that takes advantage of the commonalties of human environments to fine-tune fundamental neural networks. A related feature, he advised, is experience-dependent plasticity. Whereas your experience-expectant brain exercises a "sculpting" effect in pruning and refining neural networks, your experience-dependent brain exercises an influence on the growth and strengthening of new neural networks. This plasticity is what allows your brain to learn from unique experience in specific environments. It is the brain's mechanism for creating networks from experience that is not expected—an important quality given that the brain must acquire and adjust knowledge across its lifespan in whatever environment it happens to find itself. Notably, the experience-expectant and experience-dependent requirements of your brain are not limited to your childhood development. You will recall that brain development is a lifelong event, that neural networks are constantly being refined and adjusted at the bidding of environmental experience. What is a matter of development in the child becomes a matter of refinement and maintenance in the adult.

At any age, interpersonal interaction is important to the effective engagement, refinement, or creation of neural networks associated with your senses, movement, thinking, emotions, and use of language. The sensory and cognitive stimulation you received through prolonged interpersonal relationships with your parents or other adults was absolutely critical to the development of your adult brain and its intelligence capacity. But your adult brain continues to respond to social intimacies of touch, voice, facial expression, and shared thoughts. In fact, direct social interaction with other humans is the primary means by which you develop, maintain, and adjust your emotional and cognitive competencies throughout your lifetime (supplemented, as we shall discuss in the following section, by various indirect media for interpersonal interaction). Interaction with the physical environment is also necessary and important to the experience expectation and dependency of the brain, but social interaction is the foil that most effectively sharpens your exotic neural circuitry. Simply put, social interaction is what the brain expects and depends on—no less than lungs expect and depend on oxygen.

The brain seeks ways to expand its opportunities to interact with other brains. The influence of social experience on human evolution produced the big neural breakthrough of complex language capacity. This endowment was of tremendous value to the communication of information in early human communities and a defining factor in the further advancement of human intelligence. But this evolutionary gift was applied to even greater effect when your ancestors invented written language more than 5,000 years ago. In effect, the human brain that evolved the capacity for verbal language came to appreciate this advantage so much that it created a means to transfer it to graphic form, thereby extending its reach and power. Through this development, human communication moved beyond direct face-to-face interaction to an expanded society of minds—a society that included the recorded knowledge and ideas of brains that were distant in space and time. This communication innovation also demonstrated the brain's capacity and disposition to take charge of its experience dependency. By creating written records of ideas and knowledge, the brain enriched its prospects for new learning and neural growth.

The invention of written language has been followed by other initiatives to affect the scale and quality of human interactions. Such initiative is demonstrated in the technologies of print, photography, telephone, radio, film, television, and—most recently—the Internet. These communication vehicles, augmented by the invention of transportation technologies and a wide variety of art forms, have greatly expanded the means by which humans have access to one another's minds and, as observed by Friedman (2005, p. 8), continues to do so: "Clearly, it is now possible for more people than ever to collaborate and compete in real time with more people on more different kinds of work from more different corners of the planet and on a more even footing than at any previous time in the history of the world."

It is the nature of your brain to continually search for means by which it can be more social. This nurture is demonstrated by the progressive development of media for social interaction—from language to global computer networks. It is a nature that arises from the survival mission of the brain. There is safety and survival advantage in social membership. That advantage is enhanced by social interactions that network the collective knowledge of all members, whether they be present, distant, or deceased.

Social experience provides moral orientation. The human measure of what is right and what is wrong is influenced by millions of years of species evolution in a social context. As Pinker (2002, p. 59) observed, "Morality, after all, did not enter the universe with the Big Bang and then pervade it like background radiation. It was discovered by our ancestors after billions of years of the morally indifferent process known as natural selection." That is, the golden rule is neither chance observation nor the enlightened discovery of world religions that universally embrace it. It is a good and golden rule because it is good for the survival of the species, as discovered over long evolutionary time in pervasive social context. Your moral perception of what is good and what is bad reaches back to the social origins of what is good and just for all: to be safe, sheltered, fed, loved, and free. As humans, we have evolved to a profound prosocial nature in which "moral judgments are mediated by an unconscious process, a hidden moral grammar that evaluates the causes and consequences of our own and others' actions" (Hauser, 2006, p. 2).

Social experience actualizes human intelligence. In adult life, interaction with the brains of others—whether through direct face-to-face encounters or indirect media—continues to be the primary means by which you exercise and refine your intellectual capacities. You engage the knowledge and ideas of others through observation, conversation, dialogue, debate, reading, writing, and artistic representations. Social interaction creates a flow of energy and information within and between the neural networks of individuals. Such interaction stimulates emotional attention, pattern recognition, cognitive dissonance, and reflective reasoning. It physically affects electrochemical activity in participating brains and, in response to a quantity and quality of stimulation, stimulates neural network growth and rewiring. It is how you refine your emotional being, resolve your beliefs, and think your best thoughts.

ESSENCE

We live in towns, work in teams, and our lives are spider works of connections—linking us to relatives, colleagues, companions, friends, superiors, inferiors. We are, misanthropes notwithstanding, unable to live without each other. . . . We are far more dependent on other members of our species than any other species of ape or monkey. We are more like ants or termites that live as slaves to their societies. We define virtue almost exclusively as pro-social behavior.

—Ridley (1996, p. 6)

Human affinity for interactive systems is observed not only in the brain but also in the genes. The human organism is composed and maintained as a system of interactive molecular and cellular relationships. The brain is disposed to replicate the pattern of its own interactive molecular and cellular organization by establishing interactive relationships with other brains. The pattern of colonies of interactive neurons forming brains is thus replicated as colonies of interactive brains forming social systems.

Social existence is a survival strategy that is common to animals and a strong environmental influence on the evolution of intelligence (e.g., as observed in dolphins, dogs, and primates). The influence of social experience in human evolution is unique in relation to collateral developments such as bipedalism, scavenging efficiency, division of labor, diversification of diet, adaptation to temperate climates, extension of lifespan, and prolonged juvenile development. This mix of evolutionary development within social experience ultimately generated a larger brain structure with highly refined neural capacities.

The general scenario is that social proximity stimulated expansion of neural capacity for constructing and storing patterns of information. This expanded capacity for information patterns facilitated neural awareness of the emotional states and behaviors of others, which prompted a conscious neural awareness of self. Refined awareness of self in relation to others, in turn, encouraged neural networking that enabled language and reflective reasoning. This species progress was synergistic as different advancements (e.g., capacities for language and reflective reasoning) evolved together and stimulated further developments.

All this is to say that despite appearances to the contrary, a human brain is extremely social. Granted, at times people exhibit shy or withdrawn behavior but seldom to the exclusion of all interaction with other minds in the media forms of books, newspapers, magazines, radio, television, telephones, or the Internet. The social nature of your capacity to think, learn, and achieve is commanding. It both requires and facilitates interaction with other brains. Denied such opportunity, a brain will not unfold according to its genetic program, nor will it perform to its potential. Operating a brain without social experience is like operating a flashlight without batteries.

What, then, is the bottom line, the meaning of all this for leadership? What qualities of the social brain are particularly worth understanding and nurturing? It is suggested here that a leader might be particularly mindful that brain capacity for learning and achievement is socially hyper, expectant, dependent, extended, and virtuous.

Hyper

Born of rich social experience over millions of years, the human brain is endowed with hyper social instincts: natural and powerful abilities for memory, language, empathy, sympathy, collaboration, and reasoning. The brain's social instincts are constantly engaged through the senses of sight, hearing, taste, smell, and touch. You directly read, watch, listen, ingest, inhale, move, feel, and touch to gather information from the environment. At more refined levels, moreover, you observe an expression, detect a pattern of behavior, read between the lines, note an inflection, hear what is not said, feel the tension, smell the excitement, taste the fear, and otherwise detect nuances that richly inform your understanding and reasoning.

Expectant

The unfolding of brain capacity to think, learn, and achieve is expectant of the same social experience that constructed it. Social interaction is a critical attribute of environmental information experienced by your brain. It is a primary means by which its neural circuitry is activated and reinforced.

Dependent

Social experience is the great provocateur of thinking and learning. Beyond fulfilling the brain's expectations for social experience, interpersonal relationships are the foils by which its neural networks are productively maintained and refined. Thus, your capacity to think, learn, and achieve profits immeasurably from associations with provocative people, ideas, and events.

Extended

To satisfy its overarching need and disposition to interact in a society of mind, the human brain has invented a variety of media that extend social interaction beyond face-to-face encounters. Whether direct or indirect, social interaction engages a flow of energy and information through a collective human intelligence. It is through interpersonal neural networking on a grand scale that the best ideas are generated, critiqued, and refined, and collective human potential to think and learn is realized in the process. It is such networking that both generates and disseminates art, philosophy, and moral perspective. Most important, communities of mind emerge from such networking to solve difficult problems, create better systems, and invent new technologies.

Virtuous

The brain has an instinctive moral orientation to prosocial behavior. The human measure of what is right and what is wrong arises from millions of years of species evolution in a social context. The golden rule is neither chance observation nor the exclusive property of world religions that universally embrace it. Your moral perception of what is good and what is bad reaches back to the social origins of humanity. What you would like to happen to you is the bottom-line measure of what is socially good and just for all: to be safe, sheltered, fed, loved, and free. You may not always act in accordance with this perception, but your brain always knows whether your behavior is in line with what is fundamentally right and wrong.

IMPLICATIONS

> *Intelligence, in one of its most basic senses, is the capacity to solve problems, meet challenges, or create valued products. In this sense, organizational intelligence represents that capacity as it emerges from the complex interplay of people and relationships, culture and roles within an organization.*

> —Goleman (1998, p. 297)

To be human is to be a hypersocial animal, an extrovert who has high social expectations and needs and will go to great lengths to satisfy them. Knowing this is important to constructing a conceptual sense of social intelligence, one that observes that intelligence is a phenomenon that operates within individuals *and* systems. Therefore, there is a necessary social relationship between leadership, intelligence, and the achievement of organizational purpose. Simply put, intelligence is enabled and operates within the individual, but it is also exercised within groups as a collective capacity for acquiring and applying knowledge in diverse and novel situations. Subsequently, leadership involves a relationship with the intelligence of the individual (i.e., both of self and others) and the collective intelligence of the membership of the organization (i.e., the system).

Knowing that nature has endowed you and your kind with extraordinary social capacity for acquiring and applying knowledge implies that such capacity should be appropriately nurtured at home, school, or work. Of particular interest might be what can be done to counter the capacity-sapping conventions of cubicles, desks, and workstations. To that end, a leader would attend to the interneural networking of the members of an organization. For example, one would seek to promote social relationships by facilitating meetings of minds, cultivating common purpose, and extending the mind's reach (Figure 6.2).

Facilitate Meetings of Minds

Social interaction is a survival strategy that has advanced the intelligence capacity throughout human evolution. As a result, the brain is

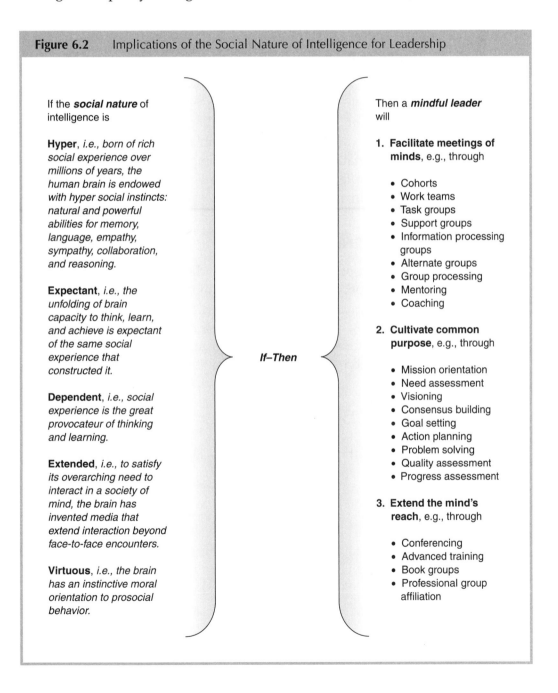

Figure 6.2   Implications of the Social Nature of Intelligence for Leadership

If the **social nature** of intelligence is

Hyper, *i.e., born of rich social experience over millions of years, the human brain is endowed with hyper social instincts: natural and powerful abilities for memory, language, empathy, sympathy, collaboration, and reasoning.*

Expectant, *i.e., the unfolding of brain capacity to think, learn, and achieve is expectant of the same social experience that constructed it.*

Dependent, *i.e., social experience is the great provocateur of thinking and learning.*

Extended, *i.e., to satisfy its overarching need to interact in a society of mind, the brain has invented media that extend interaction beyond face-to-face encounters.*

Virtuous, *i.e., the brain has an instinctive moral orientation to prosocial behavior.*

If–Then

Then a **mindful leader** will

1. **Facilitate meetings of minds**, e.g., through

   - Cohorts
   - Work teams
   - Task groups
   - Support groups
   - Information processing groups
   - Alternate groups
   - Group processing
   - Mentoring
   - Coaching

2. **Cultivate common purpose**, e.g., through

   - Mission orientation
   - Need assessment
   - Visioning
   - Consensus building
   - Goal setting
   - Action planning
   - Problem solving
   - Quality assessment
   - Progress assessment

3. **Extend the mind's reach**, e.g., through

   - Conferencing
   - Advanced training
   - Book groups
   - Professional group affiliation

expectant of and dependent on a social unfolding of its potential. Social interaction is the foil by which human intelligence is encouraged to construct meaning and engage complex reasoning. When one brain meets another brain, the exercise of thinking and learning inevitably follows. Two or more heads are better than one in socially adept groups. Accordingly, a leader will contemplate ways to facilitate the organization of cohorts, teams, and other groups as appropriate to specific responsibilities and tasks.

Cultivate Common Purpose

Social interactions between humans always occur in a moral context, and making a contribution to the common good is what counts to the social orientation of the brain. The collective capacity of human intelligence is tapped when the brains within an organization are enticed into collaborative relationships by clear, compelling, and mutually held goals. Accordingly, a leader will contemplate ways to facilitate dialogue about purpose, vision, action, and progress.

Extend the Mind's Reach

The strongest ropes are woven from diverse fibers. Diversity of experience and perspective in social interactions enhance the prospects for productive thinking and learning. This is particularly important in resolving challenging problems and tasks. Accordingly, a leader will promote diversity of background in task groups, access to distant brains through media, and on-site and off-site professional growth experiences.

READER REFLECTION

- What is essential to know and do about the social nature of intelligence?

7 Emotional Nature

When we and other animals have to make decisions, we must do so with partial information, conflicting aims, and limited time. Under these pressures, it is simply impossible to undertake a logical search through all the possibilities and identify the optimal course of action.

—Mithen (2006, p. 87)

THIS EMOTIONAL LIFE

The human brain is awash in emotion, and the proof is in the behavior. Consider the joke attributed to investigators of our emotional attributes. "Look at the things people do—they get married, go on family vacations, and buy lottery tickets, none of which they would do if they were completely rational." Jokes aside, research about our emotional nature has been very productive in recent decades. It is revealing how the brain is emotionally attentive, judgmental, motivating, and manageable (Figure 7.1).

THE GIST OF IT

While conscious control over emotions is weak, emotions can flood consciousness. This is so because the wiring of the brain at this point in our evolutionary history is such that connections from the emotional systems to the cognitive systems are stronger than connections from the cognitive systems to the emotional systems.

—LeDoux (1996, p. 19)

Figure 7.1   The Emotional Nature of Intelligence

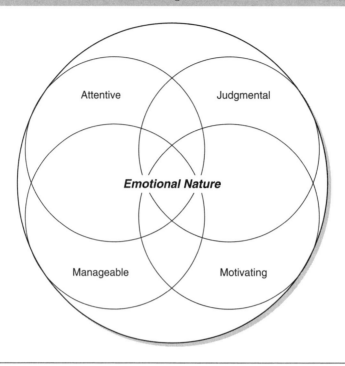

The *emotional nature* of intelligence is

Attentive: *Emotion involves neural and glandular systems that trigger changes in mind–body states, reflexive changes that arouse brain attention to what is important.*

Judgmental: *Reflexive arousal systems associated with emotion interact with rational reasoning systems in the brain to evaluate the merits of events and options.*

Motivating: *Emotion both arouses and sustains passion about things that matter.*

Manageable: *The brain is able to recognize and mediate emotional responses after the fact, a capacity called emotional intelligence.*

Feel the Power

As a means to initiate your examination of the emotional nature of human intelligence, please pick up a pen and write down what immediately comes to mind when you complete the following sentence stem:

One of the happiest moments in my life was when _____.

Now, put this book down, close your eyes, and for one full minute revisit the particular moment of happiness you have identified.

~ *Reflection Time* ~

Memories of joyous moments will vary, of course, according to individual life experience. One person may revisit a childhood adventure, first love, or professional triumph. Another might recall a particular act of kindness, the birth of a child, or the excitement of travel to an exotic environment. There will be a consistency among all brains that entertain strong memories, however, in that all such recollections will evoke emotion related to the event held in mental focus. That is, your brain recalls not only the event but also associated emotional states. In fact, in spending a few minutes revisiting a memorable moment of happiness, you experienced this phenomenon in one or more of a wide range of possible expressions. Perhaps you experienced a sense of calm or pleasure, change in body temperature or posture, alteration of facial expression—a slight upward turn of your lips?

There is also the possibility that your recollection of a happy event was not entirely pleasant. In remembering something good that happened, your brain may have activated neural networks that associate sadness with the happiness remembered. That is, your mental images expanded from the initial reconstruction of a joyful event to reflection about related events that have subsequently transpired—perhaps the loss of youth, opportunity, or loved ones. Most assuredly, if you were to reflect on a particularly unpleasant life experience, you would also evoke the emotional status associated with that recollection, perhaps anxiety, a chill, restricted breathing, tightness in the stomach, or tension in the face.

The point is that whatever the memory, some sense of mental and body state—whether subtle or strong—will be associated with the meaningful experience recalled. What you sense or feel during such a recollection is the effect of emotion associated with the event remembered. You are similarly aware of emotion-charged states in your body and mind during some events as they happen or are anticipated. For example, you might notice changes in your mind and body when you observe colored lights flashing in the rearview mirror of your car, sway to the music of a slow dance, answer an unexpected late-night phone call, plan an exotic vacation, or contemplate a major financial investment. Thus in its multiple forms, the pervasive and enduring power of emotion in your brain and body is occasionally revealed to you. The question then arises, what exactly is the nature of this powerful influence on your mind and body?

What Are Emotions?

Emotions have mostly been studied psychologically in modern times. Such efforts have provided insights, to be sure, but they also have a couple of drawbacks. One is that, in effect, everybody knows what an emotion is, but no one seems to be able to define it. The other is that there are as many theories of emotion as there are workers in the field. But studies of the brain can provide new insights into how a psychological process like emotion might work and are a valuable approach.

—LeDoux (1999, p. 124)

On becoming aware of a phenomenon, humans find it natural to attach a name to it as a precursor to figuring out exactly what it is and how it works. Thus human intrigue about a collection of forces experienced in mind, body, and behavior led to the identification of a phenomenon labeled emotion (*bodily humors* was an earlier label popular in the Middle Ages). This label reflects the common definitional interpretations of the effect of the phenomenon: agitation of the passions or sensibilities, often involving physiological changes; any strong feeling, as of joy, sorrow, reverence, hate, or love arising subjectively rather than through conscious mental effort (from Old French *esmovoir*, "to excite," and Latin *emovere*, "to move out, stir up, act; impulse to act").

Over the centuries, awareness of the phenomenon of emotion prompted ongoing theoretical and clinical investigations into its nature. Such studies have contributed many insights about the role of emotion in humans and other animal organisms. Most recently, however, inquiry into the nature of emotion has benefited substantially from applications of new neuroscience technologies in combination with clinical studies. Accordingly, science is beginning to reveal the biological underpinnings of emotion. This new information, though not yet definitive, significantly advances our understanding of the role of emotion in human intelligence and behavior. In effect, scientists are beginning to "see" emotion in the form of neural and chemical processes—emotion in action at a cellular and molecular level. From this vantage point, refined interpretations of the nature of emotion are emerging.

- Emotions are collections of patterned chemical and neural responses that regulate an organism in a manner advantageous to its survival (Damasio, 1999, p. 51).
- An emotion is a given mental state mediated by a specific neural system as a response to particular assessments of internal and external information that, in turn, give rise to measurable physiological states as well as observable behaviors (LeDoux, 1999, p. 125).

- Emotions represent dynamic processes created within the socially influenced, value-appraising processes of the brain that ready the brain and body for action (Siegel, 1999, pp. 123–124).

So what are emotions? Generally speaking, emotions are biological processes that regulate mind and body responses to subjective evaluations of internal and external information. This simple interpretation aligns well with the emotions you know so well when you feel and see them, such as fear, anger, happiness, sadness, surprise, and disgust—processes that, when activated, trigger immediate transitions in mind and body.

Feeling Emotion

Emotion involves subconscious processes that become known to the conscious brain through effects on mind and body states. As described further in later sections, emotion operates as a subconscious arousal system that, if sufficiently active, may escalate to a point that activates conscious feelings—what Damasio (1999, p. 8) calls "the feeling of that emotion and knowing that we have a feeling of that emotion." Perception of this process is critical because it establishes the reflexive nature of emotion. Such perception also establishes the relation of emotion to other dimensions of intelligence. Specifically, refinement in brain capacity to feel transitions in body states is thought to have been a critical factor in the evolution of a mental awareness of self and hence capacity for conscious reflection and construction of knowledge. Accordingly, at this point in your examination of emotion, it is important to be aware of the distinction between emotions and feelings, two words that are sometimes used synonymously. A feeling is generated by emotion and is something that you become aware of and can do something about. Emotion, on the other hand, will do what emotion will do, and you will not be aware of it until its work becomes manifest in the form of a feeling.

Stretching Emotion

There are many manifestations of emotional processes in human organisms, but the aforementioned primary emotions (i.e., fear, anger, happiness, sadness, surprise, and disgust, sometimes called categorical emotions) are universally observed across all cultures (Ekman, 1984). Variations and combinations of these primary emotions are also observed and organized by scholars into secondary classifications. For example, variations in fear would be anxiety, concern, or nervousness. Similarly, happiness might be modified to mental and physiological states associated with pride, rapture, or whimsy.

To get a better sense of the range and subtleties of human emotions, you might make a quick reference to a specific event, such as a recent political election. Based on personal voting activity in relation to the election outcome, you might experience any number or combination of emotional responses as the final vote counts are announced—perhaps satisfaction, terror, relief, concern, embarrassment, guilt, despair, joy, consternation, amusement, panic, amazement, wonder, or indifference. But whatever the nuance, the emotion experienced is a biologically determined process that is directed by an ensemble of subcortical brain devices that regulate and represent body states (Damasio, 1999). Moreover, it matters not whether the stimulation comes from an election result, hazardous weather, or winning the lottery; emotions are in the business of affecting transitions in body and mind states as induced by mental or sensory information. As such, emotions are bioregulatory responses that attend to the basic and subtle requirements of human survival—which is, of course, the reason that emotion is in the brain.

Why Be Emotional?

> *Survival depends on finding and incorporating sources of energy and on preventing all sorts of situations that threaten the integrity of living tissues.*
>
> —Damasio (1999, p. 23)

What would your life be like if you were not emotional? Think about that for a minute. What would it be like if you were not susceptible to fear, anger, happiness, sadness, surprise, disgust, or any of the infinite blendings of primary emotions? Would your life be better or worse if you were completely unemotional?

Your reflection on this question might have led to the quick conclusion that life would be pretty boring if you were never happy or if there were no surprises. You might also have flirted with the allure of a life without fear or anger. As you may have already surmised, however, without emotion, you would not have a life—literally—because emotion is an integral element of survival in animal organisms.

The brain's business, you will recall, is survival, and emotion is a frontline player in the survival business of animal organisms. Emotions are processes that affect transitions in mental and body states. The transitions they affect happen for a reason: to prepare for and support action that is of survival value. In effect, emotions provide your mind and body with the means to attend to, evaluate, and act on information that warrants attention, evaluation, and action.

The key word here is *evaluate*. The human emotional processes that emerged from eons of evolutionary history rapidly assess the merits of internal and external information to determine the need for specific preparations of mind and body for action. Consider the following example:

> While walking down the sidewalk of a heavily traveled thorough-fare, your brain is informed by sensory information (i.e., visual and auditory patterns) of the presence of a large truck weaving errati-cally in your direction and about to jump the curb. This informa-tion is instantaneously made available to neural circuits associated with the emotion of fear. Given a genetic and experiential under-standing of the nature of large objects aggressively moving in the direction of its host organism, these circuits assess the implications of the given information for your welfare and determine that a full engagement of a fear response is in order. Subsequently, in a mat-ter of milliseconds, a transition in mental and body state occurs that prepares you for what you must do to survive, that is, flee the path of the oncoming truck.

It is important to note that all mind and body activity in this fictitious scenario occurred at a subconscious level. The processes associated with the emotional state of fear are ingrained in your neural networks and brain mechanisms. These processes constantly assess incoming information for indications of a need for their services. On determining such a need, they immediately trigger the mind–body state they are responsible for. Again, this occurs without consultation with the conscious you. Only after you have escaped the danger do you become aware of what your emotional processes have been up to. It is at that point that you begin to *feel* the adjustments that emotional processes associated with fear have directed within your body: the accelerated rush of blood pumping through your heart, the tightness in your stomach, and the trembling of your limbs.

Why be emotional? It is the means by which you judge what is good and what is bad as measured against your survival interests. In some instances such judgment is primitively basic and instant. A truck moving directly at you at high speed is bad; therefore, you respond with fear. The offering of a large increase in salary and benefits is good; therefore, you respond with happiness.

The benefit of basic emotional processes should become even more obvious when you rerun the runaway truck scenario from a perspective of the hypothetical *emotionless* you. Without emotional processes in place that evaluate incoming information and efficiently engage appropriate response mechanisms, you would be indifferent to the truck because you have no means to judge its relationship to your welfare. And if by chance you are tempted to make the argument that, absent all emotion, you would still be in a position to engage your rational thinking skills to determine how to deal with the truck, be forewarned: Without emotion there can be no rational thought. The reason that this is so, as will be discussed later, is that rational thought requires valuation of all manner of information, including the alternative explanations and possibilities that are generated during reflection. The reason that this is known to be so is that humans who suffer injury to areas of the brain associated with emotional processes are impaired in their capacity for rational thinking.

Even if it were possible to be unemotionally rational (and it is not), by the time you consciously gather together the relevant pieces of information and consider your options, the truck has been and gone—and probably you with it. This is another advantage of emotion. Emotional processing of information from stimulus to action is infinitely more efficient than cognitive processing of information from stimulus to action. Just as your brain has circuits that unconsciously regulate the autonomic system's operation of basic body survival activities (such as breathing and blood circulation), it also has neural circuits that subjectively screen information for patterns that immediately and subconsciously induce prescribed mind–body responses.

However, emotional processing is not limited to the organization of rapid responses to basic survival needs. Human emotion covers a wide range of refined responses to events and interests. Emotion is commonly engaged through the reflective processing of mental patterns associated with past, current, and future events. In this manner, emotions are used more subtly and gradually to affect mind–body states and behaviors. This circumstance sheds further light on why emotion is necessary to survival. Specifically, we cannot pursue all goals at once. Pinker (1997, p. 373) puts it this way: "If an animal is both hungry and thirsty, it should not stand halfway between a berry bush and a lake." That is, an animal must commit itself to one goal at a time, and the goals have to be matched with the best opportunities for achieving them. Emotions, then, are mechanisms that help the brain make decisions and establish priorities, whether they be matters of career options, personal relationships, or selecting a brand of toothpaste. The ongoing screening of internal and external information brings forward all manner of emotional assessments that "chart the course of moment-to-moment actions as well as set the sails toward long-term achievements" (LeDoux, 1996, p. 19).

To summarize to this point, emotions are not things that you can pick up, kick around, and describe as being larger or smaller than a bread box. Rather, emotions are best understood as complicated collections of neural and chemical processes that regulate a wide range of mind and body states. They perform their regulatory tasks through subjective evaluations of internal and external information that both determine and initiate mind–body responses. As such, emotions are critical contributors to your brain's survival business. Given this assessment of the importance of emotion, your brain's emotional centers might be interested in an examination of how humans are emotional.

How Are We Emotional?

The evidence suggests that the emotions of all normal members of our species are played on the same keyboard.

—Pinker (1997, p. 365)

To establish a reality reference for your subsequent examination of how humans are emotional, you are again asked to access your personal emotional experience. This time, however, the activity will expand on the scope of human emotion and require deeper reflection about the process and effect of emotion as you once experienced it. Specifically, you will reflect about what occurred in your mind, body, and behavior during specific events—that is, you will describe *how* you were emotional in specific contexts.

This activity will take only a few minutes to complete, and you will have choices as to what to reflect about within three categories. Please be advised that writing is an important component of this exercise because (as will be elaborated on in later sections on the constructive and reflective nature of your brain) it will enhance your neural reconstruction of specific events and associated emotional experiences.

But first a warning: A range of emotional experiences are purposely solicited in this exercise, some of which will probably resurface strong feelings. That is, some recollections will predictably evoke feelings of happiness and joy, and others will evoke feelings of sadness and discomfort. You will be conducting this exercise in the comfort of private reflection, and you are afforded choice in what life experiences you will recall. Nevertheless, you may be revisiting some difficult memories. So, to paraphrase the famous Bette Davis line, fasten your seatbelt, it may be a bumpy emotional ride.

This is what you are requested to do:

A. Write brief descriptions of events in your life that correspond to given categories.

B. Write brief descriptions of what was occurring in your mind, body, and behavior during the described events.

Example:

A. Description of the event: A visit to a memorial site.

> In 1973, I spent a summer working on a kibbutz near the Gaza Strip in southeastern Israel. I was there to gather information for the completion of my master's thesis. I worked on the kibbutz in exchange for room and board during my stay. I also had opportunities for traveling throughout the country on non-working days. On one occasion, I traveled to Har Hazikaron to visit Yad Vashem, the national monument to victims of the Nazi Holocaust. I recall that the buildings were located in a forest that had been planted in memory of John F. Kennedy. Inside, there were many exhibits depicting the transportation, imprisonment, and killing of millions of Jews, Gypsies, and other victims of Nazi racism. At the center of the memorial building was a large area of marble flooring bordered by a low railing. Visitors stood at the railing and looked down on slabs of dark marble set in the lighter-colored floor. Each slab was engraved with the name of a concentration camp—names such as Treblinka, Dachau, and Auschwitz. I think there were about 15 to 20 names in all. An eternal flame flickered at the center of the floor. I remember that it was very quiet, that people were crying softly, and that some visitors had numbers tattooed on their arms.

B. Description of what was occurring in mind, body, and behavior:

> I remember being attentive and somber when going through the exhibits surrounding the memorial. As a history teacher, I had a good background of information about World War II and the Holocaust, but my mind was nevertheless captured by the graphic representations of the multimedia displays. When I arrived at the marble memorial surrounding the eternal flame, however, I was suddenly overwhelmed—by the physical memorial to millions of lives subjected to unimaginable injustice, the crying of grieving people, and the presence of survivors. I felt a heaviness in the air and a constriction in my throat and chest. I think I may have stopped breathing for a moment. My jaw clenched and my eyes watered. I bent over, placed my hands on my knees, and breathed deeply. I felt both great anger and sadness. My mind was trying to comprehend the magnitude of the inhumanity and suffering and searching for answers to why and how such atrocities happen.

Now it is your turn. Remember, you have choices as to what to recall and write about in different categories. You may decide to respond to more than one suggested prompt, but it is important that you complete a written response to at least one prompt in each category. (Note: The physical organization of information into a written response is adequately served by notes jotted down on any available piece of paper.)

Category 1: An event that evoked fear, sadness, disgust, or anger

Prompts: An event that involved a visit to a memorial, the death of a loved one, failure to achieve a goal, a life-threatening experience, observation of great cruelty, witnessing a natural disaster, an encounter with human tragedy, other

Description of the event:

~Writing Time~

Description of what was occurring in mind, body, and behavior:

~Writing Time~

Category 2: An event that evoked joy or inspiration

Prompts: An event that involved observation of courage, personal achievement, artistic expression, moral victory, friendship, the beauty of nature, family events, human triumph over adversity, displays of compassion, other

Description of the event:

~Writing Time~

Description of what was occurring in mind, body, and behavior:

~Writing Time~

Category 3: An event that required an important decision

Prompts: An event that involved a decision about a relationship, children, a moral dilemma, educational options, career choices, travel opportunities, property, financial investment, other

Description of the event:

~Writing Time~

Description of what was occurring in mind, body, and behavior:

~Writing Time~

Given the events you have revisited and described, how are you emotional? What happens in your mind, body, and behavior during events that evoke stress or pleasure? Do you laugh, cry, run, perspire, fret, tremble, focus, smile, freeze, frown, scream, stammer, or squeak? What about events in your life that entail major decisions? Do you experience emotional effects in mind, body, and behavior in those situations also?

You probably have a pretty good feel for how you are emotional if you completed the prescribed reflection activity. That is the point of the activity. You feel the effect of emotional processes associated with events and are able to describe their influence on mind, body, and behavior. But why do your emotional responses vary according to events, and how are these responses generated? In other words, what are the inner workings of how you are emotional? To answer these questions, we turn to the biology that underlies emotion.

The Basic Picture: Ready, Fire, Aim

In a typical emotion, then, certain regions of the brain, which are part of a largely preset neural system related to emotions, send commands to other regions of the brain and to most everywhere in the body proper. The commands are sent via two routes. One route is the bloodstream, where the commands are sent in the form of chemical molecules that act on receptors in the cells that constitute body tissues. The other route consists of neuron pathways and the commands along this route take the form of electrochemical signals that act on other neurons or on muscular fibers or on organs (such as the adrenal gland) which in turn can release chemicals of their own into the bloodstream. The result of these coordinated chemical and neural commands is a global change in the state of the organism.

—Damasio (1999, p. 67)

Emotion is about motion and everything that the word implies—movement, change, action—in the body and mind. It is a process, like digestion or respiration, rather than a thing, like an elbow or nose. It is a process that assesses the survival merits of information moving within and about an organism to determine advantageous movement in mind and body states that, in turn, direct movement in behavior. The basic process in every instance of emotional experience (such as those you described in the preceding exercise)—whether stressful, pleasant, or decisive—is as follows:

1. Neural networks in various regions of your brain (e.g., in the amygdala and brain stem) act as *emotion centers* that are committed to the

regulation of mind and body responses to particular configurations of internal and external information. You might want to think of these neural centers as sentries that monitor information brought forth for their inspection by your senses and body movement through the thalamus and the olfactory lobe.

2. On detecting an information pattern that it judges to be important to its particular responsibilities (e.g., assessing for information that suggests danger, opportunity, or novelty), an emotion center informs other parts of the brain of its discovery and concern.

3. Thus alerted, some neural networks initiate prescribed transitions in mind and body states appropriate to the nature of the information received. These transitions occur through electrochemical communications in neural networks and chemical releases into the bloodstream to enable action or behavior judged by your brain to be in your best interest (e.g., fight, flee, focus).

4. Other neural networks become aware of the transitions that are occurring in body and mind; they *feel* the emotional response.

5. Finally, the prefrontal cortex and other cortical areas become informed of the emotional arousal, response, and feeling that have arisen subconsciously in your brain. Thus, after your brain has reflexively reacted to important sensory information, you are presented with an opportunity to consciously reflect about what is happening and what you want to do about it. It is as if your subconscious brain is reporting to your conscious brain about events that have occurred.

An important point about the sequence just described is that emotion dictates an act-first, think-later response to information. Whether the action is as extreme as physical aggression or as mild as a focusing of attention, emotion is very much in the driver's seat in determining what you will attend to and how you will initially respond to that which captures your attention. In a classic fear response, for example, neural clusters in the amygdala scan sensory information for patterns that suggest the possibility of danger. On detecting such a pattern, the amygdala sounds an alert to other brain centers. The informed neural networks act on the alert by releasing hormones, increasing heart rate and blood pressure, slowing breathing, mobilizing muscle groups, shutting down systems unnecessary to the moment (e.g., digestion), and referencing the hippocampus and other memory systems to retrieve information that may be valuable to the matter at hand.

Notably, sensory information that is presented to the amygdala is also communicated to the cortex. However, the amygdala receives the information milliseconds before the cortical areas, and if the amygdala judges said information to warrant an alarm, the brain is, in effect, hijacked to serve an emotional priority (LeDoux, 1996); that is, the reflective capacities of your cortex are put on hold while your brain attends to first things first. This phenomenon is born of the survival imperative that drives your brain. Eventually, your powers of rational thinking are brought to bear on what the amygdala and other emotional mechanisms have already acted on, but only after your brain has reflexively taken steps to ensure that you will be around to do some thinking.

The advantages of this arrangement between the reflexive and reflective qualities of you brain are obvious when you consider that it was important for your early ancestors to refrain from engaging in observations about the comparative qualities and habits of approaching carnivores until after the safety of a perch in a tall tree afforded security for such reflection. In such instances, an "attend, react, then think" approach seems necessary for participation in the gene pool. What might not be as obvious is that this arrangement for attending, responding, and incorporating reflection is at work in your brain in all instances of life experience—be they large or small, dramatic or mundane.

Additional insights about the basic nature of emotion in brain and body follow.

In the beginning, it was all about the body. Before there were brains, there were bodies without brains. Accordingly, as Pert (1997) describes, there was a body chemical nervous system before there was a central nervous system that incorporated electrochemical communications. That original body system remains in operation. It is a system that evaluates and responds to information by means of parasynaptic transmissions (i.e., transmissions that are secondary or parallel to synaptic exchanges of chemicals in neural circuitry) of ligands (i.e., neurotransmitters, hormones, peptides) through extracellular fluids to receptor molecules on cells throughout the body. This chemical communication system is the means to effect adjustments in body states, as directed by information processed directly in the body or communicated by the brain. This is an important point. As the brain evolved and assumed its system-management and decision-making responsibilities, it incorporated the existing body communication system. Thus the brain informs and affects the body, and the body informs and affects the brain. You truly do have a mind–body. This is part of the explanation for gut instinct. Your stomach acquires and acts on information and informs your brain accordingly.

Likewise, your brain acquires and acts on information that becomes known to the stomach. This two-way-street arrangement is observed when an upset stomach trips emotional centers in the brain and when emotional alerts in the brain initiate physical responses in the stomach. What happens to the body happens to the brain and vice versa—and always with emotional markers.

The nose knows. The olfactory lobe is suspected of having played a pivotal role in the evolution of higher brain structures. Specifically, the ability to detect, organize, and recall a wide range of scents became a very valuable survival skill. It was a means to determine what was good or bad to eat, be near, or do. As the mammalian brain evolved at the prodding of mobility in rich experiential environments, there was more to smell and, subsequently, decipher and organize as important information patterns. Such environmental stimulation is thought to have encouraged the beginnings of complex information processing and memory systems, including the development of a cortex. As mammals became more multisensorily adept, this brain development was accelerated. Therefore, it is helpful to remember that the sophisticated information and memory systems in your brain originate from a survival need to judge what is good for you and what is bad for you—an emotional orientation that remains deeply invested in all the information processing you engage in.

Emotion is everywhere. Damasio (1999, p. 61) advises that there is no single site for the processing of emotions. However, there are discrete systems associated with different emotional patterns. Thus, different sites induce different emotions, such as the association of sadness with the ventromedial prefrontal cortex, hypothalamus, and brain stem and the amygdala's involvement with fear and anger. LeDoux (1996, p. 16) agrees with this assessment, stating that emotion is not something that the brain has or does; rather, it is something a number of neural systems are involved with. Accordingly, there is no single brain system dedicated to emotion; the emotional system you use to defend against danger is different from the one you engage to procreate.

Like an individual neuron, emotion considers the source. Neurons fire their chemical messages based on the quality and quantity of electrochemical information that they receive from other neurons. This pattern is observable in emotion because a relevant network does not sound an alert unless sufficiently encouraged by sensory information that such attention is warranted. This explains why you are not constantly emotional in every possible way.

A strong emotion is designed to be a sprinter, not a distance runner. The primary job of emotion is to alert other brain–body systems about the need for their services. Monitoring sensory information is a low-key function of emotion, similar to the low expenditure of energy needed by sentinels standing watch at their posts. On detecting an information pattern of concern, however, emotional networks adopt a more energy-consuming posture: They literally light up with the electrochemical flow of information that alerts and enacts transitions in mind and body. Therefore, a problem arises when emotional networks are overengaged or sustained in use. It is equivalent to the problem that arises from running a car engine at top speed for a sustained period of time; such stress can damage the components of the system. In the case of emotion, neural networks are subject to damage from the extended presence of associated chemicals, such as the cortisol secretions involved in a fear response. Having performed its initial arousal service, however, an emotion network needs to adopt a lower-level maintenance role and attend to further monitoring of incoming sensory information. This is modeled in nature by the grazing animals of the African savanna that quickly revert to normal feeding and social behaviors after the emotional surge associated with escape from the attack of a predator.

The Complex Picture: The Fine Art of Emotion

There is nothing simple about emotion or any other quality of human intelligence. Beyond the marvel of the basic character and function of emotion in mind and body is the nature of its relationship to the complex thinking capacities of the brain.

Emotion is the arbiter between lower and higher brain structures. As Sylwester (2000) describes it, sensory information patterns activate emotional systems that activate brain attention and, most important, your capacity to construct understanding, solve problems, and make decisions. Emotion is in partnership with the cortex, then, not to resolve but to involve. From systems located primarily in the lower and older areas of the brain, emotion initiates a process that informs the prefrontal cortex about what it should be thinking about. The cortex, in response, acts to understand what has been brought to its attention and to generate behaviors that will relieve the concerns therein.

Emotion flows uphill. More neural communications flow from emotion systems to complex reasoning systems than from complex reasoning systems to emotion systems. The good news about this arrangement is that the prefrontal cortex is provided with many challenges that both require and sharpen its reflective, problem-solving, and decision-making capacities. The thinking cortex is also afforded many opportunities by this directional flow of information to refine its capacity for emotional intelligence, that is, to manage emotion in a manner that contributes to your welfare and quality of life.

Emotion can be turned on by the thought of you. From your experience with several exercises earlier in this section, you are already aware of your ability to engage emotion at will by conscious reflection. The significance of this ability is that you are not completely at the mercy of your emotions, that your cortex can manage and adjust your emotional state by its conscious actions. If you can turn it on, you have some leverage in turning it down or otherwise tuning it to your advantage.

Too much of a good thing co-opts the work of the best and brightest. Intense or sustained surges of emotion initiate processes that highjack the brain to a basic survival focus. In such instances, the services of the analytic and creative thinking areas of the prefrontal cortex are compromised. When emotionally overwhelmed, your brain experiences difficulty in attending, learning, remembering, or making decisions. As Goleman (1995, p. 149) relates, "Stress makes people stupid."

Emotion moves beyond the passion of the moment. Whereas less evolved life forms have a more limited range of responses to environmental stimuli, a larger and complex human neocortex enables a more expansive and nimble repertoire of emotional assessment and behavioral response (Goleman, 1995, p. 12). Thus human emotion systems are capable of influencing refined and subtle regulation of mind and body states as well as full-blown alarm exercises. This refined capacity for assessing the merits of environmental information is also the means by which emotion initiates and sustains human passion for art, philosophy, and other applications of complex reasoning.

A Popular Dance Partner

Emotion does not dance alone on the multidimensional stage of intelligence. The physiological platform of intelligence is saturated with the webs and chemicals of emotion systems, and the healthy functioning of such systems depends on the healthy maintenance of brain physiology. Social experience is a primary source of influence on emotional systems. You feel emotion well up inside you as you approach a podium, visit a gravesite, attend a wedding, cross the finish line, or engage in office politics. However, it is in the constructive and reflective dimensions of your intelligence that a particularly intimate dance of knowledge acquisition and application is engaged at the valuation lead of emotion. You construct understanding and reflect only about that which is judged to be worth knowing and thinking about. Similarly, emotion prods and reinforces your disposition to develop and habitually exercise productive thinking skills. Thus emotion moves—step for step—with other qualities of intelligence across the comprehensive landscape of human learning and achievement.

ESSENCE

We are about as effective at stopping an emotion as we are at preventing a sneeze.

—Damasio (1999, p. 49)

You are aroused in mind and body by your emotional brain to do what it takes to survive and thrive. Absent this emotional dimension, you would be unable to determine where to go or what to do.

Emotion evolved as a survival mechanism in life forms that move and therefore need to quickly screen, judge, and react to a vast array of environmental information. It is an endowment that has been highly refined in humankind by the influence of rich social experience and high mobility over a long evolutionary period. The purpose of emotion is to ensure that the organism reflexively acts first and then reflectively thinks later. The way it works is, sensory information is directed by the thalamus to emotional centers connected to memory sites in the amygdala, hippocampus, and other brain areas that, if sufficiently excited, activate the endocrine system and otherwise alter mind and body states that may generate feelings that inform the prefrontal cortex that there is something worth thinking about.

A determination is to be made, then, about what is most important to know and do regarding the emotional capacities of self and others. Knowing how the brain is emotionally attentive, judgmental, motivated, and manageable is worthy of leadership attention.

Attentive

Emotion involves neural and glandular systems that trigger changes in mind–body states: reflexive changes that arouse brain attention to what is important. The brain is emotionally attentive. The resources of mind and body are aroused and focused by emotional assessments of what merits attention. Accordingly, the brain will not easily attend to what is perceived to be insignificant or inconsequential. The brain will also find it difficult to attend to matters that are important if it is emotionally distracted by concerns for its immediate physical or social welfare.

Judgmental

Reflexive arousal systems associated with emotion interact with rational reasoning systems in the brain to evaluate the merits of events and options. The brain is emotionally judgmental. It is constantly weighing the advantages and disadvantages of every situation. Although much of this occurs at a subconscious level, it extends to reflective capacities because the brain cannot make reasoned judgments without emotional input. All efforts to rationally analyze, solve, decide, and resolve are performed in concert with emotional assessments of what is best to do.

Motivated

Emotion both arouses and sustains passion about things that matter. The brain is emotionally motivated. Beyond an initial assessment that something is worthy of attention, the continuing allocation of mind–body resources depends on ongoing dialogue between emotional and reflective brain centers about the value of the issue at hand.

Manageable

The brain is able to recognize and mediate emotional responses, a capacity called emotional intelligence. The emotional brain is manageable to the degree that it is adept at regulating emotional effects. The power of emotion must be managed to informational and motivational advantage by the rational capacity of the brain.

IMPLICATIONS

No doubt humankind's original leaders—whether tribal chieftains or shamanesses—earned their place in large part because their leadership was emotionally compelling.

—Goleman, Boyatzis, and McKee (2002, p. 5)

The brain is going to be emotional under all circumstances. Not only is it aroused and focused by emotion, it is always emotional before it is aware of a need to be rational. Give the nature of emotion, a leader will advisedly consider ways to establish a productive alliance with the powerful force that moves mind and body. The goal would be no less than that of harnessing the power of emotion. To do that, a leader would advisedly act to ease the mind, excite the mind, and evaluate states of mind in self and others as situational contexts require (Figure 7.2).

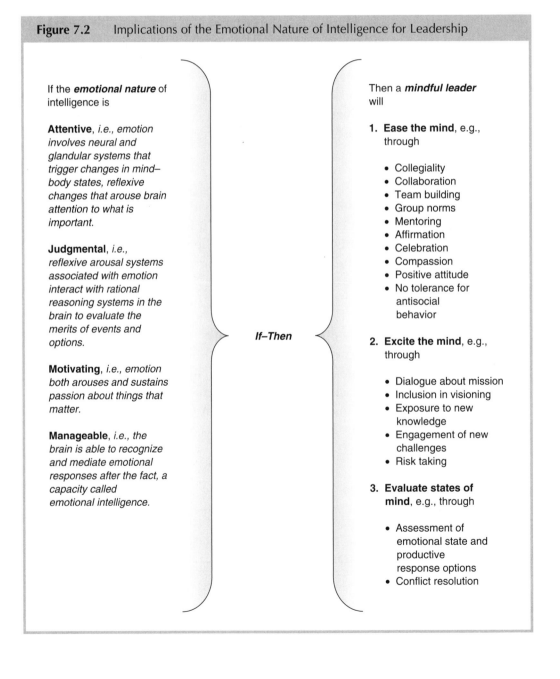

Figure 7.2 Implications of the Emotional Nature of Intelligence for Leadership

If the **emotional nature** of intelligence is

Attentive, *i.e.*, emotion involves neural and glandular systems that trigger changes in mind–body states, reflexive changes that arouse brain attention to what is important.

Judgmental, *i.e.*, reflexive arousal systems associated with emotion interact with rational reasoning systems in the brain to evaluate the merits of events and options.

Motivating, *i.e.*, emotion both arouses and sustains passion about things that matter.

Manageable, *i.e.*, the brain is able to recognize and mediate emotional responses after the fact, a capacity called emotional intelligence.

If–Then

Then a **mindful leader** will

1. **Ease the mind**, e.g., through

   - Collegiality
   - Collaboration
   - Team building
   - Group norms
   - Mentoring
   - Affirmation
   - Celebration
   - Compassion
   - Positive attitude
   - No tolerance for antisocial behavior

2. **Excite the mind**, e.g., through

   - Dialogue about mission
   - Inclusion in visioning
   - Exposure to new knowledge
   - Engagement of new challenges
   - Risk taking

3. **Evaluate states of mind**, e.g., through

   - Assessment of emotional state and productive response options
   - Conflict resolution

Ease the Mind

The brain will not attend well to other tasks if it is emotionally distracted by concerns for its physical or social welfare. Intelligence capacity is challenge motivated and threat inhibited. Furthermore, strong emotion (e.g., fear, anger) is designed for limited engagement and will adversely affect physical and mental health through associated chemical releases if sustained over time. Therefore, it is important for a leader to consider means by which the brain can be made to feel safe, valued, and supported.

Excite the Mind

The resources of the brain are aroused and focused by emotional assessment of what merits attention. For that reason, it is advisable that leaders orient the brain to matters of compelling value, vision, and purpose to create productive levels of goal tension.

Evaluate States of Mind

The power of emotion must be managed to advantage by the rational capacity of the brain. To do this, the relationship between emotion as a subconscious arousal system and the feeling of the consequence of the system (e.g., fear) must be appreciated. There is nothing to be done about the spontaneity of an emotional response. Tears and laughter come not at the bidding of conscious will but from a subconscious trigger. However, conscious awareness of an emotional effect is the gateway to reflection about how to manage emotion to advantage. Accordingly, a leader will facilitate reflection about emotional states and the means to regulate them to productive advantage.

READER REFLECTION

- What is essential to know and do about the emotional nature of intelligence?

8 Constructive Nature

The brain detects, constructs, and elaborates patterns as a basic, built-in, natural function. It does not have to be taught or motivated to do so, any more than the heart needs to be instructed or coaxed to pump blood.

—Hart (1983, p. 60)

GENIUS

In common use, the term *genius* distinguishes people who, among the masses, demonstrate great natural ability—exceptional mental ability in particular. *Genius* is also a term for describing the definitive ability of a particular group.

To further construct personal understanding of the genius of human intelligence, revisit for a moment the occasion of your birth. You may not recall the details, but, assuming a normal process, you were resting comfortably in an environment that adequately satisfied your needs for warmth and nutrition. Then things changed dramatically. After some pushing and pulling (depending in part on how accommodating you were to the process), you were thrust into a completely different environment. Cold air assailed your naked skin and shocked your untested lungs. Bright light pierced your still-closed eyelids. And the noise! Chaotic sounds swirled around your tender auditory sensing system. Indeed, the combined stress from temperature, light, and noise was probably overwhelming, causing you to cry out in distress.

Now fast-forward a few years to your first day of school. Many things have changed since that chaotic, disorienting moment of entry into human society. Most notably, you have mastered the basics of a defining human skill: language. Specifically, you have established semantic mastery of a vocabulary 5,000 or more words. You have also become adept in the syntactic arrangement of sounds, words, phrases, and sentences that underlies language communication. Thus you are able to verbally communicate easily and profusely with peers and adults as you enter the classroom, a matter that quickly becomes a classroom management challenge for your teacher.

This mastery of verbal language is both impressive and important. After all, it represents a skill base that underlies both formal and informal learning throughout your lifetime. What is most impressive, however, is that you mastered this sophisticated skill without the benefit of formal instruction. This raises a question: How did you master the complexities of verbal language between birth and age 5?

~Reflection Time~

Your reflection about your mastery of language skills will probably credit opportunities to observe, mimic, and interact with peers, siblings, and adults. Such social exposure to modeling, trial and error, and feedback is a common factor in all human learning. However, beneath this social framework beats a more fundamental rhythm of learning. To better understand this, return to your prenatal experience.

You might not recall it, but your womb experience involved exposure to many sound patterns. From the very earliest emergence of your sensory and cortical structures, you were exposed to the thump-thump of beating hearts (yours, your mom's, and those of any siblings who were in there with you at the time), the whoosh of blood through veins and air through lungs, and, yes, the distinct vibration patterns of your mother's voice. How did you master the basics of language? As you are already aware, the human brain is committed to discerning information patterns that serve its survival instincts. To that end, your brain was neurally prepared for pattern recognition in the womb. That is, you did not arrive in this world quite as helpless as it might have seemed at the time. You were armed with a neural disposition to detect and connect information patterns. Your discernment of the pattern of a heartbeat connected to the rhythmic sounds emitted by hovering adults and other environmental sources. These patterns, in turn, prompted monosyllabic and polysyllabic trials, possibly "Momma" or "Dadda." One pattern connected to another and another until the day you walked through the schoolhouse door prepared to communicate and learn with teachers and peers.

This extraordinary capacity for perceiving and endlessly constructing connections between pieces of information enables human cognition. It is pattern making, sensory, social, emotional, refined, and susceptible to a double bind (Figure 8.1). It is the foundation for all cognition engenders, be it a child's mastery of language or a physicist's formulation of $E = mc^2$— and the focus of this chapter.

Figure 8.1 The Constructive Nature of Intelligence

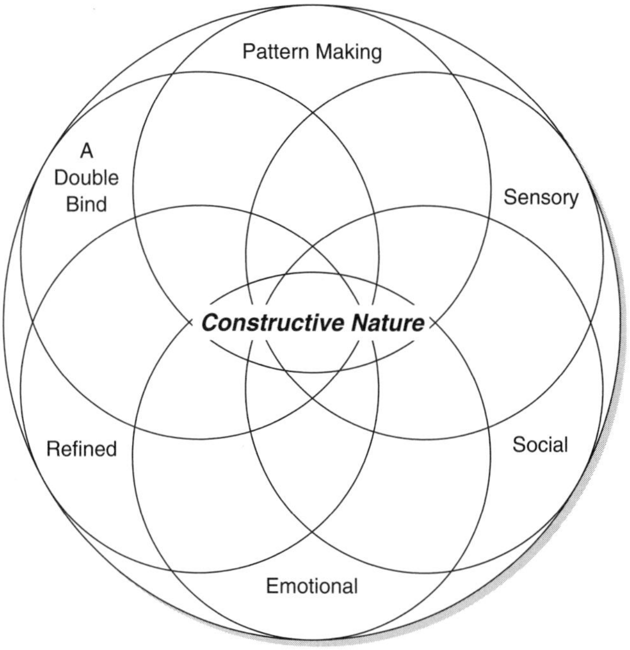

The **constructive nature** of intelligence is

Pattern Making: *The brain enables infinite capacity for constructing meaning and memory from information patterns; it is a "lean, mean, pattern-making machine."*

Sensory: *The brain constructs meaning and memory from sensory input stimulated by environmental experience, and direct experience affects quality of construction.*

Social: *Social interaction is a primary source of rich environmental experience that both stimulates and facilitates the construction of meaning and memory.*

Emotional: *Emotion influences the construction of meaning and memory through the arousal of attention and the establishment of emotional context.*

Refined: *What is constructed and remembered is reconstructed and refined by the brain through ongoing examination of relationships to new information.*

A Double Bind: *Comfort with existing patterns disregards new patterns.*

THE GIST OF IT

A Lean, Mean, Pattern-Making Machine

> *As soon as the infant can see, it recognizes faces, and we now know that this skill is hardwired into our brains. Those infants who, a million years ago, were unable to recognize a face smiled back less, were less likely to win the hearts of their parents, and less likely to prosper. These days, nearly every infant is quick to identify a human face, and to respond with a gooney grin.*

—Sagan (1996, p. 45)

Every healthy human brain possesses genius for detecting and organizing patterns that are useful to the determination of advantageous behavior. There is individual genius within this species wide genius, but every human is adept at pattern discrimination and construction to a degree that challenges the comprehension of the very intelligence that is operating it.

Consider once again the example of your early mastery of verbal language. Such accomplishment is impressive enough as a pattern discernment process that your brain engaged in to perceive relationships within and between sound, semantics, and syntax. The process becomes more impressive as one further considers all that your brain was doing to put the pieces of language together. After all, words and phrases were not coming from one source. There were different voices, pitches, inflections, accents, and a host of other language characteristics from many sources that assailed your young brain. There also were all kinds of other auditory events (e.g., bells, whistles, hammers, horns, barking dogs, instrumental music, the hum of a car engine) vying for your pattern discernment attention. Accordingly, Smith (1990) advises that an aspiring infant linguist is doing much more than merely mimicking or copying sounds in a passive or mechanical sense. Rather, the infant is engaging in a complex process of analysis that ultimately synthesizes important patterns and rules for language. This process is all the more impressive given that it occurs primarily at a subconscious level, while the infant is similarly mastering complex patterns associated with capacities such as sight, movement, and social relationships.

Patterns are the currency of intelligence in the business of survival. Your brain is designed to construct a wealth of meaning from internal and external sensory information. It does so by detecting patterns that can be assigned meaning in relation to patterns previously established in neural networks. The brain uses this process to organize information important to survival. For example, it is of survival importance for an infant to recognize the faces of primary caregivers, master communication skills, comprehend physical objects, and acclimate to cultural norms. The pattern detection and construction apparatus of the brain is the means by which a child achieves such needs. It is this same process that constructs conceptual and procedural understanding throughout the lifespan, whether it is understanding about economic principles, a new technology, or a recipe for preparing chicken curry. This, then, is the purpose of brain information processing: the acquisition and integration of highly organized and interconnected information patterns, commonly called knowledge.

The Power of Patterns

The process of learning is the extraction of patterns from confusion— not from clarity and simplicity.

—Hart (1983, p. 75)

Knowledge is power—power to survive born of constructed understanding about objects, people, events, processes, and abstract concepts. Such constructions arise from your brain's incessant detection and integration of information patterns. The following exercise illustrates the process:

Task: Memorize information about new symbols for the digits 0 to 9.

Step 1: Within 60 seconds, and using only visual observation (i.e., without the aid of pencil, paper, or other props), commit to memory new symbols for the digits 0 to 9 as presented in Figure 8.2.

Step 2: After the 60-second time period has expired, hide Figure 8.2 from your view and attempt to write a credit card number, your social security number, or a randomly selected number from the phone book using the new number symbols as you are able to remember them.

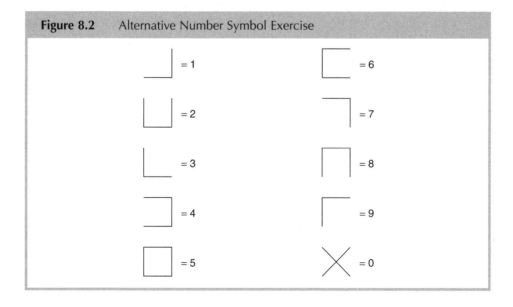

Figure 8.2   Alternative Number Symbol Exercise

You may have completed this task with little difficulty, which would certainly reflect brain capacity for organizing new information within a short period of time. Most people experience some frustration with this task, however, given the strangeness of the proposed new symbols and the limited time span in which to learn it. Therein lies an important insight about a basic principle of knowledge construction. When confronted by new information that does not immediately connect to existing neural networks, your brain (given sufficient motivation and time) searches further for relationships to established patterns. Ultimately, it will construct a pattern that incorporates the new with the familiar. Perhaps you were aware of your brain doing this as it recognized a similarity between the shape of the traditional number 7 and the proposed new symbol. If such a connection does not occur, however, your brain is stymied, confused, or simply oblivious. The new information does not have meaning because the informational pieces have not been put together in a recognizable or useful pattern. To your brain, such disconnected information takes on the qualities of a stranger passing by (i.e., "I do not know this person; this person means little to me") or not recalling something about familiar people (e.g., their names, where and when you were with them, what you did together). Thus your brain is either oblivious or frustrated until information pieces are put together in such a manner that a pattern is either recognized or created.

To more fully appreciate this proclivity for seeking and connecting patterns, take a moment to reference Figure 8.3. If your brain has not already arrived at this connection, you will gain a greater sense of its pattern connection and construction bias. That is, mastery of the alternative number symbol system is almost instantaneous when a familiar pattern establishes a relationship with the new information. Thus, an established neural pattern (i.e., the tic-tac-toe grid) serves as a framework that facilitates the neural organization of a new pattern (i.e., a new number symbol system).

Be assured that you have an infinite number of intricately constructed information patterns established in your neural networks. Indeed, some

Figure 8.3   Graphic Reference for Alternative Number Symbol Exercise

1	2	3	
4	5	6	
7	8	9	X = 0

patterns were genetically installed in your brain, such as neural networks dedicated to the recognition of geometric shapes, numbers, and the sounds for all the languages in the world—a necessity, given that you did not know where you were going to be born and what language you were going to learn. However, most of the information patterns you hold in your brain are the constructions you have been putting together throughout your life experience, in response to environmental stimuli. Such constructions represent all that you know about people, history, literature, geography, operating a business, driving a car, sports, and chocolate cake. These information patterns represent your knowledge, your personal understanding of the world you live in. It is vast knowledge that extends well beyond your conscious awareness. It is so profound and integrated that it is capable of generating patterns of information that do not exist (as you will experience a bit later in this chapter). Furthermore, given the experience of tomorrow, your knowledge then will be greater than that of today.

Given the powerful ability of the brain to construct information patterns, it is worthwhile to reflect about how humans came to possess this capacity.

The Legacy of Mobility: The Rich Get Richer

You do not need a brain if you are not going anywhere.

—Sylwester (2000, p. 41)

With locomotion, whether by foot, fin, wing, or other means, comes adjustment in the quantity and quality of life experience. It's a simple equation. Mobility expands the potential environmental experience of an organism, which, in turn, engenders more opportunity to detect and construct information patterns. Those who wander have greater opportunity—and need—to ponder.

Sylwester (2000) emphasizes mobility as a defining property of human experience and a central reason for a having a brain. Plants do not have brains, he points out, because their immobility renders a brain unnecessary to the information processing needed for survival interaction with their environment. In fact, ignorance is a blessing for an immobile organism unable to escape forces that might approach with consumption or other forms of assault in mind. What purpose would it serve to detect and construct information patterns that cannot be responded to?

On the other hand, mobile organisms have options, and options require decisions, and decisions require information—good information.

In deciding to go here or there and do this or that, an organism that moves of its own volition must constantly reference its survival interest in relation to current, prior, and anticipated experience, which places a high premium on the detection, construction, and elaboration of information patterns. This circumstance is amplified by environmental circumstances that promote mobility as a means to acquire food, safe harbor, and reproduction opportunities.

Calvin (1996) is among those who observe a correlation between varied diet, mobility, and mental versatility. Omnivores (e.g., octopuses, rats, and primates) exemplify this correlation in the construction of an extensive repertoire of sensory templates and movement options that correspond to their need to identify a wide range of environmental sounds, smells, tastes, textures, and images. The advantage that results from the construction of such an extensive library of patterns is that the organism has more pattern templates to reference and manipulate when confronted by novel information. This phenomenon is amplified further in organisms (e.g., humans) that have evolved as omnivores in diverse climates. A temperate climate is particularly provocative to the construction of mental templates that interpret patterns of changing food sources and shelter needs within cyclical seasons.

At a basic level, the effect of mobility on pattern construction can be observed in early child development. Diamond and Hopson (1998) describe the brain development that is observed in children as they begin to crawl. They note, in particular, the dramatic increase in neural activity and networking that occurs as a child uses the four-point mobility system of crawling to expand environmental reach and experience. The dramatic increase in sensory stimulation that results from such exploration provides a richness of data from which the baby detects and connects patterns, thus feeding the construction of knowledge about objects, people, language, and how things work.

The same phenomenon of knowledge acquisition and integration abetted by mobility is represented in the historic experience of humans as the most mobile life forms on the planet. Early evolutionary development of oppositional thumbs and bipedalism enabled the climbing of trees and mountains and the traversing of broad savannas and deserts. Hand dexterity also contributed to the development of basic tools that enhanced excavation and cultivation of the earth, hunting of large animals, and construction of clothing and shelter, all of which made it possible to explore and survive in all geographic regions and climates on Earth. The development of transportation systems and strategies has also played a role in the success of human mobility. From the domestication of animals and the invention of the wheel, humankind moved on to trains, planes, and automobiles.

More recently, human travel has moved to the depths of sea and space. The effect of this mobility experience is the same as that on a crawling infant. In the case of vast historic time, however, the effect is observed as a compounded influence of the interface between mobility, experience, and the acquisition of knowledge. Over time, as humans moved through diverse environments and encountered infinite new experiences, they provoked natural selection for brain capacity that was increasingly adept at detecting, organizing, storing, and retrieving information patterns important to survival. In effect, more movement generated more experience, which generated more neural networking. Thus humans have historically expanded their capacity to acquire and integrate knowledge through the aggressive exercise of their capacity to move to new experiences—and the pattern rich thereby become richer in both accumulated knowledge and capacity to generate more knowledge.

In the twenty-first century, humans still move in and out of multiple and varied environments, thus feeding the brain the raw material of experience needed to construct knowledge that promotes advantageous behavior. Movement to new experience is very much facilitated by technological developments, such as personal computers, the Internet, and other media. These technological developments in themselves represent new information patterns for the brain to entertain and interpret—to construct meaning that will influence decisions about new moves. Fortunately, the neural construction crew that has brought humanity to this point is up to the task.

Taking Care of Business: Subcontractors

The ancient Greeks surmised that the stuff of the universe was made up of tiny "uncuttable" ingredients that they called atoms. Just as the enormous number of words in an alphabetic language is built from the wealth of combinations of a small number of letters, they guessed that the vast range of material objects might also result from combinations of a small number of distinct, elementary building blocks. It was a prescient guess. More than 2,000 years later we still believe it to be true, although the identity of the most fundamental units has gone through numerous revisions.

—Greene (1999, p. 7)

The basic rule that guides your brain's pattern construction activity is that *things unknown become known when connected to things known.* Accordingly, when your brain confronts information that is unfamiliar, its task is to establish a relationship to familiar patterns as a base on which to construct new understanding. This process is observed in the construction of a vast vocabulary from a limited number of letters in an alphabet. It also reflects nature's disposition to generate great diversity from different combinations of limited elements, as observed in the wide range of physical and biological constructions that emerge from the basic building blocks of atomic and subatomic elements. Thus the human brain is endlessly interpreting the infinite array of patterns that nature puts together from basic information elements such as shape, sound, taste, smell, pressure, temperature, and movement.

Given the extent and complexity of the task, the brain's knowledge construction business is not attributable to a particular neural site, physiological structure, or dimension of intelligence. The acquisition and integration of important information involve the entire brain. Accordingly, the physiological, social, emotional, reflective, and dispositional dimensions of intelligence collectively contribute to the constructive dimension of intelligence—a dimension that detects, connects, stores, and retrieves blocks of knowledge that serve the intelligence business of making sense of what is encountered and deciding what to do about it (Figure 8.4). In effect, the aforementioned dimensions of intelligence are subcontractors that collaborate in the knowledge construction business—a knowledge construction firm, you might say. Notably, not all of the subcontractors are on the job at the same time, but they all contribute in some manner to constructions that matter.

Physiological Construction

Imagine a very small person moving among a thick maze of electrical cords and outlets in your head, incessantly connecting plugs to sockets to form circuits and networks that become increasingly more interconnected and complex. This simple visualization provides a basic perspective of *the construction site* for knowledge acquisition—construction that occurs at the cellular level of your brain. The involved processes include using sense to make sense, neurons firing and wiring together, and making memorable patterns.

Using sense to make sense. The initial key to knowledge construction is direct and multisensory input. In fact, the more direct and multisensory the experience, the more effective the construction. The explanation for this is fairly simple: The greater the intimacy and range of sensory information, the more pieces of the puzzle the brain has to work with in constructing meaning. The brain conducts this construction activity by directing sensory input through the brain stem to the thalamus, which distributes it

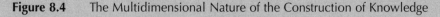

Figure 8.4   The Multidimensional Nature of the Construction of Knowledge

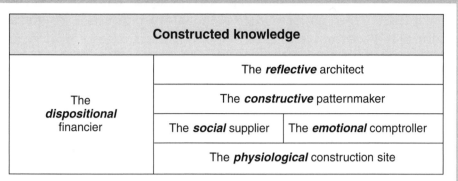

Constructed knowledge		
The **dispositional** financier	The **reflective** architect	
	The **constructive** patternmaker	
	The **social** supplier	The **emotional** comptroller
	The **physiological** construction site	

Multiple dimensions of intelligence collectively contribute to brain capacity for organizing, storing, and retrieving useful information patterns:

1. The physiology of the brain provides the construction site upon which information is sensed, organized, stored, and retrieved in neural networks that are continuously refined by the construction experience.

2. Social interaction, either direct or indirect, is a primary source of rich environmental experience from which discernment of meaningful information patterns is made.

3. Emotion is both a judge and monitor of what is worth knowing.

4. Constructive pattern discernment composes meaning and memory.

5. Reflection refines and manipulates patterns toward complex constructions.

6. Disposition determines the quantity and quality of intelligence invested in knowledge construction.

to other brain sites for further processing. The entire brain is involved in this processing, but different sites have different interests. For example, the amygdala screens information for patterns of emotional interest, the cerebellum is interested in patterns affecting procedural and automatic exercises of body or mind, and the hippocampus analyzes and indexes patterns related to words, facts, and places. Information is also processed in primary and associated cortices (e.g., visual, auditory, motor) where additional pattern connections are examined and constructed. Analysis of the merits and potential of information patterns in the frontal lobe cortex is particularly important to such examination and construction. It is in this area that your brain is consciously exploring relationships between prior knowledge and new information.

Neurons firing and wiring together. Neurons that are stimulated by sensory input form alliances that acknowledge useful information patterns (Hebb, 1949). When an established neural alliance detects a recognizable information pattern, it will respond to that pattern in some manner (e.g., initiate a standard behavior, seek more information, share the information with other neurons). If the information is new, the established neural networks will attempt to connect it to existing patterns and thereby form new alliances. The importance of this phenomenon is that alliances of neurons are formed, normed, and renormed by both quantity and quality of sensory input. Your brain is continually undergoing a synaptic sculpting process as neural affiliations grow and diminish under the influence of environmental experience. This is the working of plasticity in the brain, the means by which you continually reinforce and reconstruct your knowledge in response to a continually changing environment.

Making memorable patterns. An information pattern constructed is a pattern remembered—if it is constructed well. The basic workings of memory are the same as those of knowledge construction. Information that is attended to and processed by your brain stimulates the formation of neural networks that are responsive to that information. If neural alliances are well constructed by a quality and quantity of input, the information pattern thus organized can be recalled. The more frequently the pattern is recalled, the more often the relevant neurons access the blood, glial cell, and chemical resources that support that neural alliance. In this fashion, a network becomes more strongly established—and memorable. The more you use it, the better you build it, and the less likely you are to lose it.

Social Construction

The brain constructs its understanding of its environment the old-fashioned way: It earns it. That is, given its original base of genetically installed information patterns, each human brain is left to its own experience and initiative to make sense of the world. Interaction with the physical environment is the primary source of experience that feeds the brain's construction of knowledge. Moreover, the most important variable in our environment is social interaction. In effect, if the physiological nature of the brain is the construction site for knowledge, the social nature of the brain is the *major supplier of material and labor* for the construction process.

A simple way to test the importance of social interaction to human construction of understanding is to reflect about what you have learned in your lifetime that did not involve such interaction in some way. How did you learn about language, cooking, mathematics, etiquette, philosophy, charity, music, ethics, science, juggling, geography, racism, loyalty, poverty, love, or growing roses? The nature of exceptional human capacity to construct knowledge is born of long evolutionary experience in social communities. This is not to say that you do not learn when physically alone through individual engagement of environmental stimuli. However, in such moments you are predictably reviewing or preparing knowledge that has a social origin or target through a social medium of some sort, such as a conversation, book, lecture, film, report, meeting, or work of art. Furthermore, the more significant the knowledge construction, the more likely it is to be the product of teamwork. Even such an apparent construction of singular insight as Einstein's $E = mc^2$ was a construction born of extensive interaction between the knowledge of an individual and the knowledge of others.

As examined in Chapter 6, social interaction is the environmental experience that the developmental unfolding of your brain most expects and depends on. Your brain particularly expects opportunities to construct valuable information patterns through observing, mimicking, playing, listening, debating, and other social interactions. In fact, the quantity and quality of knowledge patterns organized by your brain depend on the quantity and quality of social experience it encounters. Again, the importance of such interaction cannot be overestimated. It is the most effective means available not only by which understanding is constructed but also by which cognitive dissonance is generated and established information patterns are challenged and refined.

The importance of social interaction in the construction of neural patterns is also reinforced by the phenomenon of mirror neurons, in which coalitions of neural networks are developed and reinforced by "sympathy" firings that mentally reflect the actions of others (Motluk, 2001). "'Mirror' neurons do just that: they reflect back an action we observe in someone else, making us mimic that action or have the impulse to do so" (Goleman, 2006, p. 41). In this social manner, the brain constructs and rehearses patterns that aid language, procedures, empathy, and anticipation of actions.

Vygotsky (1978) is among the many cognitive theorists who have concluded that strong and lasting knowledge constructions are the product of highly interactive social experience. Indeed, this theoretical position is supported by research on the positive achievement effects of cooperative learning for children and adults, as reported by Slavin (1990) and others. Such findings reinforce common perceptions, such as "Two heads are better than one," "No one of us is as smart as all of us," and "You never learn anything as well as when you teach it to others." In fact, appreciation for the influence of social experience on learning engenders a perception of a community of mind, one that is collectively constructing a shared human knowledge base through synapses that bridge the physical space between individual brains.

Emotional Construction

Emotion decides what the brain will attend to. In effect, the role of emotion in the construction of knowledge is that of *the comptroller of the construction schedule*—that is, the construction supervisor that decides what, where, and when construction will take place. This is an essential element of knowledge construction. As good as it is at physiological and social processing of information, your brain cannot attend to and process everything. Accordingly, emotional networks screen and prioritize brain attention to information judged to have potential for some degree of survival advantage.

Emotion also influences the organization, storage, and retrieval of information patterns by the association of emotional context to the construction experience (e.g., pleasure, fear, excitement, anger, fun, sadness). More specifically, the construction of knowledge is enhanced by challenge and inhibited by threat (Caine & Caine, 1991). For example, stress states raise the level of the hormone cortisol in your body, which has an adverse effect on information indexing by your hippocampus. In the other direction, the periodic release of noradrenaline in response to challenges you judge to be achievable helps to focus and sustain knowledge construction. In the best-case scenario, the establishment of a clear goal or purpose is a means to both arouse and sustain the brain's passion for knowledge construction.

Reflective Construction

There is knowledge construction, and then there is knowledge construction. That is, knowledge is inevitably constructed, torn down, and reconstructed in your brain. The role of reflection in the knowledge construction business is that of *the architect* responsible for envisioning the merits and potential of information patterns. Such reflection occurs in the frontal lobes as the brain consciously mulls over information that is arriving from sensory inputs of the moment in relation to information accessed from existing neural networks. Thus, reflection is the means for refining and extending existing knowledge. It also designs and directs the construction of original ideas from the creative interplay of the brain's wealth of diverse information.

Basically, reflection is a frontal lobe–directed examination of information toward forming hypotheses, making predictions, conducting experiments, and formulating theories about how things work or might work. It is a continuous process of exploring relationships between patterns. Constructed patterns are the building blocks for reflective thinking, which in turn stimulates the construction of more patterns.

Dispositional Construction

As will be described in Chapter 10, dispositions are inclinations or tendencies of behavior that are born of both genetic programming and environmental experience. The dispositional nature of intelligence is revealed in the disparate manners in which individuals and groups exercise their capacity to acquire and apply knowledge. More simply put, dispositional intelligence is a matter of habits of mind—the tendencies and inclinations that characterize one's thinking.

Dispositional intelligence might be thought of as the *financier* that determines the investment to be made in knowledge construction and thereby the likely return to be realized from such investment. For example, one might be disposed to maintain a healthy physiological brain state, seek out social stimulation, and engage in reflective thinking strategies, or one might be disposed to abuse the physiology of the brain, withdraw from human contact, and think about things as little as possible. The point is, dispositions habitually direct your behavior, and a disposition to broadly exercise intelligence is an important influence on the construction of knowledge. Furthermore, when specifically aligned with the exercise of reflective intelligence, a proactive learning disposition is a means to override a double bind governor on your brain's proclivity for knowledge construction.

Governing the Double Bind

> *We are constantly thinking about what the world is like, and what it is likely to be like, and even about worlds that are most unlikely. Our explanations about the world constantly change as a consequence of our experience and in the process we collect—construct might be a better word—knowledge or information.*
>
> —Smith (1990, p. 13)

Your brain is very good at constructing organized information patterns, that is, knowledge. According to Perkins (1995), it is a pattern machine that becomes attuned through experience to familiar and useful patterns in the world and adept at replaying such patterns efficiently and reflexively. This is easily illustrated though a simple exercise. To that end, take a moment to read and respond to the following scenario.

Scenario: Emily is playing with her friends when she hears the ice cream truck coming down the street. She remembers her birthday money and runs into the house.

Question: What is Emily going to do?

~Reflection Time~

If your mental response to this question entertained the thought that Emily is going to purchase ice cream with her birthday money, that is understandable from a brain-as-pattern-making-machine perspective. However, a review of the scenario reveals that there is no narrative information that supports such a conclusion. All you know for sure is that Emily hears the ice cream truck, remembers her birthday money, and goes into the house. Might the truck be a refrigerated 18-wheeler delivering its cargo to a wholesale grocery? Might such a truck rumble by an outdoor café where 33-year-old Emily is playing bridge with Bubba, Bruno, and Boris when she remembers the $5,000 birthday check she received the day before from her wealthy Aunt Ruth, causing her to run into her neighbor's house to call the local Harley-Davidson dealership to order the red Sportster motorcycle she's had her eye on? No? Maybe? The point, of course, is that each scenario is as likely as any other from the information given. What your constructive brain probably did, however, was infer an outcome from patterns of information that it is familiar with and that have served it often and well in the past.

Reflective capacity for inference is an invaluable survival asset, but Perkins (1995) advises that there is an evolutionary double bind in the constructive works. The problem is that the asset carries some baggage in the form of an inherent weakness. That is, constructive intelligence is subject to bias toward patterns that work well most of the time. Two dangers are associated with this circumstance: Inappropriate applications of ingrained patterns are made to novel situations that require new understanding and original responses, and your brain is capable of constructing deficient (i.e., inaccurate, misinformed) information patterns from limited or prejudiced experience. Fortunately, reflective and dispositional intelligence (as described in Chapters 9 and 10) helps manage the double bind that naturally shadows your brain's pattern-making business.

ESSENCE

In essence, the quality of information to which one is exposed and the amount of information one acquires is reflected throughout one's lifetime in the structure of the brain.

—Bransford, Brown, and Cocking (2000, p. 118)

Pattern construction is the core business of the brain. Without this foundational capacity, the other dimensions of brain ability to learn and achieve are hopelessly compromised. Patterns are the currency of the brain. Patterns are what the brain values, accumulates, compounds, and exchanges. Leadership attention is certainly due to this constructive quality of intelligence. In determining what is most important to know about this defining human dimension, a leader might advisedly attend to its pattern-making, sensory, social, emotional, refined, and double bind nature.

Pattern Making

The brain is a lean, mean, pattern-making machine, a biological platform that enables the construction of meaning and memory from diverse information sources. This genius for discerning useful patterns defines the human species. It underlies the cognitive processes by which all knowledge is acquired, as well as how the brain conducts the sophisticated work of language, abstraction, logic, metaphor, and imagination.

Sensory

The brain constructs meaning and memory from sensory input stimulated by environmental experience, and rich, direct experience influences the quality of construction. Beyond understanding and appreciating the pattern construction genius of the brain, it is important to respect and accommodate how that genius conducts its business. That is, to do its best knowledge construction work, the brain needs a multisensory relationship with environmental information—to see, hear, touch, move, taste, and smell. Knowledge is very much a matter of construction, not instruction. The more active and multisensory the construction process is, the better the product.

Social

Social interaction is a primary source of rich environmental experience that both stimulates and facilitates the construction of meaning and memory. There is no source more stimulating and helpful to the brain's knowledge construction interests than interaction with other brains. Whether face-to-face or over distance and time, social experience is the great provocateur of knowledge construction and refinement.

Emotional

Emotion plays an important role in the construction of meaning and memory through the arousal of attention and the establishment of emotional context. The brain constructs understanding only about information judged worthy of attention and effort. Emotion also enriches the construction information the brain has to work with. Positive tension enhances pattern construction, however, whereas excessive stress inhibits it.

Refined

What is constructed and remembered is reconstructed and refined by the brain through ongoing examination of relationships to new information. Knowledge is always a work in progress in the brain. Every environmental experience encountered is an opportunity for the brain to reference and adjust prior knowledge.

A Double Bind

Comfort with existing information engenders disregard for new information. The brain values useful patterns as the means to survive and thrive. Useful mental models present a double bind, however, when openness to alternative patterns is ignored or resisted. The danger is that a familiar pattern will be maintained beyond its usefulness or accuracy. The necessary defense against such pattern complacency is a disposition to be open to new information and to continually challenge and refine existing knowledge.

IMPLICATIONS

Perception is, in the end, a cognitive event. What we see is not simply a function of what we take from the world, but what we make of it.

—Eisner (2002, p. xii)

Humankind is endowed with extraordinary capacity for constructing meaning and memory, an ability influenced by sensory, social, and emotional experience, continually refined, and subject to a double bind. This genius for pattern making resides in everyone but must be exercised to be potent. Accordingly, a leader would naturally seek to expedite the construction of knowledge by justifying, facilitating, and extending knowledge construction by self and others (Figure 8.5).

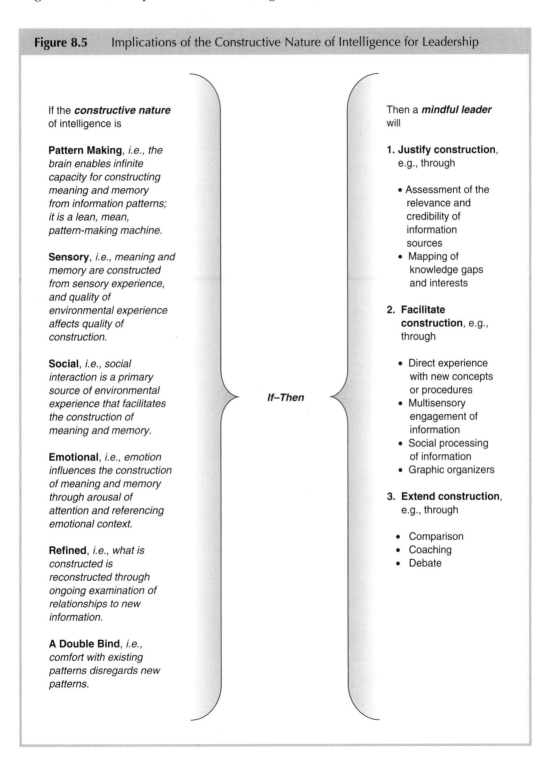

Figure 8.5 Implications of the Constructive Nature of Intelligence for Leadership

If the ***constructive nature*** of intelligence is

Pattern Making, *i.e., the brain enables infinite capacity for constructing meaning and memory from information patterns; it is a lean, mean, pattern-making machine.*

Sensory, *i.e., meaning and memory are constructed from sensory experience, and quality of environmental experience affects quality of construction.*

Social, *i.e., social interaction is a primary source of environmental experience that facilitates the construction of meaning and memory.*

Emotional, *i.e., emotion influences the construction of meaning and memory through arousal of attention and referencing emotional context.*

Refined, *i.e., what is constructed is reconstructed through ongoing examination of relationships to new information.*

A Double Bind, *i.e., comfort with existing patterns disregards new patterns.*

If–Then

Then a ***mindful leader*** will

1. **Justify construction**, e.g., through

   - Assessment of the relevance and credibility of information sources
   - Mapping of knowledge gaps and interests

2. **Facilitate construction**, e.g., through

   - Direct experience with new concepts or procedures
   - Multisensory engagement of information
   - Social processing of information
   - Graphic organizers

3. **Extend construction**, e.g., through

   - Comparison
   - Coaching
   - Debate

Justify Construction

The brain is motivated to construct meaning and memory about information that is emotionally and rationally valued. With this in mind, a leader will structure assessments that establish the relevance and potential of new information.

Facilitate Construction

The neural construction of meaning and memory is influenced by social interaction and other rich environmental experiences. Accordingly, a leader will facilitate the direct, social, and multisensory engagement of diverse information sources.

Extend Construction

Information patterns constructed and remembered are refined by connections to new information if the brain does not become too comfortable with existing patterns. A leader will therefore seek to extend and refine established knowledge by promoting exposure to new information and challenges to established perceptions.

READER REFLECTION

- What is essential to know and do about the constructive nature of intelligence?

9 Reflective Nature

Higher order consciousness involves the ability to be conscious of being conscious, and it allows the recognition by a thinking subject of his or her own acts and affections. It is accompanied by the ability in the waking state explicitly to recreate past episodes and to form future intentions.

—Edelman (2004, p. 9)

IMAGINE

To orient your reflection about the reflective nature of intelligence, access a nearby mirror (if a mirror is not available, just *imagine* your use of a mirror). Looking into the mirror (real or imagined), you will recognize the patterns your brain has constructed to represent your face and (if a full-size mirror) your body. Turning to the right or left, you will observe different perspectives of yourself. Similarly, tipping your head forward or back, smiling, frowning, or any other manipulation of posture or facial muscle will affect what is reflected back to your vision.

Thus far in this exercise, you have been engaging your constructive capacity for recognizing familiar information patterns and connecting new information worthy of attention—perhaps the status of your hair, weight, muscle tone, or a new wrinkle or suspicious blemish (which engages your emotional intelligence). However, you are able to see much more in the mirror if you elect to do so. Picture what your hair looked like 10 years ago and what it might look like 10 years into the future. How about your weight and muscle tone? Is there anything you have done in the last 10 years that has contributed to your present condition? Is there anything you might have done differently? What about the future? What are your options?

You might note that at this point you are seeing things in your mind that are not in the mirror. That is, your brain has moved from observing a present reality to envisioning what has been and what might be and what has made or will make a difference to either. This exemplifies how you re-create, explain, and forecast anything, be it as simple as a reflection about the effects of diet and exercise or as profound as John Lennon (1971) poetically imagining that the "world will be as one." Your brain constructs understanding of things the way it thinks they are, but it can also recon-struct how and why they were and how and why they might yet be. In the big survival-of-the-species picture, this capacity for conscious reflection captures the essence of what it means to be human. It is a dimension of intelligence that is manipulative, executive, unifying, and promising (Figure 9.1). We exercise it in the inductive, deductive, analytic, and cre-ative thinking involved in all decision making and problem solving. It is a capacity to see and debate answers to questions of why and how and what if within one's own mind: to imagine.

THE GIST OF IT

An Executive Function

The frontal lobes perform the most advanced and complex functions in all of the brain, the so-called executive functions. They are linked to intentionality, purposefulness, and complex decision making. They reach significant development only in humans; arguably, they make us human. . . . The frontal lobes are to the brain what a conductor is to an orchestra, a general is to an army, the chief executive officer is to a cor-poration. They coordinate and lead other neural structures in concerted action. The frontal lobes are the brain's command post.

—Goldberg (2001, p. 2)

Goldberg observes that the evolution of a cortical principle of brain organization enabled far greater complexity and connectivity of informa-tion processing than would be accommodated by a modular principle of brain organization. In effect, the brain developed a truly "dynamic topol-ogy" (2001, p. 218) as the cortex evolved. Such explosive development in capacity required the emergence of a mechanism for managing it to effect. Enter the frontal lobes of the brain.

Figure 9.1   The Reflective Nature of Intelligence

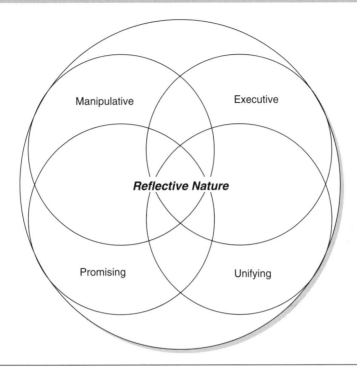

The **reflective nature** of intelligence is

Manipulative: *Reflection is the distinguishing brain capacity for consciously manipulating information and rehearsing options before action—to move beyond the construction of what is to the contemplation of what has been and might be.*

Executive: *Reflection serves an executive function that purposefully accesses, coordinates, directs, and otherwise governs the vast resources of the brain in the exercise of complex reasoning. This executive governance is particularly important when there is need to constrain, redirect, or otherwise remedy actions initiated in other brain areas, such as actions initiated in the emotional centers of the brain.*

Unifying: *Reflective problem resolution requires physiological support, social interaction, managed emotion, knowledge construction, and productive dispositions.*

Promising: *The essence of reflection is expressed in scientific inquiry, philosophy, and art; it is the capacity that empowers human versatility and future prospects.*

It is useful to reference the physiological evolution of the brain when investigating its reflective capacities because the physiology helps to explain the reflective process. Specifically, the frontal lobes of the brain represent an evolutionary development that met the need for "coordinating and constraining the activities of a vast array of neural structures at any given time and over time" (Goldberg, 2001, p. 218). You might say that, just as the brain evolved a means to coordinate the components of increasingly complex organisms, the frontal lobes evolved to coordinate the components of an increasingly complex brain. To that end, the frontal lobes are globally connected to the rest of the brain so that they might access and configure information in the manner required of any specific circumstance. The frontal lobes also have the capacity to constrain, redirect, or remediate actions initiated in other brain areas.

The bottom line is that the frontal lobes are the area of the neural landscape that humans depend on to maximize brain capacity to resolve, create, and project. As such, they justify Goldberg's (2001, p. 24) assessment of the brain as "truly the organ of civilization." They are the physiological territory that is capable of lighting up intelligence potential within individuals and organizations.

Vive la Différence

We certainly have a passion for stringing things together in structured ways, ones that go far beyond the sequences produced by other animals. Besides words into sentences, we combine notes into melodies, steps into dances, and elaborate narratives into games with procedural rules. Might structured strings be a core facility of the brain, useful for language, storytelling, planning ahead, games, and ethics? Might natural selection for any of these abilities augment the common neural machinery, so that improved grammar incidentally serves to expand plan-ahead activities?

—Calvin (1996, p. 95)

If information patterns are the currency of intelligence, reflection is the compounding of returns on the original investment in their construction. That is, reflection is the ultimate stringing together of patterns of information through serious consideration—a conscious bending back—of constructed knowledge to proactively explore further configurations, implications, and applications thereof. In effect, the reflective qualities of your brain engage in examination of how that which is mentally constructed might best be invested—*exploited* might be a better word—to the advantage of survival interests.

Calvin (1996) advises that the neural mechanisms that enable the stringing together of meaningless phonemes to form meaningful words is the same mechanism that underlies the stringing together of words into sentences, concepts, and narrative stories. Ultimately, this stringing together of patterns is exhibited in the unique human capacity to string together mental narratives about events, issues, possible actions, and probable effects—that is, the capacity to analyze, plan, and predict. This capacity emerged from the strong influence of social experience that marked human evolution. A culminating effect of such experience was enhanced brain physiology for the construction of information templates. This base of neural capacity for extensive experiential knowledge served the evolution of conscious empathy for the experience of others, which in turn enabled mental narratives strung along the lines of "why," "how," and "what if." It is simple narratives such as these that eventually lead to the more complex narratives that accompany the invention of religion, art, philosophy, and scientific inquiry—ultimate expressions of human desire to explain and influence environmental experience.

Capacity for conscious reflection, then, is the distinguishing dimension of human intelligence, a dimension that is differentiated from the construction of knowledge by its physiological complexity, social unfolding, emotional refinement, and constructive capacity. As Damasio (1999) advises, it is how we know of ourselves in the past and future as well as the present.

The Mirrors of Your Mind

Even when we carry out high-level abstract thinking, it is likely that sensory and motor areas of the brain give our thoughts concrete meaning. This form of conceptual representation may underlie the appeal of metaphorical arguments so common to discourse.

—Posner and Rothbart (2007, p. 208)

Reflection is a term that many would immediately associate with intelligence. Indeed, mental images of Rodin's *The Thinker* might come to mind when one contemplates the defining nature of intelligence. From such a perspective, intelligence is the capacity to reflectively contemplate, to think deeply with fist to chin and elbow to knee in search of answers to challenging problems and issues of human existence. However, such capacity does not stand on its own. As in the case of the construction of knowledge, your capacity for reflective manipulation of information patterns is intimately enmeshed with the collective qualities of other dimensions of intelligence.

Returning for a moment to the mirror exercise presented at the beginning of this chapter, the reflective nature of intelligence can be interpreted as the conscious bending back of information patterns to discern potential relationships of peril or promise. This bending back and replaying of information occurs in the cortex and subcortical regions during reflective thought. In effect, your brain performs as a house of mirrors as it plays the light of new and established information along infinite neural networks to create and explore different perspectives. That is, your reflective brain is not content to stare into the mirror and accept what is immediately revealed. Rather, in its reflective mode, your brain is moving information at will to generate alternative images.

Reflective intelligence, then, is about enhancing the perception potential of information by organizing alternative poses from multiple information sources. Such reflection might be envisioned as a laser light show occurring within your brain, involving electrochemical messages flashing between trillions of synapses in incredibly complex arrangements of incoming, recalled, and reconstructed information patterns—the physical reality of brainstorming. Evidence of this neural activity is observed in chess players planning 12 moves out, scientists planning a landing on the moon, and coaches planning for a big game. It is also observable in the creativity and problem solving of artists, politicians, and entrepreneurs. The same process is at work in evaluating a personal relationship, planning a vacation, or pondering a career move. Most of all, it is a process that unifies the multidimensional nature of your intelligence in the act of meaningful real-world thinking and learning. As Senge (1990, p. 14) observes, such thinking "gets to the heart of what it means to be human"—to re-create ourselves, perceive the world and our relationship to it, extend our capacity to create, and be part of the generative processes of life.

A Unifying Intelligence

The prefrontal cortex plays the central role in forming goals and objectives and then devising plans of action required to attain these goals. It selects the cognitive skills required to implement the plans, coordinates these skills, and applies them in a correct order. Finally, the prefrontal cortex is responsible for evaluating our actions as success or failure relative to our intentions.

—Goldberg (2001, p. 24)

It is possible for you to reflect on anything, including your navel. Your reflective intelligence is usually reserved for more interesting and challenging situations, however, such as making decisions or resolving problems of consequence to you and others in the context of work, home, or play. Such reflection naturally draws together other dimensions of knowledge acquisition and application (Figure 9.2).

Figure 9.2   The Unifying Influence of Reflection on Multiple Dimensions of Intelligence

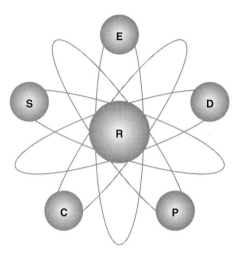

The engagement of **R**eflection through meaningful problem solving, decision making, or other tasks involving complex reasoning requires

1. **P**hysiological engagement of the brain's comprehensive network of cells, circuits, and chemicals
2. **S**ocial interaction in processing information toward shared purpose
3. **E**motional attention, judgment, motivation, and management
4. **C**onstruction of relevant knowledge
5. **D**isposition to exercise productive thinking

Physiological involvement: Conscious reflection about concepts, events, and options lights up your brain—literally. Functional magnetic resonance imaging scans of your brain while it is engaged in problem solving or other reflective exercises will detect extensive electrochemical activity as neural networks are activated in cross-referencing available information patterns. This is particularly evident in the cortex, the crowning glory of human brain evolution, the neural field in which brainstorming physically occurs. Such neural communication is most dramatic when the reflective task is novel to your brain, thus placing greater demands on the working memory functions of the prefrontal lobe and access to undedicated neural space in various associative cortices that accommodate the storage, retrieval, and continual sculpting of information.

Social involvement: Reflection seeks out interaction with the knowledge of other brains, through either direct or extended means. Such interaction is an essential source of dissonance and options for your brain's reflective efforts. Social experience is the great provocateur of reflection, the foil that challenges and refines existing patterns in the quest for the better pattern. It is an element of reflection born of highly social communities, one that supplies new information and encourages the asking of who, what, where, when, why, and how.

Emotional involvement: Reflective intelligence is not engaged unless the emotional centers of the brain have judged a situation or circumstance worthy of your brain's conscious attention. Once they are engaged, however, reflective pursuit of an answer, solution, or original product or idea is itself an influence on your emotions. In effect, confrontation with a meaningful, real-world challenge both arouses and fans the passions of the mind, thus engaging reflective focus and perseverance. The danger that lurks is that the reflection challenge is of a magnitude that overwhelms or intimidates, thus stimulating an emotional decision to withdraw.

Constructive involvement: Reflection about a meaningful problem or other challenging task provides your brain with the greatest motivation and opportunity to construct knowledge. One cannot reflect about alternatives and options without relevant information. Accordingly, information must be retrieved from existing neural networks, or new patterns of understanding must be constructed. The building blocks of knowledge must be available for your reflective intelligence to play with if it is to compose its virtuoso performances of thought and deed.

Dispositional involvement: Habits are formed, not born. The exercise of reflective intelligence requires a disposition to analyze, create, and resolve. Furthermore, the development of such disposition is the product of reflective thinking experience. To that end, to cultivate productive dispositions toward the effective exercise of reflective thinking strategies, the old adage applies: Practice, practice, practice.

Intelligence Most Conscious

The combinatorial nature of language and thought allows us to entertain an explosion of ideas even though we are equipped with a finite inventory of concepts and relations.

—Pinker (2007, p. 436)

Human intelligence is made distinct by a unique capacity for mental visioning and rehearsal of behavior options before action. This specific capacity for the reflective review and manipulation of information is of particular survival advantage when confronted by novel environmental challenges—when guessing well is, indeed, the game, and pressure is on your brain.

If the genius of human intelligence rests on an extraordinary capacity to construct useful information patterns, then reflection is the exhibition of virtuosity in the application of that genius. This is observed in the fact that the resolutions of problems or tasks often are the products of mentally massaging existing information. A brief exercise illustrates this point:

1. Extend your right arm in front of you at chest level with the palm of your hand facing down and make a fist.

2. Think of a controversial issue that is being hotly debated in the nation, your community, your home, or your place of work.

3. Identify the pro and con positions of the issue you have identified (e.g., for or against a large tax cut, for or against physician-assisted suicide, for or against drilling for oil in wilderness areas, for or against a pending school referendum).

4. Indicate your position (i.e., for or against) by extending the thumb of your extended fist up or down. You may think about this for a moment, but you must take a thumbs-up or thumbs-down position on the issue.

5. Put your arm down, grab a pen, and jot down your rationale, that is, your reasons for your position on the issue.

6. Now write down what you believe advocates of the position opposite yours would write as their rationale for their position.

7. Question: What was happening in your brain as you completed Steps 1–6?

~ Reflection Time ~

This exercise becomes more stimulating of the reflective circuitry in your prefrontal cortex, and its interaction with the rest of your brain, if you have access to someone who advocates an opposing position. You would be able to compare what you anticipated about each other's reasoning to each one's actual arguments. You might also be prompted to reflect further about evidence and opinions that support or detract from either position; you might even change your position. What you should be aware of, in any case, is that your neural circuitry was able to

- access existing information that has been stored throughout your brain by prior information constructions,
- articulate a position on the issue that you reconstructed in your mind,
- articulate a second perspective about the same issue, and
- in the seventh step of the exercise, analyze what your brain was doing as it was doing it.

As simple as this exercise was, it reveals the essence of the reflective difference in your brain compared with the brains of other life forms—the capacity to replay information sequences and patterns in your head at will, to think 12 steps out on a chess board or in career planning, or to construct deeper understanding of an issue, process, or concept. This is what your brain does when it is performing at the high end of its evolutionary endowment. It is the quality of human intelligence that draws on all other dimensions of mental capacity to orchestrate the phenomenal success of the species. It is also the quality that will determine future success. Incredibly, as will be observed in Chapter 10, the effective exercise of this powerful capacity for analytic and creative thinking is optional, to be used at the disposition of those who are blessed with it.

ESSENCE

The creative process arises from the ferment of ideas in the brain turning and colliding until something new emerges. At the neural level, associations begin to form where they did not previously exist.

—Andreasen (2005, p. 128)

The core business of the brain is pattern construction. Reflective reasoning is the executive function that applies that business to exceptional advantage. Indeed, the reflective capacity of the brain defines the biological niche of humankind. The ability to consciously review and reconfigure relationships within and between established patterns is what makes us unique. It is the capacity by which individuals and groups can aspire to unravel any mystery, resolve any problem, and meet any challenge. It is what we turn to when the going gets tough, there are no set answers, and we have to guess well. What, then, is most worth knowing about this dimension of intelligence? The suggestion here is that leaders everywhere—whether in the schoolhouse, medical center, manufacturing plant, financial institution, or any other human enterprise—should understand how the brain is manipulative, executive, unifying, and promising.

Manipulative

Reflection is the distinguishing brain capacity for consciously manipulating information and rehearsing options before action—to move beyond the construction of what is to the contemplation of what has been and might be. The brain is always working information to review actions and project events. This ability is the essence of the essence of intelligence, the most potent asset to be nurtured in any human system.

Executive

Reflection serves an executive function that purposefully accesses, coordinates, and directs the vast resources of the brain in the exercise of complex reasoning. The frontal lobes of the brain enable reflection about what is worth reflecting about and how the rest of the brain will be involved. This is the capacity by which neural assets are allocated and managed to a greater or lesser advantage. Notably, reflection constrains, redirects, or otherwise remedies actions initiated in other brain areas, particularly actions initiated in the emotional centers of the brain. This is evident when reasoning is used to harness the power of emotion to a productive advantage. It is also the means for consciously engaging new information and options to counter the seductive control of established knowledge (i.e., the double bind).

Unifying

Reflective reasoning is observed at the neural level in the outer layers of the prefrontal lobe of the cortex. Microtechnology can further locate specific aspects of complex reasoning processes, such as problem solving, in the lateral prefrontal cortex. However, reflective capacity is intimately connected to the entire brain system. Reflective attention to a meaningful problem or decision requires physiological support, social interaction, emotional tension, knowledge construction, and productive thinking dispositions. Reflective reasoning comprehensively engages the integrated neural networks of the brain. When confronted with a real-world challenge, the brain is physically engaged, emotionally focused, and socially disposed toward the construction and refinement of information patterns that will resolve the issue.

Promising

The essence of reflection is expressed in scientific inquiry, philosophy, and art; it is the capacity that empowers human versatility and future prospects. Reflective analysis, experimentation, and imagination hold the keys to human survival and success.

IMPLICATIONS

Except for the neural engine we carry under our skulls, the experiential and reflective intelligence housed by that engine, and the products of past intelligence in the form of an immense support structure of culture and language and artifacts that lets each generation capitalize on the advances of the previous, we human beings are unimpressive organisms.

—Perkins (1995, p. 319)

The reflective capacity to consciously manipulate information backward and forward and inside out is the crowning glory of human intelligence. It is a capacity that directs the complex thinking involved in solving problems, improving programs, and creating new products and procedures. What approaches, then, would be used to cultivate a culture of reflection? Two suggestions for how a leader might connect to the reflective powers of the prefrontal cortex would be to structure and challenge the thinking of self and others (Figure 9.3).

Structure Thinking

The brain will more efficiently engage its capacity for manipulating information when facilitated by templates that support the natural structures of human thinking. Accordingly, a leader will use structured steps in problem solving, decision making, and organizational planning.

Challenge Thinking

The best thinking takes place at the edge. The analytic and creative capacities of the brain are brought into play by serious questions in need of answers. The brain will not bring forth its greatest assets unless pressed by the environment to do so. For that reason, a leader will challenge the thinking of self and others through debate, innovation, and invention.

READER REFLECTION

- What is essential to know and do about the reflective nature of intelligence?

Figure 9.3 Implications of the Reflective Nature of Intelligence for Leadership

If the **reflective nature** of intelligence is

Manipulative, *i.e., reflection is the distinguishing brain capacity for consciously manipulating information and rehearsing options before action—to move beyond the construction of what is to the contemplation of what has been and might be.*

Executive, *i.e., reflection is an executive function that accesses, coordinates, and otherwise governs brain resources in the exercise of complex reasoning, governance that constrains or redirects actions initiated in other brain areas (e.g., in emotional centers).*

Unifying, *i.e., reflective problem solving requires physiological support, social interaction, managed emotion, knowledge construction, and productive disposition.*

Promising, *i.e., the essence of reflection is expressed in scientific inquiry, philosophy, and art; it is the capacity that empowers human versatility and future prospects.*

If–Then

Then a **mindful leader** will

1. **Structure thinking** by self and others, e.g., through

   - Investigation
   - Analysis
   - Synthesis
   - Analogy
   - Projection
   - Brainstorming
   - Inductive reasoning
   - Deductive reasoning
   - Critiquing
   - Defending
   - Role plays
   - Case study

2. **Challenge thinking** of self and others, e.g., through

   - Problem solving
   - Decision making
   - Force field analysis
   - System analysis
   - Scenario planning
   - Debate
   - Analysis of perspective
   - Metaphor
   - Invention
   - Lateral thinking
   - Improvisation
   - Artistic interpretation

10 Dispositional Nature

If it ain't in your heart, it ain't in your horn.

—Attributed to legendary
saxophonist Charlie Parker

DISPOSITION FAIR AND FOUL

Think about a friend, colleague, or family member whom you hold in high esteem. What do you appreciate most about that person? Similarly, what qualities do you admire in people whom you know less well, such as people you encounter in the process of conducting your work, shopping, engaging professional services, or dining out?

~ Reflection Time ~

Attributes that you admire in the people who cross your path—whether through long relationships or brief encounters—are almost limitless in possibility. It is nonetheless predictable that such qualities as being *positive, proactive, kind, productive, creative, friendly, organized, sincere, open-minded, modest, conscientious, resilient, fun loving, considerate, confident, dedicated, responsible,* or *compassionate* come to mind when you are envisioning an admirable person.

Unfavorable attributes will also readily emerge when you are reflecting on a close relationship or passing encounter with a person held in low esteem. How would you describe the qualities of a person whom you find to be less than admirable in some way?

~ Reflection Time ~

Again, the range of attributes that could be used to describe undesirable qualities in people is endless. Terms such as *negative, reactive, cruel, lazy, unimaginative, cold, disorganized, insincere, closed-minded, conceited, inattentive, morose, dull, rude, indecisive, uncommitted, irresponsible,* or *insensitive* are common candidates.

What of you? What attributes—be they admirable or unfavorable—come to mind when you contemplate your qualities? The test for this reflection is to assess how you might commonly respond in given situations. For example, how would you respond to:

- Another driver cutting you off in heavy traffic?
- Criticism from a colleague of an idea you have proposed?
- The announcement of a major restructuring of your organization?
- An innovative idea that proposes radical change in existing policy or practice?
- A news report describing a social injustice committed against an individual or group of people?
- Winning the lottery?
- Responsibility for organizing an investment portfolio, family vacation, political campaign, construction project, wedding, or other major planning activity?
- A decline in market share for your organization due to new competition?
- A problem that has not been resolved after several efforts to find a solution?
- Required training in how to use a new technology?

How do you see yourself responding to these situations? Would others see you in the same light? Would you resist the allure of road rage, persist in the face of a daunting problem, or be open to critical review from a colleague? What do your projected responses reveal about admirable human qualities—or qualities judged to be less than admirable?

~ Reflection Time ~

What might be concluded from these exercises? It should be clear that humans adopt characteristic behaviors. It should also be clear that you know what you appreciate and do not appreciate about other people, just as they know what they appreciate and do not appreciate about you. Indeed, we determine defining qualities of self and others through valuation of habitual behavior in social contexts. We come to know one another by our characteristic behavior. Of course, we would not make such distinctions if we were not inclined to habitual behavior—behavior that reveals dispositions of mind and character. This chapter explores the macro, mandatory, malleable, and minimizing and maximizing nature of dispositions (Figure 10.1).

Figure 10.1 The Dispositional Nature of Intelligence

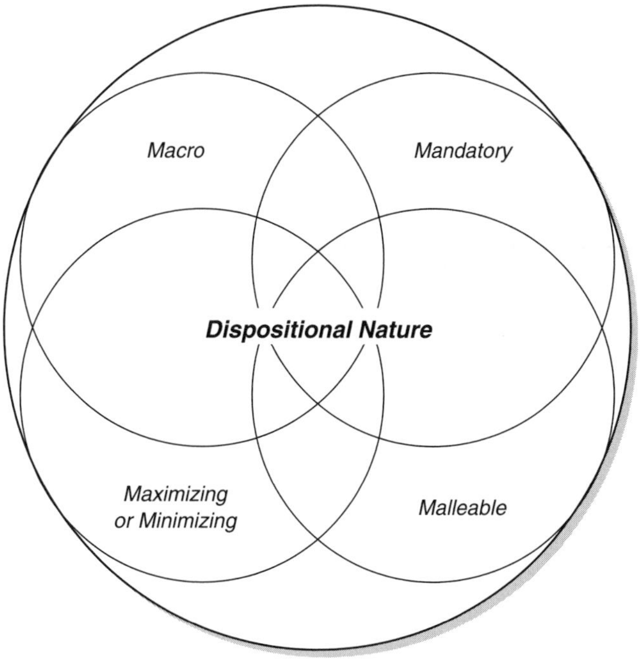

The **dispositional nature** of intelligence is

Macro: *The brain adopts patterns of thinking—mental tendencies or inclinations—that are habitually applied on a broad scale as the brain conducts its survival business.*

Mandatory: *The brain has no option other than to develop and exercise habits of thinking, but there are options regarding the quality of habits developed.*

Malleable: *Thinking dispositions are genetically introduced and environmentally influenced.*

Maximizing or Minimizing: *Thinking habits are determining factors in how far and well one travels the neural byways of the brain; human capacity to think, learn, and achieve is realized to the degree that there is a productive disposition driving it.*

THE GIST OF IT

The Disposition of Disposition

Dispositions shape our lives. They are proclivities that lead us in one direction rather than another within the freedom of action that we have.

—Perkins (1995, p. 275)

There are many levels and facets of understanding disposition (i.e., a habitual inclination; a tendency) that invite investigation. However, the proclivity of human intelligence to engage and cultivate itself is of particular interest to this narrative. Specifically, how are qualities of mind and character arranged as tendencies and inclinations that affect the exercise of intelligence? The answer to this question, predictably, is that it is a matter of brain nature and nurture.

Dispositions evolve from the electrochemical compositions, allocations, and interactions that mediate all human behavior. That is, dispositions are ultimately the product of electrochemical activity in the neural networks of the brain. Accordingly, at birth, an infant has genetically established neural circuits that are disposed to engage particular behavior patterns in particular situations. Some of these dispositions are so universally demonstrated—for example, crying when hungry or otherwise physically distressed—that they are hardly distinguishable between infants. As every parent of more than one child well knows, however, individual infants almost immediately demonstrate dispositions that mark their unique character as human beings. Thus infants are evaluated as being more or less irritable, anxious, or easygoing by the habitual behaviors they exhibit. Parents, teachers, and other observers of child development will also note that initial dispositional exhibitions may strengthen, diminish, or otherwise change over time under the influence of environmental experience.

The bottom line is that some dispositions are factory installed in the brain by virtue of the genetic endowment of the human species as passed on from parent to child. This inheritance accesses the common dispositional attributes of the human species as evolved over millions of years of natural selection. Some of these dispositions are immediately evident, whereas others become more apparent at later developmental stages. Gopnik, Meltzoff, and Kuhl (1999) speak to such inherited species attributes when they describe children's natural interest and behavior in making sense of the people, objects, and language that they encounter as analogous to the disposition and behavior of scientists. That is, children naturally seek to construct understanding by forming hypotheses, making predictions, conducting experiments, and formulating theories about how

people, things, and language work. However, a disposition that is origi-
nally installed is also immediately and continually influenced (commenc-
ing in the womb) by the specific environmental experience of the individual.
Thus human disposition is disposed by both nature and nurture—as are
all other qualities of human organisms. The challenge and potential, of
course, lie in the nurture.

Why Dispositions?

*Humans are prepared by their biology to form friendships, fall in love,
cope with fear, and try, continually, to move toward their prized goals,
despite early experiences that might make these attainments hard to
accomplish. These urges are remarkably difficult to subdue.*

—Kagan (1998, p. 109)

Returning once again to the primary business of the human brain, dispositions can be interpreted as habitual patterns of behavior that the brain
at some level—consciously, or subconsciously, disposed by nature or nurture or a combination thereof—judges to be of survival value. This does
not mean that a particular behavioral pattern is indeed a good one; it just
means the brain at some level believes that it is somehow useful to behave
in a certain manner (e.g., to be habitually positive or negative, open- or
closed-minded, timid or adventurous, trusting or suspicious, active or
lethargic). The discernment of such patterns is consistent with the basic
information processing operations of the brain that determine patterns of
advantageous behavior—whether determining patterns pertinent to object
recognition, feeding, communication, or any other advantage. The discernment of dispositions is, in effect, the organization of behavior patterns
at a broad level, patterns that are established and exhibited as habits, tendencies, or inclinations. Such patterns reflect the brain's decision that it is
of value to cultivate a tendency to behave in a certain manner. Notably, the
discernment of preferred dispositional patterns engages physiological,
social, emotional, constructive, and reflective dimensions of intelligence.
That is, the physiological platform enables the construction and reflective
adjustment of dispositional patterns that unfold within social and emotional experience.

Kagan (1998) speaks to the nature and nurture of human disposition in
his analysis of transitions that occur in initial exhibitions of high- and low-
reactivity temperaments by infants. He speculates that infants inherit different neurochemistries in brain structures that mediate avoidance
reactions to novelty. However, subsequent developmental stages combined
with nurturing environmental experiences assert a changing influence on

the initial high-reactivity dispositions of many infants. This effect is most dramatically demonstrated by the resiliency of war orphans who, by virtue of nurturing adult care, progress from anxious and subdued dispositional states to normal psychological profiles.

So it is with humans over the lifespan. Dispositions—loosely and variously referred to as habits, tendencies, inclinations, attitudes, personality, character, or temperament—are rooted in genetic blueprints but malleable by experience. The malleability of disposition is observable in the adolescent who breaks or reverses an established dispositional pattern and the adult who is dispositionally transformed by significant changes in professional or personal circumstances. Dispositions bloom and sour at the experience of new schools, jobs, challenges, relationships, and other life experiences—as well as the cumulative effect of more subtle everyday experiences. They are also affected by conscious reflection about dispositional status and what actions might engender the attainment of preferred states, as will be discussed shortly.

Why dispositions? It is nature's way to organize and adapt patterns. Dispositions are habitual behavior patterns that are observable in every arena of human activity. They serve as behavior templates that affect hygiene, exercise, diet, interpersonal relations, work, and almost any other activity that presents an option as to how to act. In fact, it is difficult to imagine human existence without the element of habitual behavior. Life would be much more difficult to manage on a moment-to-moment basis if one had to continually pause to reflect about every behavior option. The establishment of habitual behavior patterns relieves the brain of such mundane preoccupation with how to act in every instance (e.g., to be positive or negative, open-minded or closed-minded). The trick, of course, is to establish productive dispositions that generally guide advantageous behavior over the wide range of human activity, thus freeing the reflective powers of the brain for more momentous tasks.

The advantage of a productive disposition (and, conversely, the disadvantage of a detrimental disposition) is that it provides ready propensity for behavior by which you might more efficiently and effectively conduct your survival business. Nowhere is this more significant than in the disposition to engage and exercise intelligent behavior.

Disposition of Mind

A disposition is a propensity to act in a certain way. Viewing intelligence dispositionally says that intelligence is expressed as characteristic patterns of intellectual behavior in everyday situations.

—Tishman (2000, p. 43)

All forms of disposition matter, whether they are genetically ingrained or experientially cultivated. Disposition to consciously exercise the multiple dimensions of human intelligence is of particular importance. In effect, it is the nature of human intelligence to adopt habitual patterns for the engagement of its diverse and powerful properties. Significantly, it is disposition to consciously engage intelligence that holds sway over all other possible human dispositions, good or bad. Furthermore, such disposition might be exercised on both broad and specific levels of engagement.

Broad Disposition to Exercise Intelligence

Humans are gifted by nature with extraordinary intelligence capacity. This capacity is available on demand for use and development as individuals and organizations choose to engage it. There lies the rub. Capacity does not equate with effective use or realization of potential. Natural capacity to walk, talk, or create visual images does not automatically evolve to ballet, opera, or the *Mona Lisa*. Likewise, human capacity for intelligence does not automatically translate into intelligent behavior. Humans are genetically disposed to engage the

- *Physiological nature* of brain capacity for monitoring and processing information through a biological platform of cells, circuits, and chemicals that is intimately integrated with the entire physiology of the body
- *Social nature* of brain capacity for interacting with other brains to learn and achieve
- *Emotional nature* of brain capacity for arousing mind and body to advantageous responses and actions
- *Constructive nature* of brain capacity for discerning and storing useful information patterns from the richness of environmental experience
- *Reflective nature* of brain capacity for consciously assessing objectives, obstacles, and options
- *Dispositional nature* of brain capacity for organizing broad patterns of thinking and behavior that are perceived to be of some survival advantage

There is no choice in this matter. It is our nature to acquire and apply information in such multidimensional fashion. It is as natural as breathing. Human intelligence must be consciously and regularly exercised if it is to realize its potential, however. Conscious engagement of intelligence is key to maximizing intelligence. What might such broad disposition toward intelligence look like? Examples follow.

- A disposition to optimally exercise the *physiological dimension* of intelligence might be expressed through propensities for physical exercise, healthy diet, water consumption, fresh air, natural light, novelty, and stimulating environments.
- A disposition to optimally exercise the *social dimension* of intelligence might be expressed through characteristic propensities for seeking opportunities for interaction, collaboration, and the sharing and challenging of ideas.
- A disposition to optimally exercise the *emotional dimension* of intelligence might be expressed through characteristic propensities for mediating emotion in a manner that contributes to the quality of one's life (i.e., emotional intelligence), proactive management of detrimental stress factors, and orientation to compelling professional and personal purpose.
- A disposition to optimally exercise the *constructive dimension* of intelligence might be expressed through characteristic propensities for constructing personal understanding through direct sensory information experiences such as writing, speaking, drawing, enactment, assembly, experimentation, or demonstration.
- A disposition to optimally exercise the *reflective dimension* of intelligence might be expressed through characteristic propensities for engaging specific thinking strategies associated with planning, analysis, problem solving, decision making, conflict resolution, and creativity.
- A disposition to optimally exercise the *dispositional dimension* of intelligence might be expressed through characteristic propensities for metacognition (thinking about one's thinking) as it pertains to other dimensions of intelligence (i.e., physiological, social, emotional, constructive, and reflective).

Specific Disposition to Think

Beyond a broad disposition to engage intelligence lies the opportunity to use specific strategies that maximize the phenomenon. This perception is reflected in a wide range of research about effective thinking, the findings of which point to specific qualities and behaviors of effective thinkers. Notably, scholars in this arena argue for the distinction between human capacity for intelligence and specific thinking strategies that take full advantage of said capacity. They also acknowledge the importance of thinking disposition, that is, the disposition to both learn and, subsequently, apply thinking skills.

Perkins (1995) advises that a thinking disposition is a tendency, habit, or commitment toward thinking in a certain way, such as the disposition to be open-minded, the disposition to think in an imaginative and adventurous way, or the disposition to seek out evidence. Perkins further points out that although the cultivation of intelligence certainly involves skill development (e.g., in problem-solving, decision-making, or creative thinking strategies), the disposition to exercise learned skills needs attention also. That is, people can become reasonably skilled at an activity such as swimming, selling, or thinking without being especially disposed to engage in it. Examples of the dispositions of effective thinkers, as identified by Perkins and others, follow.

- Paul (1990) proposes seven interdependent traits of mind that are important to critical thinking: intellectual humility, courage, empathy, good faith (integrity), perseverance, reason, and a sense of justice.
- Facione and Facione (1992) suggest that there are seven general thinking dispositions: truth seeking, open-mindedness, analyticity, systematicity, self-confidence, inquisitiveness, and maturity.
- Perkins (1995, pp. 284–285) describes seven core dispositions of good thinking:

  1. *Disposition to be clear,* coherent, precise, specific, and well organized

  2. *Disposition to be broad,* adventurous, flexible, and independent while appreciative of other perspectives and committed to the discovery of connections

  3. *Disposition to seek deep understanding* of underlying unities in the form of laws, theories, frameworks, principles, causes, and other governing factors of ideas, things, and events

  4. *Disposition to be sound,* accurate, thorough, fair, knowledgeable, logical, and well supported by evidence

  5. *Disposition to be curious,* questioning, probing, and inquisitive

  6. *Disposition to be strategic* and organized in thinking

  7. *Disposition to be metacognitively aware* of one's thinking pattern and progress

Aside from an obvious affinity for seven items, these lists suggest some common themes (e.g., openness to new information and alternative views). It is understandable that different scholars come to different conclusions about core thinking dispositions, although we may find it disconcerting that they use different terms and phrases to describe elements that they do agree on. This problem is attributable in part to the nature of scholarship, but it also raises an important point about thinking dispositions: Determining the exact thinking skills to be mastered is not the matter of greatest concern or difficulty. What matters most is a disposition to seek, master, and use effective thinking strategies. This statement may appear to be a bit reckless at first blush, but it embodies a critical perspective of thinking dispositions. Perkins (1995) captures this relationship in his metaphor of "mindware" (i.e., mental software) programs that are run in the mind to make the best use of intelligence—that is, to solve problems, make decisions, understand difficult concepts, or perform other difficult intellectual tasks. Thinking skills are mindware programs, and there are many such programs. Disposition is the element that interprets the nature and value of a particular thinking skill program and—most important— determines whether, when, and how it will be run.

The Dispositional Difference

Some people are better mental pilots with a more elevated point of view.

—Perkins (1995, p. 99)

How important is the dispositional dimension of intelligence? Simply put, it is disposition that holds sway over all other dimensions of intelligence. It is the arena in which intelligent behavior (i.e., the referencing and engagement of multiple intelligence capacities and strategies) is either advanced or diminished. This is particularly true for the conscious engagement of thinking strategies appropriate to the reflective nature of human intelligence—the dimension that is most defining of the human capacity for acquiring and applying information to survival advantage. Ultimately, disposition is the means to grow physiological, social, emotional, constructive, and reflective intelligence.

Perkins (1995) is among the theorists who discern a learnable human intelligence as demonstrated by people who engage specific strategies for the best use of their minds. Such people are more likely to monitor their own thinking and pilot it in effective ways. They cultivate and use more strategies for intellectually challenging tasks, including dispositions to be proactive, persistent, and creative. The point Perkins makes is that people can learn to think and act more intelligently; good thinkers are made, not born.

As to the matter of thinking strategies that merit dispositional consideration, help is close at hand from composite lists that draw on the collective findings of scholars.

Winning Dispositions

A mind is like a parachute. To work well, it has to be open.

—Bumper sticker

Costa and Kallick (2000) articulate 16 habits of mind that are displayed by intelligent people in response to problems, dilemmas, and enigmas: persisting, managing impulsiveness, listening with understanding and empathy, thinking flexibly, thinking about thinking (metacognition), striving for accuracy, questioning and posing problems, applying past knowledge to new problems, thinking and communicating with clarity and precision, gathering data with all senses, creating and innovating, responding with wonderment and awe, taking responsible risks, finding humor, thinking interdependently, and remaining open to continuous learning.

Covey (1989) advises that habitual dispositions ultimately determine personal effectiveness. He contends that people become more effective as they progress from dependent to independent and interdependent states through mastery of the dispositions to be proactive, look to the end, put first things first, seek first to understand and then be understood, seek win–win solutions, synergize, and sharpen the saw (i.e., continually pursue self-renewal in the physical, social–emotional, mental, and spiritual domains).

Winning dispositions are not of benefit to individuals only. Organizations also benefit from productive dispositional qualities. Senge (1990) speaks to this in his articulation of five disciplines that characterize the dispositions of a learning organization: systems thinking, personal mastery, mental models, shared vision, and team learning.

Endgame: Mindful Disposition

Mental habits, whether good or bad, are certain to be formed.

—Dewey (1933, p. 89)

In examining what he calls the intelligence paradox (i.e., how can we be so smart and yet so dumb), Perkins (1995, pp. 152–153) concludes that humans are subject to default thinking, that is, they fall into the intelligence traps of:

- Hasty thinking, characterized by impulsiveness and mindlessness—people reacting and acting without thinking about what they are doing
- Narrow thinking, marked by bias and fixed, limited patterns of information

- Fuzzy thinking that fails to seek clarity, precision, and distinctions in information
- Sprawling thinking that wanders in a disorganized way without ever converging

People are susceptible to falling into these traps when they are not engaged in what Ellen Langer (1989) calls *mindfulness,* that is, a mindful state of being that creates new categories, is open to new information, and is aware of more than one perspective. Mindlessness, on the other hand, is like being on automatic pilot and inattentive.

How shall you be disposed to use and optimize your intelligence? The answer, it appears, is that you will do it if and how you wish to do it. What seems more certain is that productive habits of mind are the product of initiative and effort—a disposition to cultivate dispositions. Another way to say this is to once again apply the maxim that if you want a good disposition, you have to earn it. Covey (1989) speaks to the nature of habit formation in a similar manner when he stipulates the interactive effects of knowledge, desire, and skill over time in the construction of preferred dispositional behavior. A final exercise in this chapter will illustrate this point.

Scenario: Amy, Emily, and Abby are each holding an identical plastic cube in their hands at waist height. They all release the cube they are holding at the same time. When they do so, Amy's cube descends, Emily's cube ascends, and Abby's cube does not move.

Question: What is your explanation for this phenomenon: Three people release three identical plastic cubes at the same time and each cube responds to the release in a different way.

~ Reflection Time ~

Your brief reflection about possible explanations for this scenario undoubtedly produced a plausible explanation. You may have thought of an explanation immediately, or perhaps you thought about it for a bit, but you did come up with an explanation—perhaps several explanations. Now go an extra step in this exercise. Come up with *one more* explanation for the scenario. The only requirement is that it must be a different explanation from what you thought of in your first attempt.

~ Reflection Time ~

The assumption is that you have now thought of at least two explanations for the described mystery. A further assumption is that if you were asked to go back to the scenario and come up with yet another explanation, you could do so. You might even become more analytical and imaginative each time you had a go at it. Indeed, you might become quite good at generating alternatives. Should you happen to be conducting such reflection in the company of others, the explanations might never stop, given the many hundreds of billions of neurons networked in the investigation of all possible alternatives. That, of course, is the point of the exercise. The goal is not the quick answer—that one person is on land, one person is under water, and one person is on a space shuttle orbiting the Earth; or that one person is standing upright, one person is standing on her head, and one person is lying on her side on the ground; or that one person is above water, one person is under water, and one person is standing in water at waist depth; and so on. The possibilities are endless, are they not, once you start thinking?

And what is the product of such thinking? Obviously, it is a means to generate alternatives, a process of problem solving or decision making. More important, it is an exercise that builds and refines a productive disposition of mind—to be inclined to generate and consider possible alternatives in given situations. This, then, is the endgame of mindfulness: to be disposed to exercise the physiological, social, emotional, constructive, and reflective qualities of your brain to greatest advantage.

ESSENCE

Disposed toward independence and individualism, creativity nevertheless benefits from direct nurturing in the form of training and emotional and intellectual support.

—Andreasen (2005, p. 131)

The brain is disposed to conduct its business in ways that are both prescribed by nature and subject to nurture. At any given time, the brain is working to establish a cohesive state of mind among the integrated mental processes that define it. To that end, it is disposed to exercise intelligence in a habitual manner that corresponds to valued patterns of internal and external survival information. The value of dispositional intelligence is assessed by its value to survival (e.g., disposition to be accurate, organized, persistent, open-minded, analytic, or creative). Accordingly, a useful disposition is a means for standardizing automatic responses to stimuli—an alternative to constantly making moment-to-moment decisions about how to respond to the environment. Without such disposition, the brain would be hopelessly bogged down by overload and indecision.

Is this matter of dispositions of interest to leaders? More to the point, what should they be disposed to know about disposition of self and others? The suggestion here is that, among other things, they would know that the dispositional nature of the brain is macro, mandatory, malleable, and maximizing or minimizing.

Macro

The brain adopts patterns of thinking—mental tendencies or inclinations—that are habitually applied on a broad scale as the brain conducts its survival business. The brain interprets and organizes useful information patterns on all levels of scale. Thinking dispositions are products of the brain's pattern making at a macro level. They are neural constructions designed to process broad categories of environmental experience.

Mandatory

The brain has no option other than to develop and exercise habits of thinking, but there are options regarding the quality of habits developed. Every healthy brain is genetically and environmentally disposed to the broad physiological, social, emotional, constructive, and reflective exercise of intelligence. The instinctive and habitual application of natural capacity is essential to the brain's survival business. Furthermore, habits of mind are means for efficiently allocating the neural resources of the brain as it goes about its daily business.

Malleable

Thinking dispositions are genetically introduced and environmentally influenced. Beyond basic genetic prescriptions, the human disposition to exercise intelligence to greater or lesser effect is malleable. That is, habits of mind are responsive to the influence of physical environment, culture, and conscious reflection throughout the lifespan. As a result, each brain becomes experientially unique in its disposition to exercise intelligence.

Maximizing and Minimizing

Thinking habits are determining factors in how far and well one travels the neural byways of the brain; the human capacity to think, learn, and achieve is realized to the degree that there is a productive disposition driving it. Sustained states of dispositional intelligence are defining elements of individual and organizational character. They are the means by which the potential of intelligence is explored and realized. Thinking dispositions are primary influences over the exercise of all other dimensions of intelligence (e.g., physiological, social, emotional, constructive, and reflective).

IMPLICATIONS

Only when we do something to keep our thinking in order do we escape the potholes of cognition.

—Perkins (1995, p. 154)

A fundamental understanding of the dispositional nature of intelligence conjures up the classic wisdom about teaching a man how to fish so that he might feed himself for a lifetime versus giving a man a fish to feed him for a day. If thinking dispositions are mandatory yet malleable influences on how well the brain exercises its multidimensional capacity for acquiring and applying knowledge, a leader is well advised to cultivate productive patterns of thinking. Moreover, a leader will advisedly do so by cultivating broad habits as well as targeting specific habits (Figure 10.2).

Cultivate Broad Habits

Productive habits of mind do not just happen; the brain is disposed to engage a way of thinking to the degree that it has experienced it. Ergo, exercise the brain broadly to habituate disposition toward fitness, collaboration, self-motivation, knowledge acquisition, and reasoning.

Target Specific Habits

Effective thinkers have productive thinking habits—habits that maximize their capacity to learn and achieve. Target and practice the habits that matter most (e.g., questioning, clarifying, persisting, and being curious and open-minded).

READER REFLECTION

- What is essential to know and do about the dispositional nature of intelligence?

Figure 10.2 Implications of the Dispositional Nature of Intelligence for Leadership

If the *dispositional nature* of intelligence is

Macro, *i.e., the brain adopts patterns of thinking —mental tendencies or inclinations—that are habitually applied on a broad scale as the brain conducts its survival business.*

Mandatory, *i.e., the brain has no option other than to develop and exercise habits of thinking, but there are high-quality options.*

Malleable, *i.e., thinking dispositions are genetically introduced and environmentally influenced.*

Maximizing or Minimizing, *i.e., thinking habits are determining factors in how far and well one travels the neural byways of the brain; human capacity to think, learn, and achieve is realized to the degree that there is a productive disposition driving it.*

If–Then

Then a *mindful leader* will

1. **Cultivate broad habits**, e.g., through

   - Physical stimulation
   - Social interaction
   - Emotional management
   - Construction of knowledge
   - Reflective reasoning
   - Metacognition

2. **Target specific habits**, e.g., through

   - Listening
   - Collaborating
   - Striving for accuracy
   - Seeking clarity
   - Questioning
   - Researching data
   - Persisting
   - Open-mindedness
   - Empathy
   - Flexibility
   - Innovation
   - Creativity

Part III

Following Through

Unprecedented opportunity to understand and effectively engage human capacity creates a compelling case for leadership that is mindful (attentive and thoughtful) rather than mindless (unaware and heedless) of the nature and nurture of *intellgence*.

Chapter 11 examines the purpose and principles of mindful leadership. It specifically models how perception of the nature of intelligence is applied and adjusted to leadership practice. Chapter 12 addresses the need for twenty-first-century leaders to confront, push, and step beyond prevailing perceptions of leadership.

11 Mindful Leadership

No leader is ever fully realized; at most, one can observe individuals who are in the course of attaining greater skills and heightened effectiveness.

—Gardner (1995, p. 36)

Gardner's observation about the road to effective leadership reflects a broad view of human experience. Few would challenge the assertion that humankind has yet to realize its potential. At the same time, most would acknowledge progress in advancing from cave dwelling to space traveling. It is apparent that we are a story in progress, participants in an ongoing journey of distance covered and promising destinations ahead. Moreover, what is certain within the journey is that the evolution of leadership perspective and skill affects how and to what extent we move forward. The question then is, in what ways do leaders need to evolve to become more effective at this point in the story? More to the point, what do leaders need to be most mindful of in the process of influencing human progress in the context of the near and distant future?

THE MINDFUL LEADER

The essence of mindful leadership is being mindful about mind in self and others. The idea is conceptualized in a simple statement: *A mindful leader is attentive to the nature and nurture of intelligence in the process of influencing others toward the achievement of goals.* Pieces of this portrayal of a mindful leader have been sketched out across the preceding 10 chapters. The picture that emerges is that of a leader who adheres to mindful purpose and principles (Figure 11.1). That portrait is brought into sharper focus in this chapter.

Figure 11.1   Attributes of a Mindful Leader

Mindful Purpose: Nurture of intelligence

Mindful Principles:

Attend to information about the nature of intelligence.
Articulate perception of the nature and nurture of intelligence.
Apply perception of the nature and nurture of intelligence to behavior.

   A. Application as standard practice:

      1. Support the physiological platform that enables intelligence
         a. Attend to brain fitness
         b. Stimulate neural networking

      2. Promote social relationships
         a. Facilitate meeting of minds
         b. Cultivate common purpose
         c. Extend the mind's reach

      3. Harness the power of emotion
         a. Ease the mind
         b. Excite the mind
         c. Evaluate states of mind

      4. Expedite the construction of knowledge
         a. Justify construction
         b. Facilitate construction
         c. Extend construction

      5. Build a culture of reflection
         a. Structure thinking
         b. Challenge thinking

      6. Cultivate productive dispositions
         a. Cultivate broad habits
         b. Target specific habits

   B. Application as prescribed practice (i.e., to self, systems, and situations)

Adjust information, perception, and behavior from application experience.

MINDFUL PURPOSE

Purpose is that deepest dimension within us—our central core or essence where we have a profound sense of who we are, where we come from, and where we are going. Purpose is the quality we choose to shape our life around. Purpose is a source of energy and direction.

—Leider (1997, p. 1)

Antecedents

Your path to leadership purpose naturally draws on personal experience, experience that includes people who have influenced your leadership perceptions on a subconscious, if not conscious, level. The following exercise illustrates that influence.

1. Reflect for a moment about people whom you respect as leadership exemplars. They might be historic or contemporary figures, members of your family, or others you judge to be effective leaders— whether in positions associated with social, government, business, education, or other organizations.

   ~ Reflection Time ~

2. Select three of the leaders you admire to join you at the council table represented in Figure 11.2. Identify each of the invited leaders by name in the three "Leader" chairs to the right of the table.

3. Assign yourself to the chair marked "Heir to Wisdom."

4. Moving from chair to chair, write down one or two distinguishing attributes of leadership character or values for each leader seated at the table.

   ~ Reflection Time ~

5. Moving around the table once more, ask each of your distinguished guests to share his or her best advice about leadership. Again, in the space provided on the seat locations, jot down what you think your guests' advice would be.

   ~Reflection Time~

6. Finally, in the space provided in the middle of the table, record what you have learned about leadership from these leaders—from their example and their advice. That is, what is your inheritance? What

leadership wisdom has been passed on to you? How have your perceptions of leadership been influenced by important people in your life experience?

~*Reflection Time*~

Regardless of the mix of people sitting at your table—your mother, third-grade teacher, high school coach, Joan of Arc, Gandhi, whoever—your perceptions of effective leadership can be traced to the values and behaviors modeled by people you know and have observed. Similarly, you

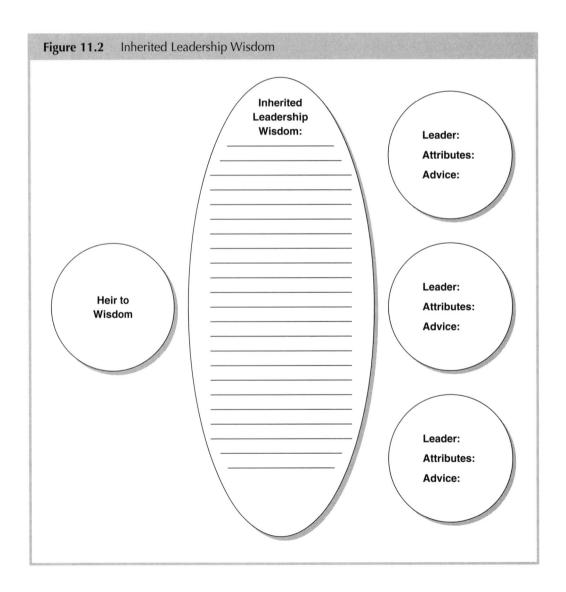

Figure 11.2   Inherited Leadership Wisdom

have also probably been influenced by encounters with the general literature about leadership, literature that espouses tenets of organizational wellness, collaboration, common vision, stress management, empowerment, team learning, quality management, and win–win negotiations. What advice came forth from the leaders huddled around your council table? Were you advised about the importance of clear goals? Do your leadership mentors value common vision, empowerment of others, collaboration, commitment to quality, or team learning in their orientation to leadership?

The point is, your development as a leader (or person) did not begin with the reading of this book. Your reflection about the nature of leadership did not start today, nor has it occurred in a vacuum. You come prepared for further contemplation by virtue of the past experience of self and others. Indeed, the inherited insight you laid out on the council table probably describes leadership qualities that are intuitively attentive to the nature and nurture of intelligence—qualities that naturally favor physiological, social, emotional, constructive, reflective, and dispositional dimensions of human capacity. An instinct for connecting to the capacity of others is not new to leadership. However, the opportunity to be consciously informed and mindfully disposed about said connection is.

Affirmation

Perception of compelling purpose is key to mindful leadership. Without a compelling reason to be mindful of the nature and nurture of intelligence, a leader lacks the motivation to pursue relevant principles and practices. Moreover, a mindful sense of purpose influences leadership on multiple levels.

A *focused purpose*, in the form of a goal associated with a particular task or problem, provides a specific reason as to why a leader would commit thoughtful attention to the nature and nurture of intelligence. The motivation in this instance is to better understand and influence human capacity toward the achievement of a particular end.

A *fundamental purpose* presents a broader reason for why a leader would commit thoughtful attention to the nature and nurture of intelligence. Contemplation of such larger purpose is encouraged by the contextual challenges that confront leaders at the beginning of the twenty-first century. It envisions a big-picture role for mindful leadership, one that aspires to shape organizational capacity beyond an immediate goal. The fundamental purpose of leadership is understood to be mindful cultivation of intelligence itself. This is demonstrated through the comprehensive nurturing of organizational capacity for achieving an important mission. It becomes even bigger than that, however, when perceived as a responsibility to exercise the intelligence of humanity toward greater growth and effect in general.

In life, those who figure out the answer to the challenge of the moment get to move on to the next challenge. Intelligence is the means to figure it out—to resolve problems and achieve goals—and leadership is the means to actualize intelligence in organizations, whether that intelligence is exercised toward focused or fundamental purpose. Consider further that the challenges of the future are largely unknown and that intelligence is the means for resolving any challenge. This circumstance appears to place a premium on cultivation of the powerful resources of mind that are at the disposal of all human beings. Although mindful attention to the intelligence required to achieve specific, focused purposes is appropriate and necessary, there is a more fundamental purpose in nurturing intelligence toward the advancement of meaningful missions—and in the process, nurturing the mind itself toward ever greater survival advantage.

Ultimately, mindful leadership aspires to the purpose of building and sustaining a mindful culture—a culture that collectively attends to the cultivation of intelligence. Within such pervasive attention to human nature, the nurture of intelligence is clearly perceived as the compelling purpose of leadership.

MINDFUL ATTENTION

How a leader adheres to the mindful principle of attending to relevant information was modeled across Chapters 5–10. It is a matter of consciously turning brain attention to substantive information to distill essential understanding about the nature of human capacity for acquiring and applying knowledge.

Is this an important principle (i.e., standard rule of behavior) that leaders should adhere to? Given current scientific revelations, we might find it unacceptable that a leader would be either unaware or unsupportive of the ubiquitous nature of human intelligence. We might deem it past time that leaders rise above society's intrigue (fed by the mass media) with perceived displays of prowess and success by the famous and powerful. Are we going to continue to be dazzled by the brilliance of the scholar, CEO, politician, or artist who excels yet blind to the intelligence that glows within every human being? At what cost does society sustain such limited vision of where and how intelligence shines? What excuse do we have for maintaining such a myopic view, given the quantity and quality of knowledge about the nature of species intelligence available to us? Ultimately, the price of being oblivious of such rich knowledge is to be denied insight into that which defines humankind—and the guidance therein for how best to conduct human affairs.

In the end, your interest in knowing more about the nature of intelligence has to stem from your interest in being an effective leader. If attending to information about how people acquire and apply knowledge will give you an edge in your efforts to influence others toward the achievement of goals, you have reason to be interested. You have to be proactive about this, however, because your brain encounters a lot of things that compete for its attention. Accordingly, you have to make the effort to attend to information sources that provide practical summarization and interpretation of intelligence research and theory. You will also seek opportunities to participate in professional conferences that cover the topic. Other than that, you might make it a point to associate with peers who, like you, are motivated to continually improve their leadership capacity. If there is anything happening out there that might make the leadership difference, those who are looking for it are going to discover it first.

MINDFUL ARTICULATION

Given appropriate attention to the knowledge base, the principle of articulation comes into play as conscious examination of the essence of nature in relation to implications for nurture. To not engage in this construction is to forgo personal perception of what is most essential to know and attend to when influencing others toward the achievement of purpose. You have to go beyond just knowing things about the brain to understanding the nature of intelligence in a reality context of how you as a leader will engage it. To that end, asking and answering *if–then* questions is a productive exercise. For example, *if* the knowledge construction and reflective reasoning capacities of the brain are both stimulated and facilitated by social interaction, *then* leaders should structure frequent opportunities for individuals in an organization to interact with others as they engage new information, set goals, solve problems, complete tasks, and the like (Table 11.1).

MINDFUL APPLICATION

Through mindful processing of substantive information (i.e., through attention and articulation), your brain constructs informed perceptions about the nature and nurture of intelligence. Mindful application of that constructed knowledge to standard and prescribed leadership practice

Table 11.1   Articulating Perception of the Nature and Nurture of Intelligence

Nature of Intelligence	Perception of Nature & Nurture	Nurturing Behavior
The *physiological* nature of intelligence is big, mind–body connected, high maintenance, and malleable.	←——— If – then ———→	• Attend to brain fitness (e.g., movement, nutrition, hydration). • Stimulate neural networks (e.g., humor, music, novelty, strange encounters).
The *social nature* of intelligence is expectant, dependent, extended, and virtuous.	←——— If – then ———→	• Facilitate meetings of mind (e.g., dyads, triads). • Cultivate common purpose (e.g., base groups, consensus). • Extend the mind's reach (e.g., professional affiliations).
The *emotional nature* of intelligence is attentive, judgmental, motivating, and managed after the fact.	←——— If – then ———→	• Ease the mind (e.g., group norms, affirmations). • Excite the mind (e.g., anticipatory set, mission dialogue, inspirations). • Evaluate states of mind (conflict resolution).
The *constructive nature* of intelligence is pattern making, sensory, social, emotional, reflective, and susceptible to a double bind.	←——— If – then ———→	• Justify knowledge construction (e.g., knowledge mapping). • Facilitate construction (e.g., multisensory engagement). • Extend construction (e.g., coaching).
The *reflective nature* of intelligence is manipulative, executive, unifying, and promising.	←——— If – then ———→	• Structure thinking (e.g., brainstorming, problem solving, decision making). • Challenge thinking (e.g., debate, analysis of perspective, projection).
The *dispositional nature* of intelligence is macro, mandatory, malleable, and either maximizing or minimizing.	←——— If – then ———→	• Cultivate broad habits (e.g., collaboration, reflection, metacognition). • Target specific habits (e.g., open-mindedness, questioning, persistence).

follows. Both approaches—standard and prescribed—draw directly from your perception of the essential nature of intelligence and compatible ways to nurture that nature.

Standard Practice

One way of acting on what you know about intelligence is to mindfully apply it as standard operating procedure—the way you do leadership. It is a matter of translating informed understanding about nature to compatible behavior. In effect, it is taking *if–then* articulation of the nature and nurture of intelligence to the street and acting it out in everyday practice. This is the endgame for mindfully connecting leadership to the brain, an internalized understanding of intelligence that broadly and naturally guides compatible leadership behavior. Referencing the standard practice examples presented in Figure 11.1, this application of knowledge practice would look something like what follows.

Standard Practice 1: Support the Physiological Platform That Enables Intelligence

I know that attending to physiological needs helps people function effectively. Balancing work with rest, healthful diet, and exercise reaps payoffs in productivity. Excessive or prolonged stress (e.g., physical or psychological harassment, overwhelming workloads, pressure for change, confusing directives) generates negative effects on neural health and efficiency. The bottom line is that it is important to create environments that are physiologically supportive of the members of an organization. Given what I know, **my standard practice will attend to brain fitness** through actions that support access to drinking water, healthful food, fresh air, and natural light; physical movement while working; participation in fitness and wellness programs; work that is meaningful and challenging but not overly stressful; flexible work schedules; collaborative team structures; open and frequent communication; positive disposition, humor; fun; celebration of achievement; physically safe facilities and surroundings; and intolerance of harassment in any form.

I also know that environmental experience modifies brain capacity throughout the lifespan. Routine and repetitious tasks are not stimulating to neural development. An environment that is rich in novelty and sensory stimulation supports neural development—the cultivation of bushy dendrites. Such development is enhanced when opportunity to learn and grow becomes a valued part of organizational life. Given what I know, **my standard practice will stimulate neural networking** through actions that support meaningful and challenging work; social interaction in the processes of planning, performing, evaluating, and resolving; diversity of experience in work teams and cross-department task groups; access to information; variety of roles and responsibilities embedded in job descriptions; individual and group goal setting and self-assessment of progress; on-site and off-site professional growth opportunities (e.g., workshops, seminars, study groups, conferences, retreats, sabbaticals); sensory enrichment within the design of the physical environment (e.g., color, music, artwork, furnishings, space).

Standard Practice 2: Promote Social Relationships

I know that the brain expects and depends on social experience as the critical means for unfolding and developing its potential. Simply put, when one brain meets another brain, the exercise of multidimensional intelligence inevitably follows. Given what I know, **my standard practice will facilitate meetings of mind** through actions that support the organization of teams, cohorts, and other groups as appropriate to general responsibilities and specific tasks and interests; time and grouping formats that support dialogue; alteration of group compositions to change the dynamics of ideas and experience; training in group processes; structured interaction between departments; flow of information throughout the organization; professional growth in the company of colleagues; collaboration in the resolution of problems, decisions, or other challenging tasks; mentoring of new members; and peer coaching of performance goals and assessments.

I also know that social interaction most effectively benefits organizational capacity when focused by a shared vision of meaningful purpose. Such vision strengthens a culture of collaboration in which common purpose transcends individual ambition. Making a contribution to the common good becomes what counts. The collective capacity of human intelligence is tapped when the brains within the organization are enticed into collaborative relationships by clear, compelling, and mutually held goals. Given what I know, **my standard practice will cultivate common purpose** through actions that support formal and informal conversations about purpose and progress, organizational visioning, strategic planning, quality circles, and action research and planning.

I also understand that the strongest ropes are woven from diverse fibers. Similarly, diversity of perspective within social interactions increases the prospects for productive thinking, particularly in instances involving challenging tasks. Two or more heads are better than one when engaged in socially adept collaborative groups. Such benefit is realized to the degree that every brain feels comfortable and valued in making contributions. It is equally important that the brains within an organization are exposed to diversity of experience through interactions with brains outside the organization. Given what I know, **my standard practice will extend the mind's reach** through actions that support access to diverse viewpoints, diversity of experience and perspective in task groups, diversity training, training in group skills, access to distant brains through media (e.g., books, video, Internet), and access to off-site professional growth experiences.

Standard Practice 3: Harness the Power of Emotion

I know that the emotional mechanisms of the brain adjust mind and body states through ongoing assessments of survival interests. Therefore, the brain does its best work when challenged to achieve meaningful purpose in safe and supportive environments. Given what I know, **my standard practice will ease the mind** through actions that support a spirit of collaboration; inclusion in solution seeking; collegial relationships through team building, mentoring, interpersonal skill training, and social events; civility and positivism; zero tolerance for harassment, intimidation, or other antisocial behavior; self-confidence and celebration of achievements (individual and organization); value for diverse perspectives and experiences; risk taking; and resolution of personal challenges.

I also know that the brain continually screens sensory information to determine what is worthy of the investment of its resources. Simply put, if the brain is not emotionally excited about something, it is not going to effectively engage in social interaction, construction of knowledge, reflective reasoning, or productive thinking dispositions, all of which stimulate the physiological refinement of neural networks. The engagement of intelligence is motivated most by novel and challenging tasks related to significant purpose. Given what I know, **my standard practice will excite the mind** through actions that support dialogue about personal and organizational purpose; inclusive visioning and planning; inclusion in planning, implementing, and assessing vision-aligned actions; formal and informal conversations about progress toward achieving purpose; referencing of organizational purpose in decision making and problem solving; modeling of passion for purpose; and professional growth relevant to the achievement of purpose.

I further understand that emotional intelligence is the capacity to be aware of and regulate one's emotional state in a manner that contributes to the welfare of self and others. Given what I know, **my standard practice will evaluate states of mind** through actions that support awareness of the motivating role of emotion in maintaining commitment to the achievement of purpose, reflection about emotional state in relation to issues and events, structures and strategies for the reflective processing of emotional states and productive responses, and skill in conflict resolution.

Standard Practice 4: Expedite the Construction of Knowledge

I know that the brain is motivated to construct meaning and memory by its judgment of value for specific information. Assessing the qualities of an information target promotes discernment of knowledge that is pertinent to organizational purpose and therefore worthy of a knowledge construction effort. Given what I know, **my standard practice will justify the construction of knowledge** through actions that support mapping of prior knowledge; articulation of knowledge status, need, and progress; alignment of knowledge acquisition to organizational purpose and goals; and decentralized decision making to promote personal judgments about what is worth knowing.

I also know that the brain has phenomenal capacity for discerning, storing, and retrieving meaningful information patterns (knowledge). The exercise of this capacity relies on the quantity and quality of sensory stimulation received from environmental experience. The acquisition of knowledge is a brain-by-brain process of connecting new information to prior knowledge. Knowledge is physically constructed through the neural networks of an individual brain as the result of sensory experience. Given what I know, **my standard practice will facilitate the construction of knowledge** through actions that support access to rich information sources (e.g., print, video, news media, Internet, workshops, seminars, interactive conferencing, natural environments); direct hands-on experience with new concepts or procedures; visualization of concepts and procedures through graphic representation and model construction; use of metaphor and analogy; jigsaw processing of new information; reciprocal teaching, peer coaching, and mentoring of new concepts and procedures; and environments for dialogue (e.g., conference rooms, nature settings).

I further understand that the brain's survival business is predicated on the discernment of useful information patterns. The double bind within that work is the danger of relying on patterns that have proved useful in the past. Thus seduced, the brain resists exploring new information, to its ultimate disadvantage. It is important to challenge conventional knowledge and entertain the construction of new and refined perception. Given what I know, **my standard practice will extend the construction of knowledge** through actions that support knowledge updates, coaching of knowledge extension and refinement, debate, novelty of experience, and creative thinking.

Standard Practice 5: Build a Culture of Reflection

I know that the brain responds to problems and tasks by consciously manipulating information related to action options. It does this reflective work best when afforded the time, place, and tools that support deliberate reasoning. This manipulation of information and rehearsal of options underlies analytic and creative thinking. Given what I know, **my standard practice will structure thinking** through actions that support journal writing, metaphor, analogy, scheduled time for reflection about issues relevant to purpose, environments conducive to reflection (e.g., natural light, fresh air, comfortable furniture, access to information resources, opportunity for movement, freedom from distractions), formal thinking processes (e.g., articulated steps for problem solving, decision making, system analysis, conflict resolution, investigation, case study, analysis of perspective, debate, comparison, inductive and deductive reasoning), and group information processing (e.g., ordered processing, nominal group process, brainstorming, fishbowls, role plays).

I also know that reflective reasoning is exercised by provocations that bring analytic and creative thinking into play to detect causal relationships, link seemingly unrelated information, generate alternative views, and construct new understandings and products. Given what I know, **my standard practice will challenge thinking** through actions that support social debate about controversial and challenging issues, systems thinking, scenario planning, construction of support for positions, analysis of errors in positions, reverse perspective, force field analysis, divergent and lateral thinking, improvisation, and invention.

Standard Practice 6: Cultivate Productive Dispositions

I know that intelligence capacity does not automatically translate into intelligent behavior. We are genetically programmed to exercise physiological, social, emotional, constructive, and reflective dimensions of intelligence. That multifaceted nature must be productively engaged, however, if its potential is to be realized. One might say that intelligence is developed and refined to the degree that there is a disposition to use it. Given what I know, **my standard practice will cultivate broad habits** through actions that support propensity for exercise, nutritious diet, novel experience, and other means to optimize the physiological base of intelligence; propensity for social collaboration, sharing of ideas and purpose; propensity for the management of emotional states; propensity for rich sensory experience and construction of personal understanding; propensity for reflective reasoning; and propensity for metacognition.

I also know that there are ways of thinking that merit conscious development. Given what I know, **my standard practice will target specific habits** through practices that support the use of data, collaboration, creativity, open-mindedness, persistence, accuracy, empathy, curiosity, listening, questioning, risk taking, metacognition, and humor.

Prescribed Practice

If the endgame for connecting leadership to the brain is the translation of internalized knowledge about the nature of intelligence to standard leadership practice, that translation is obviously going to happen at different times to different degrees for different leaders, assuming effort is made to make it happen. Before and after such transformation, there is need for mindful application of knowledge about intelligence to leadership practice in a prescribed manner. This prescriptive approach involves the conscious laying out of a course of action to be followed in a given context affecting *self*, a *system*, or a *situation*. However, prescriptive application does not replace application of knowledge as standard practice. Again, application of knowledge to standard practice aspires to internalize and translate knowledge about intelligence to everyday behavior. Prescribed practice complements and extends that standard practice as a more formal and staged reflection about what and how things should be done. It is the overt prescribing of intelligence-informed leadership behavior when circumstances call for it.

To engage your brain in a physical sense in prescribed applications of knowledge about intelligence to leadership practice, envision the four concentric circles of the prescriptive application model (Figure 11.3) laid out on the floor of a familiar room—your office or a room in your home will do. Now picture yourself standing in the center circle. Better yet, stand in the middle of the room you are located in as you read this (if reading this while a passenger in a car, plane, or train, you will of course forgo the kinesthetic experience and stick with the visualization). Thus positioned in the prescribed application program, your leadership practice is centered by the first of four steps.

Prescribed Practice Step 1:
Clarification of Need (Purpose or Goal)

In the case of an application of the prescription process to self, the answer to this question for a leader is always the same by virtue of the very definition of leadership. The purpose of leadership is always to influence others toward the achievement of a goal. The value of asking this question is that it serves as a valuable reminder. It is a means to

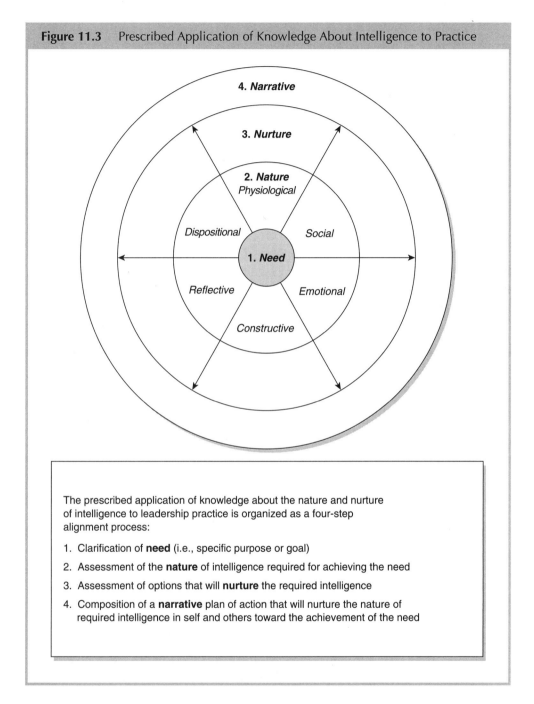

Figure 11.3 Prescribed Application of Knowledge About Intelligence to Practice

The prescribed application of knowledge about the nature and nurture
of intelligence to leadership practice is organized as a four-step
alignment process:

1. Clarification of **need** (i.e., specific purpose or goal)

2. Assessment of the **nature** of intelligence required for achieving the need

3. Assessment of options that will **nurture** the required intelligence

4. Composition of a **narrative** plan of action that will nurture the nature of
   required intelligence in self and others toward the achievement of the need

reorient and avoid confusion about your purpose as a leader—to reaf-
firm that leadership is a matter of helping others discern and achieve a
compelling purpose.

Questions for You: As you stand at the center of the prescription
circle, what is your understanding of the universal purpose of

leadership? What is the compelling purpose (goal) that currently motivates your leadership?

Clarification of need in systems or situations is a different matter because there is no universal answer to the question. In fact, it is critically important to clarify and communicate the unique purpose or goal of any system or situation. This is the prerequisite step too often overlooked, whether from ignorance or neglect: that of garnering the emotional commitment of intelligence capacity. In the case of large organizational systems (i.e., educational, commercial, governmental, nonprofit) or subsystems (e.g., units, departments, divisions), need is often described in terms of mission, purpose, or charge. A targeted need in a given situation is expressed as a goal, such as a material gain, performance improvement, or the resolution of a problem or important decision.

Again, clarification of need is the essential first step in the mindful prescription of leadership practice. It is what centers leadership and generates passion for acting on important purpose. In all cases, be it a matter of self, a system, or a situation, leadership is not leadership unless it influences the achievement of a need.

Questions for You: What is the mission or purpose of an organizational system you are associated with? What is a current situation confronting that organization (e.g., a new project, specific problem, unique opportunity)? What is the goal related to that situation?

Prescribed Practice Step 2: Assessment of Required Intelligence

This step occurs as you move outward from the center of the prescription circle. It is the same prescription step whether applied to self, system, or situation: a conscious reflection about the nature of intelligence in relation to an achievement need. This involves questions about the status and requirements of different dimensions of intelligence that are important to the achievement of an identified purpose or goal: What are the apparent physiological demands and effects of the targeted need (i.e., purpose or goal)? What are the requirements and opportunities for social interaction? What are likely and preferred emotional responses to the defined need? Is there a need to construct new knowledge? Is reflective reasoning required? What thinking dispositions will be important to achieving this need?

A Question for You: Think back to your responses to prior questions about the purpose of leadership, the mission of an organization you are associated with, or a goal associated with a situation confronting that organization. What is your assessment of the intelligence required (e.g., physiological, social, emotional, constructive, reflective, dispositional) for achieving any or all of those needs?

Prescribed Practice Step 3:
Assessment of Options for Nurturing Intelligence

Moving outward to the next ring of the circle, a leader assesses options for favorably influencing dimensions of intelligence deemed relevant to the achievement of an identified need. In a very real sense, leaders at this step are conducting a conversation with themselves. They reflect on the desired outcome, qualities of intelligence important to achieving the outcome, and interventions that will nurture said qualities to positive effect. This step prescribes application of knowledge about intelligence to leadership behavior affecting self, systems, or situations. It draws on articulated perception of nature and nurture to ascertain how to best influence the achievement of targeted need in a particular context. For example, if you perceive that a given need will place high demand on capacity for exercising emotional intelligence while under pressure to construct new knowledge toward the reflective resolution of a challenging problem, you will explore options for supporting those dimensions of intelligence. Such support might involve the facilitation of emotional release, collaborative processing of relevant information, and brainstorming innovative alternatives in problem-solving processes.

A Question for You: Given your prior discernment of intelligence requirements for achieving leadership purpose, the mission of a system, or a preferred outcome in a particular situation, what specific leadership practices would you prescribe to support the required dimensions of intelligence?

Prescribed Practice Step 4:
Composition of a Narrative Plan of Action

Thus far there has been a simple logic to this application process. There is basic rhyme and reason in the sequence of clarifying a desirable outcome, assessing resources that are important to achieving that outcome, and then exploring means by which said resources might be most effectively secured and deployed. Given clarity of a need and assessment of the nature of the intelligence required to achieve it, it makes sense that leaders would concern themselves with the nurture of the nature that will achieve the need. If left at this stage, however, the prescriptive application process probably will fall victim to the classic demise of many failed leadership ventures: *the failure to act*. It is from this concern that a fourth important step in the prescription process is added to translate reflection and assessment into action. To that end, Step 4 in the process solicits the composition of a narrative plan of action from the intervention options considered in Step 3. The importance of this step cannot be overstated. Too often good insights and ideas come to naught for lack of an implementation plan (as observed in the "then a miracle occurs" story described in Chapter 4). Accordingly, the leader steps into the outer ring of the prescription circle to compose—mentally or physically—a plan of action for nurturing the intelligence required for achieving a targeted need. This might be a very focused and concise plan prescribing specific practice for a one-time, specific effect. An example of a more far-reaching application would be a prescribing a long-term commitment to developing team skills and habituating collaborative dispositions that favorably influence multiple dimensions of organizational intelligence (e.g., physiological, social, emotional, constructive, reflective, dispositional).

> *A Question for You:* Given your assessments of need, nature, and nurture across the first three rings of this prescriptive application process, what plan of action for nurturing the intelligence required for achieving the targeted need would you prescribe?

As you step out of the outer circle and look back at the four steps of the application structure, you are in a position to observe the unity of the process. It is not a complicated or unknown process. After all, this is what successful leaders do, be they CEOs, generals, coaches, philosophers, or politicians. It matters not whether the goal is to put the ball in the end zone or resolve a social injustice, the process is the same in the leaders' brain: What is the goal? What knowledge, skills, or attitudes are important to the achievement of this goal? What are my options for influencing the required knowledge, skills, or attitudes? Which options will I act on?

What is different—the new twist in the context of twenty-first-century knowledge—is that leaders have both the motivation and the means for more effectively aligning their behavior to what is known about human nature. Assuming clarity about purpose and commitment to act, leaders who are informed about the nature of intelligence are in a position to more effectively prescribe nurturing behavior.

MINDFUL ADJUSTMENT

As described in Chapter 4, a framework provides skeletal structure for the organization of ideas and processes. Whatever the specific framework, however, it must be assembled in your mind before being put to use. Furthermore, any framework might be awkwardly engaged at first. Over time, however, it will be progressively internalized and more naturally engaged.

Leaders who engage this framework to mindfully apply knowledge to standard and prescribed leadership practice will expect to progress from a mechanical application of its components to refined disposition and skill. In doing so, they will mindfully process feedback from application experience to continually adjust informed perceptions of effective leadership behavior.

Feedback from application experiences informs and reforms the information base that informs the perceptions that inform behavior. The old maxim "Experience is the best teacher" applies to this matter. It is just that simple: You learn by doing. In the case of mindful leadership, you attend to and articulate knowledge about the nature and nurture of intelligence and then apply that knowledge to how you influence others toward the achievement of goals. One can hardly help but learn about what works and what doesn't work from such experience. The key to this, as you would expect, is mindful processing of the experience. There are two simple yet powerful means to that end: individual reflection about what is and is not working in an application experience, as it proceeds and after it is completed, and the same reflection process in the company of colleagues, particularly those involved in the achievement of the identified goal or purpose.

Individual Practice

As observed in Chapter 4, the time-honored means for mastering any skill or disposition is to practice it until we have it right, working at doing whatever we aspire to do in a progressively competent and productive fashion (e.g., if learning to ride a bike, that would involve practicing the process until you are not tipping over while proceeding from Point A to Point B). In like fashion, mindful leadership evolves in understanding of the nature and nurture of intelligence from applications to standard practice, as well as prescribed applications to self, systems, and situations. Conscious application of well-informed knowledge to practice occurs until it becomes second nature—a natural and effective means for attending to the nature of intelligence in the process of influencing others toward the achievement of goals.

There is more to productive practice than just doing things over and over, however. If you are learning how to ride a bike or hit a baseball and not making progress, you will reflect about what you are doing, what is working and not working, and what alternatives you might try. The same holds true for the evolution of mindful leadership. A leader must mindfully reflect about what is and is not working in an application experience as it proceeds and after it is completed. Mindful practice designed to nurture the nature of capacity in self and others toward the achievement of a need will naturally work to a lesser or greater extent to the degree it is consciously assessed and adjusted.

Coached Practice

Engaging in collaborative inquiry with colleagues is a logical and powerful means for making mindful adjustments to leadership practice. As described in Chapter 6, social engagement is natural and productive in the constructive and reflective exercise of intelligence. Collegial inquiry about the nature and nurture of intelligence is also a means for promoting mindful leadership throughout an organization. It is a particularly productive means for compounding insight about what is and is not working in an application experience as it proceeds and after it is completed.

It comes down to acknowledging that two heads are better than one at some point in attempts to do just about anything. In other words, the more mindfulness, the better. Mindful leadership isn't something that is done best alone in an organization. In fact, the best approach would be to involve every stakeholder in some fashion in each component of the framework, particularly in a prescriptive application process. In that way, everyone is focusing on what needs to get done, the intelligence requirements for getting it done, and how to nurture those capacities. In coaching each other through the application process, colleagues also have opportunity to access what is working and what needs to adjusted at that time and in the future. In this fashion, a group is constantly upgrading its knowledge about the nature and nurture of intelligence. There is ongoing contemplation about what further adjustments might be made to effectively influence natural capacities toward the achievement of important purpose.

MINDFUL CONCLUSIONS

Given the description of mindful leadership presented in this chapter, you should be informed to the point of drawing your own conclusions about the nature and merits of the concept. The following summary observations might help focus your conclusions.

Mind the Nail

For want of a nail, the shoe was lost;

For want of a shoe, the horse was lost;

For want of a horse, the rider was lost;

For want of a rider, the battle was lost;

For want of a battle, the kingdom was lost.

—Anonymous

What people bring to the table as members of any organization is the same intelligence package that masters language, creates art and philosophy, eradicates disease, designs political and economic systems, and enables travel to the moon, planets, and stars beyond. It is this same capacity that holds the promise of solutions for major problems that continue to challenge humankind, such as issues of equity, peace, and environmental stewardship. The very existence of this potent capacity is encouraging, but to be fully realized it must be understood, engaged, and managed in a productive fashion. Most important, the nature of intelligence must be recognized as the force that underlies all human achievement. Not to be mindful of the nature and nurture of intelligence is, in effect, to be mindless of the nail that enables the shoe that enables the horse that enables the rider that enables the battle that enables the kingdom.

Informed Sailors Have an Edge

If a little bit of knowledge is a dangerous thing, then who among us is completely out of danger?

—Anonymous

A little bit of knowledge can be dangerous, particularly if that knowledge is superficial or questionable. Nevertheless, partial knowledge is often what successful human behavior operates on. We successfully incorporate basic understanding of such things as electricity, germs, and balanced diet in the conduct of our lives without the benefit of the extensive information known to the physicist, biologist, or nutritionist. We do have to have the basics right, however, whether gleaned from acculturation over time or by proactive investigation of good information sources.

Ultimately, knowing the nature of something holds the key to a favorable relationship. Understanding the nature of fire, for example, positions you to use it to your advantage rather than being terrorized or victimized by the phenomenon. Similarly, knowing the nature of intelligence enables an advantageous relationship.

In the event of the emergence of a rich new reservoir of knowledge, such as that currently emerging from brain science, there will be inevitable cultural assimilation of the essence of that knowledge. Important breakthroughs in knowledge present a moral imperative for proactive investigation, however, to the degree that they might improve the conduct of human affairs. Historic examples of that inquiry are the proactive translation of new knowledge about microorganisms into campaigns for preventing diseases such as smallpox, polio, malaria, and AIDS. The point is that people in positions of power and influence do not have the luxury of having all the answers to all questions before applying knowledge for the benefit of those whom they serve.

As a case in point, leaders at the beginning of the twenty-first century cannot know all that is known or will be known about the human brain and its capacity for intelligence, yet they must lead—now. What leaders can and must do in this circumstance is proactively engage knowledge about human intelligence as it emerges, and thereby progressively construct personal understanding that will inform their leadership behavior. To that end, the use of a framework for mindfully attending to and articulating that knowledge base toward applications and adjustments in leadership practice is useful. In making the effort to be thus informed, as daunting as the sea of information may appear to be, we might observe that the informed sailor stands the best chance of a successful navigation—one that serves the interests of both oneself and fellow voyagers.

Reverse Perspective

Humans have evolved as a species to a point where they can reconstruct their mental models at will. As knowledge about the brain and the nature of intelligence is revealed, leaders can reflect on their current perceptions of leadership and engage in personal change processes that will further assess appropriate behavior. What is there to grasp is a new mental model of leadership, one that mindfully connects with capacity within the organization toward the achievement of purpose.

If this concept of mindful leadership is not yet clear, contemplate the alternative. What is the cost to organizational purpose—not to mention the frustration for all people involved—when leadership is mindless in its relationship to human capacity? Consider the qualities and effects of leadership that, out of either ignorance or ill-informed perception, promotes stress, isolation, exclusion, confusion about purpose, limited information, passivity, toxic competition, conflict, top-down planning, redundancy, lack of confidence, complacency, and closed minds. To reflect a bit further about this, refer to Figure 11.4 to assess how you would personally respond to being employed in

The mindful organization. This an organization in which leaders consciously connect to capacity through actions that support the physiological platform that enables intelligence, promote social relationships, harness the power of emotion, expedite the construction of knowledge, build a culture of reflection, and cultivate productive dispositions.

The mindless organization. The leaders in this organization are clueless about capacity and thereby create physical and mental stress, promote isolation and confusion, generate passivity and anxiety, provide limited and redundant access to information, encourage complacency, and cultivate closed minds.

Our guess is that you would opt for being employed by the mindful organization rather than the mindless organization. This might be expected for many reasons. Not to be overlooked, however, is that you would naturally appreciate an organizational culture that is mindful of your nature.

Figure 11.4   Effects of Mindful and Mindless Leadership

Mindful Leadership	**Mindless Leadership**
1. Supports the physiological platform that enables intelligence	1. Creates physical and mental stress
2. Promotes social relationships	2. Promotes isolation and confusion
3. Harnesses the power of emotion	3. Generates passivity and anxiety
4. Expedites the construction of knowledge	4. Provides limited and redundant access to information
5. Builds a culture of reflection	5. Encourages complacency
6. Cultivates productive dispositions	6. Cultivates closed minds

Bring It Home

As a last exercise in drawing conclusions about the nature and merits of leadership that is mindfully attuned to how people best achieve results, reflect for a moment about an instance—an actual case—when a leader (you or another) attempted to engage the members of your organization in the achievement of a goal. Take a few moments to describe for yourself the essential components of that leadership story. What was the goal to be resolved? What did the leader do to influence resolution, and how did she or he go about doing it? How did members of the organization respond to the challenge of resolving the goal and to the behavior of the leader?

With your personal leadership case in mind, reflect further about the relevance of mindful leadership to how that real-life story played out. Referring back to the examples in Figure 11.4 and using the space provided below to record your observations, how was the leader either mindful (i.e., attentive) or mindless (i.e., heedless) of capacity relevant to the achievement need? Specifically, in what manner was the leader mindful or mindless about:

- The nature and nurture of the physiological platform that enables intelligence?
- The nature and nurture of social relationships?
- The nature and nurture of the power of emotion?
- The nature and nurture of the construction of meaning?
- The nature and nurture of a culture of reflection?
- The nature and nurture of mindful dispositions?

Evidence of Mindfulness   Evidence of Mindlessness

_____   _____

_____   _____

_____   _____

_____   _____

SUMMARY OBSERVATIONS

- Mindful leadership is a concept that, like all others, is necessarily constructed in the individual brain.
- The concept of mindful leadership described in this chapter portrays a leader who is attentive to the nature and nurture of intelligence in the process of influencing others toward the achievement of goals.

- Mindful purpose establishes the necessary value orientation (both emotional and rational) for engaging mindful behavior. It is important to view purpose in this sense, lest a leader fall into a trap that will dissipate leadership energy and effect. Compelling purpose motivates the investment of effort. Progress toward the achievement of purpose, in turn, assumes behavior that adheres to principles (standard rules) and practices (customary actions). The trap to avoid is mindless circumvention of principles that guide practice. A leader who pursues purpose in an unprincipled and ill-practiced manner runs the risk that the effort will be superficial, ineffective, and short-lived, probably in that order.

READER REFLECTION

- What is the rationale for mindful leadership?
- What is the difference between mindful applications of knowledge about intelligence to standard practice and prescribed practice?

12 Mindful Shift

Of all the species on earth, we humans are the ones who specialize in voluntary mind change: we change the minds of others, we change our own minds.

—Gardner (2004, p. 199)

We humans are creatures of habit, but we are also able and willing to make adjustments at the prodding of new experience and knowledge. In our better moments, we consciously engage this ability to learn and adjust. Thus might leaders proactively engage emerging knowledge about the nature of intelligence to better inform their leadership perception and practice.

CONFRONTING THE BOX

It is common to hear people admonish themselves or others to "think outside the box." The implication is that old ideas are trapped inside a box of established ways of thinking, whereas new challenges require new ideas that can emerge only from unconventional ways of thinking, that is, from thinking outside the box. Another way to pose this is that thinking outside the box is a matter of seeing the box, and then reshaping it, and then seeing it and reshaping it again and again and again.

It's What We Do

"Why reshape the box?" you may ask. The answer to that, simply, is that it is what we naturally and necessarily do to survive. Patterns and relationships are the currency of our mental world. This is necessarily so because patterns and relationships define the nature of the physical world that we belong to. The brain is always taking in information and making sense of it to construct understanding of its environment.

Complexity theory proposes that order comes out of chaos, that a natural order emerges from relationships within the whole to create momentary equilibrium in both immediate and far-removed environments. Advised by said theory, we will observe that as our brain engages new information, new patterns and relationships are discerned, and a new order of understanding emerges. Wheatley (1992) speaks to this in observing that information both informs us and forms us. What knowledge is taken in and how it is made sense of actually re-creates who people are, what they think, and how they behave.

Perhaps changing the expression "think outside the box" to "think about the box and adjust it accordingly" is more appropriate. "The box" is fundamental to human nature because we must construct mental patterns by which the world is understood. There is no option but to create and modify patterns in relation to surrounding influences. However, we also have the capacity to reflect on the nature of a particular mental model and to actively structure and restructure it as new information and circumstances inform and reform. In fact, it is imperative that a continual reshaping of the box occurs to adapt to an ever-changing world. This reshaping is what the brain naturally does over time when confronted with new information. Notably, it does this more quickly and to greater advantage when consciously applied to that end.

A Need to Do It

More mindful (i.e., attentive and thoughtful) alignment of the leadership process that marshals human resources toward the achievement of desired results is now possible. Twenty-first-century knowledge enables a tightening of the leadership connection to the intelligence capacity that underlies all human achievement. It is a breakthrough opportunity that projects capacity-connected leaders—leaders who are more aligned in perception and practice to how individuals and groups best learn and achieve. For this shift in perception and practice to happen as expeditiously and productively as the times require, however, a proactive approach is in order. Leaders can and should push forward the perceptual shift that will reshape the leadership box according to what is now known about human nature.

PUSHING PERCEPTION

We are not only aware, and aware of our awareness, but we are now also aware of how and why we are aware and how and why we are aware of our awareness.

—Hobson (1999, p. xi)

Humankind has long sought to understand the process by which it sees and understands the world. Given that interest, the word *perception* is well established in the English vocabulary. The origins of the word can be traced to the Latin *percipere,* which means "to see wholly or see all the way through." Basically, we understand the phenomenon behind the word to be a process through which we make sense of the world (Runyon, 1977). It is a process by which we receive information through our five senses and assign meaning to it (Wells, Burnett, & Moriarty, 1995). We also know it to be a very powerful force in how we behave (Figure 12.1).

Respect the Power

As a means to organize and distill meaning from the universe of information that confronts us, perception represents our judgment of useful and important patterns of thinking, that is, serviceable mental models. Senge (1990, p. 8) describes mental models as "deeply ingrained assumptions, generalizations, pictures, images, or stories that influence how we understand the world and take action." He further observes that we are not often consciously aware of our mental models or the effect they have on our behavior. The good news is that our perceptions provide serviceable—and usually positive—templates for how to conduct our affairs. Perception leads us to extend courtesy, exercise, balance our diet, protect individual rights, aspire to fairness, educate the young, engage in hygienic practices, work hard, and so forth. Indeed, the attributes of any human culture represent common understanding of patterns important to survival and the quality of life.

The rest of the story is that is that perception *will* direct behavior, regardless of the quality of the perception. At best, perceptual formations contribute to a positive and productive worldview. However, mere formation does not ensure that a pattern of understanding is accurate, serviceable, or even good. Argyris (1990) argues that people live in a world of self-generated beliefs, which remain largely untested. Beliefs are adopted because they are based on conclusions drawn from personal observations and past experience.

Figure 12.1 The Dynamic of Influence Between Information, Perception, and Behavior

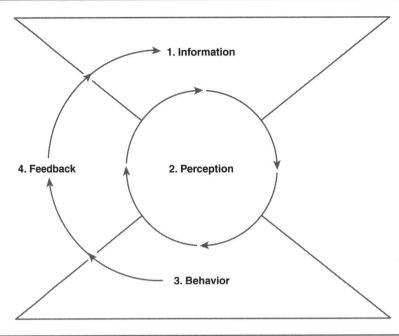

1. A body of information is engaged and processed by the brain.
2. The processing of information influences the formation of perception (i.e., essential understanding).
3. Perception influences choice of behavior within all possible options.
4. Behavior experience provides feedback that influences (i.e., further expands) information that influences perception.

It's a dilemma. When faulty perceptions are embraced, whether because of inadequate effort, misinformation, or unreasoned attachment to existing views, compatible behavior follows. In this sense, racism, war, genocide, and global warming might be observed as the result of faulty human perception at work on a grand scale.

The power of perception has another, more subtle downside: rigidity. Barker (1993) describes this as the seductive power of a successful mental model or paradigm. It is the paradigm paralysis mind-set of "If it ain't broke, don't fix it" or "We've always done it this way." This reluctance to rethink an established perception occurs naturally as we explore our world through a filter of emotions, values, and existing mental models. It is through our emotional filters that we subconsciously decide what is worth perceiving. Perceptual construction is also affected by our world-view (Gardner, 1983). Composed of prior knowledge and experience, values, beliefs, social relationships, and context, worldview is a powerful filter for incoming information and an equally powerful translator as new patterns of understanding are formed. As Fitzgerald (1998) observed, the result is that no two people see the world in exactly the same way; to every individual, a thing is what he or she thinks it is—not a thing, but a think.

Expect Stages

Understanding the nature of perception provides reason for respecting the power it holds over how we understand and behave in the world we live in. With that due respect (and given that you have an established perception of leadership), it should be clear that any meaningful shift in how you see and do leadership can happen in only one of two ways. In the first instance, you merely have to wait until the weight of new information becomes so pervasive and solid that a change in perspective and subsequent behavior naturally evolves over time (which may or may not occur in your lifetime). In the second instance, you are required to engage in overt and proactive efforts to make the shift happen sooner (e.g., by actively engaging the framework described in Chapters 4 and 11). Assuming you elect this second option, you should be aware that such effort probably will not produce a fast shift forward. Rather, you should expect that the shift would happen in stages.

Contemporary models of behavioral change suggest that three key elements are necessary to understanding a shift in thought and, ultimately, in deed (Bandura, 1995).

1. Knowledge is necessary but not sufficient to produce behavior change. Changing understandings, motivation, skills, and factors in the social environment also play important roles (e.g., leadership does not occur in a vacuum; change in leadership behavior is mediated by evolving understanding but also by perceived needs and skills for implementing the change as leaders interact with those they lead).

2. Behavior is mediated through cognition; that is, what we know and think affects how we act (e.g., for a leader to change leadership behavior, a change in the construction of the leader's understanding of leadership must occur first).

3. People and their environments interact continuously, influencing the resultant behavior change (e.g., the specific system or situation in which leadership is attempted influences the leader in deciding which behavior to select).

Bandura's assessment finds that change is a commonly observed fact of life, but that does not imply that it is welcomed or easy. Furthermore, Gardner (2004, p. 9) observes that changing minds "ultimately involves changes in behavior" that demonstrate a shift in individuals' "mental representations" of the world. He describes seven factors that leverage shifts in perspective followed by changes in behavior:

1. Reason (analytic assessment of options)

2. Research (collection of relevant data)

3. Resonance (affective response, feeling)

4. Re-descriptions (numerical, linguistic, graphic representations)

5. Resources and rewards (psychological and material reinforcement)

6. Real-world events (push toward alternative or new paths)

7. Resistances (comfort, familiarity, fear, control, emotional resonance, publicly held perspective) (pp. 14–18)

Gardner's (2004, p. 18) conclusion about the paradox of mind changing is that "we develop strong views and perspectives that are resistant to change," and "a mind change is most likely to come about when the first six factors operate in consort and the resistances are relatively weak. Conversely, mind changing is unlikely to come about when resistances are strong and the other factors do not point strongly in one direction."

Knowing that meaningful shifts in established perception are not easily made, a behavioral change model is helpful to understanding the process of pushing perception forward toward action. Figure 12.2 is a version of a widely used model that does that.

Precontemplation is characterized by lack of awareness that new information is available and relevant to one's context. For example, a leader may not be aware of a wealth of new knowledge about how the brain enables intelligence or possible implications thereof for leadership behavior. In this stage, behavior remains static or only slightly modified by factors in the environment that create a need. This type of reactive state supports stagnation in practice and missed opportunities to enhance effectiveness. In other words, the established perception of leadership (i.e., "the box") remains as formed, with tight boundaries restricting thought and behavior.

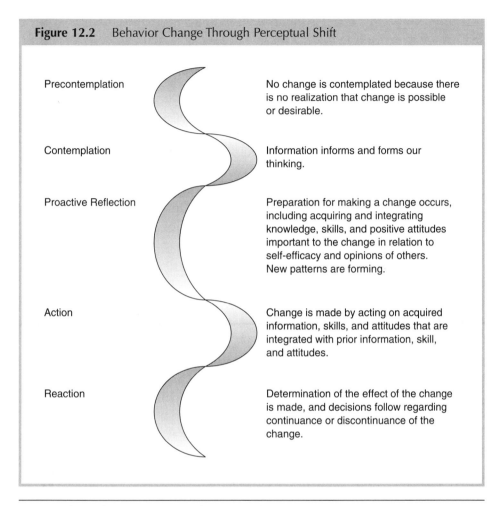

Figure 12.2 Behavior Change Through Perceptual Shift

Precontemplation	No change is contemplated because there is no realization that change is possible or desirable.
Contemplation	Information informs and forms our thinking.
Proactive Reflection	Preparation for making a change occurs, including acquiring and integrating knowledge, skills, and positive attitudes important to the change in relation to self-efficacy and opinions of others. New patterns are forming.
Action	Change is made by acting on acquired information, skills, and attitudes that are integrated with prior information, skill, and attitudes.
Reaction	Determination of the effect of the change is made, and decisions follow regarding continuance or discontinuance of the change.

Source: Adapted from Prochaska, DiClemente, and Norcross (1992).

Contemplation occurs when learning opportunities arise and are seized on as means to understand ways to be more effective. For example, as new information about the nature and nurture of intelligence becomes available, a leader seizes the opportunity to acquire insight about how he or she might better influence others toward the achievement of goals. This is the information gathering and processing stage in which new knowledge is beginning to be integrated with prior learning to challenge established perception (i.e., the sides of the box are starting to become malleable).

Proactive reflection is where cognitive dissonance accelerates with the realization that past and current understanding, beliefs, and behaviors may not be consistent with emerging insights and understandings. For example, at this point leaders will find it necessary to critically analyze their current leadership behaviors for compatibility and alignment with new information about the nature and nurture of human capacity for acquiring and applying knowledge toward the achievement of goals. Another critical development at this stage is the leader's conscious sense of self-efficacy, or perceived ability to make the changes that are now understood to be necessary (i.e., the sides of the box are being adjusted to accommodate new understandings and the implications thereof for adjustments in behavior).

Action and reaction occur simultaneously as new behavior is engaged and feedback is fielded from the impact of that behavior. As is the case whenever we are trying something new, be it a golf swing, exercise program, or professional practice, we are interested in results. If the results are as anticipated and satisfying, the new behavior probably will be continued and otherwise extended. On the other hand, if negative feedback is received in relation to the new behavior, it will be further examined, adjusted, or simply discontinued. For example, a leader who has translated articulated understanding about the nature and nurture of intelligence to compatible practice (standard and prescribed) will be interested in feedback about the impact of that new behavior (as garnered from involved stakeholders and assessments of goal achievements) and make further adjustments in behavior accordingly (i.e., at this point the box has taken on a different shape and is being tested for how well it stands up in reality). An important observation about this stage in the behavior change process is that things may not go smoothly at first. Fullan (1991) and others caution awareness about the "implementation dip" that occurs when things may get worse in reaction to a significant change in behavior before they get better (i.e., the box may resist the new shape and try to return to its former dimensions).

Be Willing and Ready

Perceptual shift and accompanying behavioral change are processes that occur over time. The process of learning new information, filtering that information through our worldview, and modifying our existing mental models is fluid and fragile. It is fluid in the sense that many thousands of connections are being made and reorganized as learning occurs; it is fragile in the sense that new learning is vulnerable to interference and forgetting.

Are you ready to take on a meaningful shift in how you see and do leadership? It is a good idea to conduct a self-assessment of how ready you are to embark on that journey. One way to do so is to reflectively process Fishbein's (2001) observation that performing a given behavior requires that one or more of the following be true:

- There is a strong positive intention (commitment) to perform the behavior.
- There are no constraints that make it impossible to perform the behavior.
- The person has the knowledge and skills necessary to perform the behavior.
- The person believes that the advantages (benefits, positive outcomes) of performing the behavior outweigh disadvantages (costs, negative outcomes).
- The person perceives more social (normative) pressure to perform the behavior than to not perform the behavior.
- The person perceives that performance of the behavior is more consistent than inconsistent with his or her self-image and does not violate personal standards.
- The emotional reaction to performing the behavior is more positive than negative.
- The person perceives that she or he has the capabilities to perform the behavior.

Are you ready for a shift? This text presents the case for mindful leadership. That case argues that now is an opportune and necessary time for leaders to consciously assess their mental models of leadership in view of emerging knowledge about the nature of intelligence. It's time to adjust the leadership box. Whether such adjustment happens is very much a matter to be resolved in the minds of individual leaders. Furthermore, there is no getting around the fact that real shift entails stepping out of the box you are in and moving on to new dimensions and forms of practice.

STEPPING OUT

The fantasy film *The Truman Show* (Pleshette, 1998) tells the story of an orphan named Truman who is raised from infancy in an environment that is contrived and controlled by an entertainment enterprise. In this artificial world, constructed as an elaborate movie set, all the people other than Truman are actors who play the roles of every imaginable member of a small-town community: mother, father, friend, teacher, coach, wife, minister, banker, baker, and candlestick maker. The basic storyline of the film is that Truman is the unaware star of *The Truman Show,* the ultimate soap opera. Truman's life is monitored by hidden cameras operating 24 hours a day to capture events prompted by the director of the show—a show that is broadcast to a large and loyal audience in the "real" world. As the film progresses, the adult Truman becomes increasingly suspicious that something is not quite right, which leads to perilous travails and, ultimately, confrontation with the truth and the creators of his contrived existence. The film comes to an end when Truman's sailboat reaches the border of his artificial world. He then must decide whether to return to the security of what has been or to step through the exterior door of the movie set to encounter a new and foreign world.

All good stories aspire to connect with people's sense of the tragedy, joy, and the dilemmas of life. *The Truman Show* might hit the mark with its play to confronting new ideas and realities. This is not unusual to human experience; our species is familiar with dramatic shifts in perception about religion, government, and gender roles, to name but a few.

Does the emergence of significant new information about the nature of human capacity challenge established perceptions about how people think, learn, and achieve? And if a shift in understanding about the nature of intelligence is in progress, does this prompt a shift in perception about the nature of leadership? If we answer "yes" to those questions, it appears that we are poised at the edge of an old reality. It is a place and moment that requires a decision: to adhere to the status quo or, like Truman, open the door and step through to a new paradigm of leadership.

Anticipate Transition

The story is told about a driver who, lost on a country road, stops to ask a local farmer how to reach the next town. The farmer responds, "You're almost there, it's just two sees away." "Pardon me. I don't understand," says the driver. "Well, it's easy," says the farmer. "You just go down the road as far as you can see from here, and then go again as far as you can see from there."

Perceptual shift and a resulting modification of leadership behavior are not only possible but essential to the context of leadership in the new millennium. A convergence of new insight about human intelligence enables proactive reflection about the implications thereof for leadership purpose and practice. Such reflection holds great promise for more effective alignment of leadership behavior to the nature and needs of human systems.

As described by the two-sees story, nevertheless, perception is incremental. Any understanding that is formulated establishes a new position from which, if one chooses, one can look deeper and farther to formulate the next level of understanding. At the same time, perceptual shift follows the organizing of information into new patterns, thereby facilitating the ability to see things more clearly while simultaneously seeing things differently (de Bono, 2001). Thus perceptional shift is the means by which the human quest for understanding is kept "movin' on down the road."

Yet some might caution leaders to wait until more is known about the nature of intelligence before they attempt more mindful alignment of their behavior to it. This position may appear to have merit at first blush, given that knowledge about the brain and the nature of intelligence is evolving at a rapid pace, with new discoveries often contradicting prior understanding. The paradox appears to be that one must wait to act until one is certain about what it is to be intelligent. This is a false paradox, however, because there really is no choice in the matter. To be a leader, one must necessarily exercise intelligence in self and others, and being mindful of what is known about the phenomenon as it is known can only be an asset to the exercise. Nevertheless, the journey to mindful leadership requires a proactive disposition to step beyond the comfort of existing norms.

Ray and Anderson (2000, pp. 48–58) describe a process that people go through in making a transition to a new cultural perspective.

1. *Inner departure:* Previously accepted explanations and practices are found to be questionable or unacceptable.

2. *Setting out:* New understandings and ways of doing things are created as we begin to act on what has been found to be unsatisfactory.

3. *Confronting the critics:* Emerging perceptions are inevitably challenged by both self and others.

4. *Turning new values into a way of life:* Established patterns and views are let go in favor of thinking in new and creative ways and seeing the big picture.

By stepping out of an established leadership box, one will necessarily proceed from inner departure to a new way of leadership life. The only means of guidance on that journey—and in all meaningful explorations—is seeing what there is to see from where you are, and then moving further from what is seen to see more.

Anticipate Competence

Whether one is riding a bike, performing brain surgery, or preparing a gourmet meal, various stages of competence are experienced as knowledge, and skills evolve from a novice stage to that of an expert. Hunter (1982) calls such stages ways of knowing. Accordingly, progressive stages of competency are a likely scenario for the development of mindful leadership perception and behavior. Consider the following competency stages as they might reflect your status as a mindful leader.

Stage 1: Unconscious Incompetence. At this stage, one would be unaware of emerging knowledge about the human brain, and few if any leadership decisions would be based on knowledge of individual and organizational intelligence. This is the blissful state of not knowing what you don't know. (You might have been at this stage before reading this book, but you are not there anymore.)

Stage 2: Conscious Incompetence. On becoming aware of emerging insights about the brain and the intelligence it enables, one begins to see implications for behavior. At this stage, leaders might become painfully aware of what they should be doing but perhaps feel unprepared to do it. This is a distressing stage because you see the discrepancy between where you are and where you want to be. Some call it controlled floundering, others disequilibrium. It is a necessary route brains must take to begin to reorder neural networks into new understandings and practices. (You may be here.)

Stage 3: Unconscious Competence. This is the stage of intuitive knowledge developed through trial and error. This level of expertise is difficult to pass on to others because actions have often become automatic and internalized, and one may not be able to articulate the thought processes engaged in creating a result. Furthermore, when behavior is organized and exercised at an intuitive level, replication is not guaranteed (i.e., your leadership instincts may often serve you well, but instinct often comes up short when there is a need for consistency and sustained execution of effective practice).

Stage 4: Conscious Competence. Informed by personal knowledge, one is able to reflect on experience and modify behavior based on results. This is a very mindful state in which you are conscious of the translation of your knowledge base into practice. This is a stage of awareness that allows you to consciously replicate and adjust behavior to influence a desired outcome. (This is where you want to be.)

Commune With Council

It is ill advised to be oblivious of emerging knowledge that offers to incite a Copernican shift in leadership perspective and behavior. It is a moment to be seized to advantage. It is an opportunity for leaders to become more intelligent about intelligence in both thought and deed.

At the close of this text, the question is, "What are you going to do about this opportunity?" One option, of course, is to maintain course and do nothing. Then again—assuming some influence from the contents of these 12 chapters in addition to your prior knowledge and experience—you might be more than ready to move forward toward applications of what you are mulling over about the merits and means of mindful leadership connections to the capacity of self and others. Betting on the latter assessment of status, we invite you to engage in a final reflection at the end of this text. To engage that reflection, you will return to the council table that you visited at the beginning of Chapter 11, but this time you will reverse the flow of insight in the following steps (Figure 12.3).

1. Invite your leadership exemplars back to the council table and have them sit in the three chairs marked "Judge."

2. Join your leadership exemplars at the table by sitting in the chair marked "Leader."

3. Assume that the purpose of your meeting with this collection of esteemed leaders is to describe your approach to mindful leadership—to lay it on the table for critical review by the assembled judges.

4. In presenting your mindful leader perception and behavior, specifically describe:

   a. The purpose of being a mindful leader

   b. The framework you use to cultivate the knowledge, skills, and dispositions required of mindful leadership

   c. Examples of how you apply what you know about the nature and nurture of intelligence to your standard (i.e., everyday) leadership practice

   d. Examples of how you apply what you know about the nature and nurture of intelligence as prescriptive practice in a particular system or situation

   e. How you collaborate with colleagues for the purpose of coaching each other toward greater expertise and effect as mindful leaders

Upon completing this exercise, you are visiting the understanding your brain has constructed about why and how leaders mindfully connect leadership to the brain. It is a visit to personal wisdom about leadership—part of the leadership legacy that you will pass on to those who call you to their council table.

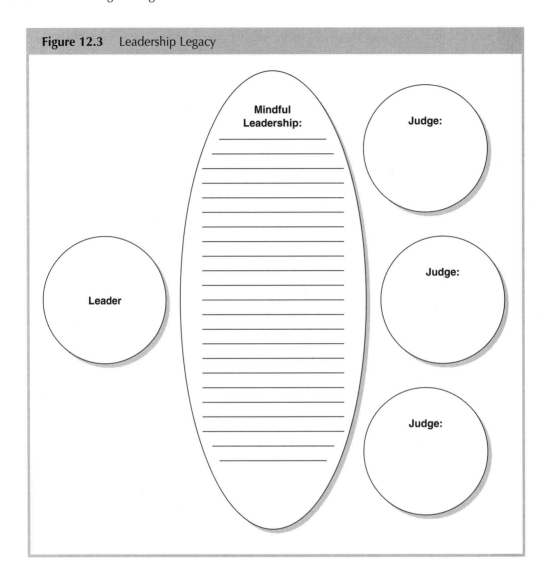

Figure 12.3   Leadership Legacy

SUMMARY OBSERVATIONS

- Perception is the process by which the brain makes sense of the world.
- Perception both prescribes and compromises behavior.
- Perceptual shift is inevitable due to the integration of new knowledge over time.
- Perceptual shift can be accelerated through proactive construction of knowledge.
- Accelerated perceptional shift prompts parallel acceleration of changes in behavior.

- Emerging knowledge about the nature and nurture of intelligence compels proactive perceptual reflection about implications for compatible leadership behavior.

READER REFLECTION

- What is perception?
- What is the relationship between perception and behavior?
- What is perception altered by?
- Why might leaders want to proactively reflect about their established perceptions of leadership?

Glossary

acetylcholine. A neurotransmitter involved in long-term memory and muscle movement.

action potential. An electrical impulse traveling down a neuron's membrane along the axon to communicate signals to other neurons at synapses.

adrenaline. A hormone released from the adrenal gland into the bloodstream during times of stress, stimulating the release of glucose for rapid energy.

amygdala. An almond-shaped structure, connected to the hippocampus, that processes sensory information, catalogues emotional memories, and initiates emotional responses.

automatic memory. Our reflexive memory that is located in the part of our brain called the cerebellum, the lower area of the brain that coordinates and integrates balance, posture, coordination, and muscle movements.

axon. Long fibers, extending out of brain cells called neurons, that carry signals away from one neuron to another. There is only one axon per neuron, but axons connect with many dendrites.

basal ganglia. A cluster of subcortical nuclei at the center of the forebrain that communicate with other brain structures to regulate subconscious actions and coordination with conscious actions.

brain stem. The lowest and earliest-formed part of the brain at the top of the spinal cord, often called the lower brain. It receives sensory input and monitors vital functions.

Broca's area. Area in the left frontal lobe where thoughts are converted into sounds and spoken words.

cell. The smallest unit of an organism capable of functioning independently.

central nervous system. Composed of the brain plus the spinal cord.

cerebellum. A cauliflower-shaped structure located in the hindbrain; coordinates and integrates balance, posture, coordination, and muscle movements.

cerebral cortex. Neocortex, the quarter-inch-thick outer layer of the cerebrum, which is densely packed with neurons (gray matter) and divided into four lobes: frontal, temporal, parietal, and occipital.

cerebrum. The largest part of the brain, consisting of the brain's right and left hemispheres. It has frontal, parietal, temporal, and occipital lobes.

cingulate gyrus. Lying directly above the corpus callosum, it is the part of the brain that facilitates communication between the midbrain and the cortex.

corpus callosum. A 4-inch-long, thick band of axon fibers that connects the right and left hemispheres of the brain.

cortisol. A hormone released from the adrenal glands during times of stress. The release of too much cortisol can damage the hippocampus, a part of the brain involved in learning and long-term memory.

dendrite. A branched fiber extension from a neuron that receives impulses from another neuron or axon through a synaptic connection. A single neuron has many dendrites.

dopamine. A neurotransmitter associated with movement and pleasure.

endorphin. A neurotransmitter that protects against excessive pain.

epinephrine. Adrenaline.

episodic memory. Memory that involves location; stored in the hippocampus.

excitatory neurotransmitter. The chemical in the brain that causes neurons to fire.

explicit memory. Type of memory that involves memories of words, facts, and places; associated with the hippocampus.

frontal lobe. One of the four main areas of the cerebrum; controls voluntary movement, verbal expression, planning, problem solving, decision making, and willpower.

gamma-aminobutyric acid (GABA). A neurotransmitter that prevents electrical impulses from moving down the axon of a neuron.

glial cells. Supporting cells in the brain and nervous system that help maintain neurons by providing oxygen and nourishment; 90% of the brain's cells are glial.

glutamate. An amino acid found in every cell in the brain; used in the nervous system as a fast excitatory neurotransmitter.

gray matter. Areas of the brain and spinal cord where neurons and dendrites are abundant.

hemisphere (cortical). Half of the cerebral cortex; each half is subdivided into four lobes.

hindbrain. Lower brain emerging from the spinal cord that consists of the medulla, pons, and cerebellum.

hippocampus. The part of the brain that encodes working factual memory to long-term storage; located under the temporal lobes.

hormone. A substance produced by one tissue and sent into the bloodstream to affect a physiological activity such as growth or metabolic rate.

hypothalamus. Located in the forebrain and concerned with basic acts and drives such as eating, drinking, and sexual activity. The hypothalamus plays an important role in emotional behavior through its influence on the pituitary gland.

implicit memory. Memory that is not voluntary and occurs automatically, such as procedural, emotional, and automatic memories.

inhibitory neurotransmitter. A chemical in the brain that prevents neurons from firing.

limbic system. A description of the midbrain area associated with memory and emotion. The limbic system includes the hypothalamus, amygdala, thalamus, hippocampus, and cingulate gyrus.

long-term memory. Process by which the brain stores memories for weeks, months, or longer.

lower brain. Also known as the hindbrain; the lower portion of the brain composed of the upper spinal cord, medulla, pons, and reticular formation. The lower brain sorts information from our senses and regulates functions of survival such as breathing and heart rate.

magnetic resonance imaging (MRI). Technology that produces an image of the brain by using a large magnetic field to map the structure of the brain.

medulla. Located in the hindbrain; controls heart rate and respiration.

melatonin. Neurotransmitter associated with the cycles of waking and sleeping.

midbrain. Associated with vision and located between the hindbrain and the forebrain.

mind. All conscious and unconscious processes originating in the brain that collectively direct all behavior.

mirror neurons. Neurons that activate to represent or mimic in the brain the observed behavior by another person.

myelin. A fatty shield that covers and insulates axons for smoother and faster transmission of messages.

neural pruning. The removal of synapses that are not being used.

neuromodulator. A chemical substance released at a synapse that causes biochemical changes in a neuron.

neurons. Cells that compose the neuron system, consisting of the cell body, axons, and dendrites.

neuropeptides. Small proteins, released at synapses, that act as neuromodulators.

neuroscientist. A scientist who studies the structure and function of the brain.

neurotransmitter. A chemical substance released in a synapse by the electrical impulse of a neuron to carry a coded message to another neuron.

noradrenaline. A neurotransmitter involved primarily in states of fight or flight, metabolic rate, blood pressure, emotions, and mood.

occipital lobe. The lobe of our brain that processes vision; located in the rear of the cerebrum.

parietal lobe. Region of the cerebral cortex found between the frontal and occipital lobes that participates in recognition of threat and opportunity; concerned primarily with processing sensory information such as pain, pressure, temperature, and touch.

peptides. Hormones that travel and carry messages throughout the body.

pineal gland. Gland that regulates the release of neurotransmitters that regulate sleep.

pituitary gland. Located at the base of the brain, a gland that releases a variety of hormones into the bloodstream and runs the endocrine system.

pons. A structure that is a critical relay station for sensory information; located in the hindbrain. The pons relays information from the cortex to the cerebellum.

positron emission tomography (PET) scanning. Technology that detects increases in activity levels in parts of the brain by tracing the metabolism of glucose.

reptilian brain. Brain stem.

reticular activating system (RAS). System that controls and regulates the amount and flow of information that enters the brain.

reticular formation. Responsible for attention, arousal, sleeping and waking, and consciousness; located at the upper brain stem and bottom of the midbrain area.

semantic memory. Memory of words, concepts, and numerical systems.

serotonin. Neurotransmitter that regulates mood and sleep and causes relaxation.

short-term memory. Temporary memory where information is processed briefly and subconsciously.

synapse. The gap across which a nerve impulse passes from an axon of one neuron to a dendrite receptor of another neuron or to a muscle or gland cell.

temporal lobes. Located in the middle of the upper brain near our ears and responsible for hearing, senses, listening, speech, language, learning, and memory.

thalamus. Located in the forebrain and responsible for relaying and sorting incoming information to the cerebral cortex.

triune brain. A model of the brain that describes three systems: forebrain, midbrain, and hindbrain.

Wernicke's area. Located in the temporal lobes and responsible for the comprehension of language necessary for reading, spoken language, and writing.

white matter. Areas of the brain and spinal cord where there is an abundance of myelinated axons, giving this area of the brain a white appearance.

working memory. A process in which information is temporarily processed consciously until it is either dropped or stored in long-term memory.

References

American Heritage dictionary of the English language (4th ed.). (2000). Boston: Houghton Mifflin.

Andreasen, N. C. (2005). *The creating brain: The neuroscience of genius.* New York: Dana.

Argyris, C. (1990). *Knowledge for action: A guide to overcoming barriers to organizational change.* San Francisco: Jossey-Bass.

Bandura, A. (1995). *Social foundations of thought and action: A social cognitive theory.* Englewood Cliffs, NJ: Prentice Hall.

Barker, J. (1993). *Paradigms: The business of discovering the future.* New York: HarperCollins.

Barlow, H. (1987). Intelligence: The art of good guesswork. In R. L. Gregory & O. L. Zangwill (Eds.), *Oxford companion to the mind* (pp. 381–383). New York: Oxford University Press.

Barnes, L. B., & Kriger, M. P. (1986). The hidden side of organizational leadership. *Sloan Management Review, 28*(1), 15–26.

Bateson, G. (1979). *Mind and nature: A necessary unity.* New York: Bantam.

Bennis, W. G. (1959). Leadership theory and administrative behavior: The problem with authority. *Administrative Science Quarterly, 4,* 259–301.

Bransford, J. D., Brown, A. L., & Cocking, R. R. (Eds.). (2000). *How people learn: Brain, mind, experience, and school.* Washington, DC: National Academy Press.

Burns, J. M. (1978). *Leadership.* New York: Harper & Row.

Caine, R., & Caine, G. (1991). *Making connections: Teaching and the human brain.* Alexandria, VA: Association for Supervision and Curriculum Development.

Calvin, W. H. (1996). *How brains think: Evolving intelligence, then and now.* New York: Basic Books.

Calvin, W. H. (2002). *A brain for all seasons: Human evolution and abrupt climate change.* Chicago: University of Chicago Press.

Calvin, W. H. (2004). *A brief history of the mind: From apes to intellect and beyond.* Oxford: Oxford University Press.

Costa, A. L., & Kallick, B. (Eds.). (2000). *Discovering and exploring habits of mind.* Alexandria, VA: Association for Supervision and Curriculum Development.

Covey, S. R. (1989). *The seven habits of highly effective people: Restoring the character ethic.* New York: Simon & Schuster.

Crick, F. (1994). *The astonishing hypothesis: The scientific search for the soul.* New York: Scribner.

Damasio, A. (1999). *The feeling of what happens: Body and emotion in the making of consciousness.* New York: Harcourt Brace.

Dawkins, R. (1991). *The selfish gene*. Oxford: Oxford University Press.

de Bono, E. (2001). *New thinking for the new millennium*. Beverly Hills, CA: New Millennium Press.

Deming, W. E., & Walton, M. (1988). *Deming management method*. New York: Perigree.

Dewey, J. (1933). *How we think: A restatement of the relation of reflective thinking to the educative process*. Boston: Houghton Mifflin.

Diamond, M., & Hopson, J. (1998). *Magic trees of the mind: How to nurture your child's intelligence, creativity, and healthy emotions from birth through adolescence*. New York: Dutton–Penguin Putnam.

Diamond, M. C., Krech, D., & Rosenzweig, M. R. (1964). The effects of an enriched environment on the histology of the rat cerebral cortex. *Journal of Comparative Neurology, 123*, 111–120.

Dowling, J. E. (1998). *Creating mind: How the brain works*. New York: Norton.

Dunbar, R. I. M. (1993). Coevolution of neocortical size, group size and language in humans. *Behavioral and Brain Sciences, 16*, 681–735.

Durant, W., & Durant, A. (1968). *The lessons of history*. New York: Simon & Schuster.

Edelman, G. M. (2004). *Wider than the sky: The phenomenal gift of consciousness*. New Haven, CT: Yale University Press.

Eisner, E. (2002). *The arts and the creation of mind*. New Haven, CT: Yale University Press.

Ekman, P. (1984). Expression and nature of emotion. In K. Scherer & P. Ekman (Eds.), *Approaches to emotion* (pp. 319–343). Hillsdale, NJ: Erlbaum.

Facione, P. A., & Facione, N. C. (1992). *California Critical Thinking Dispositions Inventory*. Millbrae: The California Academic Press.

Fishbein, M. (2001). Developing effective behavior change interventions: Some lessons learned from behavioral research. In *Reviewing the behavioral science knowledge base on technology transfer*. NIDA Research Monograph 155. Retrieved July 13, 2001, from www.nida.nih.gov/pdf/monographs/download155.html

Fitzgerald, P. (1998). *The gate of angels*. Boston: Houghton Mifflin.

Flynn, J. R. (2007). *What is intelligence? Beyond the Flynn effect*. New York: Cambridge University Press.

Friedman, T. L. (2005). *The world is flat: A brief history of the 21st century*. New York: Farrar, Straus and Giroux.

Fullan, M. (1991). *The new meaning of educational change*. New York: Teacher's College Press.

Gaarder, J. (1996). *Sophie's world: A novel about the history of philosophy*. New York: Berkley.

Gardner, H. (1983). *Frames of mind: The theory of multiple intelligences*. New York: Basic Books.

Gardner, H. (1995). *Leading minds: An anatomy of leadership*. New York: Basic Books.

Gardner, H. (1999). *Intelligence reframed*. New York: Basic Books.

Gardner, H. (2004). *Changing minds: The art and science of changing our own and other people's minds*. Boston: Harvard Business School Press.

Gazzaniga, M. (1998). *The mind's past*. Berkeley: University of California Press.

Goldberg, E. (2001). *The executive brain: Frontal lobes and the civilized mind*. New York: Oxford University Press.

Goleman, D. (1995). *Emotional intelligence*. New York: Bantam.

Goleman, D. (1998). *Working with emotional intelligence.* New York: Bantam.

Goleman, D. (2006). *Social intelligence.* New York: Bantam.

Goleman, D., Boyatzis, R. E., & McKee, A. (2002). *Primal leadership: Realizing the power of emotional intelligence.* Cambridge, MA: Harvard Business School Press.

Gopnik, A., Meltzoff, A. N., & Kuhl, P. K. (1999). *The scientist in the crib: Minds, brains, and how children learn.* New York: William Morrow.

Gould, J. L., & Gould, C. G. (1994). *The animal mind.* New York: Scientific American Library.

Green, T., Neinemann, S. F., & Gusella, J. E. (1998). Molecular neural biology and genetics: Investigation of neural function and dysfunction. *Neuron, 20,* 427–444.

Greene, B. (1999). *The elegant universe: Superstrings, hidden dimensions, and the quest for the ultimate theory.* New York: Random House.

Greenough, W. T., & Black, J. E. (1992). Induction of brain structure by experience: Substrates for cognitive development. In M. R. Gunnar & C. A. Nelson (Eds.), *Minnesota symposia on child psychology: Vol. 24. Developmental behavioral neuroscience* (pp. 155–200). Hillsdale, NJ: Erlbaum.

Greenough, W. T., Black, J. E., & Wallace, C. S. (1987). Experience and brain development. *Child Development, 58*(3), 539–555.

Hart, L. (1983). *Human brain and human learning.* Oak Creek, AZ: Books for Educators.

Hauser, M. D. (2006). *Moral minds: The nature of right and wrong.* New York: HarperCollins.

Hawkins, J. (2004). *On intelligence: How a new understanding of the brain will lead to the creation of truly intelligent machines.* New York: Times Books.

Heath, C., & Heath, D. (2007). *Made to stick: Why some ideas survive and others die.* New York: Random House.

Hebb, D. O. (1949). *The organization of behavior.* New York: Wiley.

Hobson, J. A. (1999). *Consciousness.* New York: Scientific American Library.

Hoy, W. K., & Miskel, C. G. (1987). *Educational administration: Theory, research, and practice* (3rd ed.). New York: Random House.

Humphrey, N. (1976). The social function of intellect. In P. P. G. Bateson & R. A. Hinde (Eds.), *Growing points in ethology* (pp. 303–317). Cambridge, UK: Cambridge University Press.

Hunter, M. (1982, June 20). *Increasing teacher effectiveness.* Presentation at Cardinal Stritch University.

Johnson, D. W., & Johnson R. T. (2000). *Creative conflict.* Edina, MN: Interaction Book Company.

Juran, J. M. (1988). *Juran on planning for quality.* New York: Free Press.

Kagan, J. (1998). *Three seductive ideas.* Cambridge, MA: Harvard University Press.

Kauffman, S. (1995). *At home in the universe: The search for chaos, self-organization and complexity.* Oxford: Oxford University Press.

Kipling, R. (1968). *The jungle books.* Norwalk, CT: Heritage.

Langer, E. J. (1989). *Mindfulness.* Reading, MA: Addison-Wesley.

LeDoux, J. (1996). *The emotional brain: The mysterious underpinnings of emotional life.* New York: Simon & Schuster.

LeDoux, J. (1999). The power of emotions. In R. Conlan (Ed.), *States of mind: New discoveries about how our brains make us who we are* (pp. 123–149). New York: Wiley.

Leider, R. I. (1997). *The power of purpose: Creating meaning in your life and work.* San Francisco: Berrett-Koehler.

Lennon, J. (1971). Imagine. On *Imagine* [Record]. Hollywood, CA: EMI Records.

Mithen, S. (1996). *The prehistory of the mind: The cognitive origins of art, religion and science*. London: Thames & Hudson.

Mithen, S. (2006). *The singing Neanderthals: The origins of music, language, mind, and body*. Cambridge, MA: Harvard University Press.

Motluk, A. (2001). Read my mind. *New Scientist, 227–5*(169), 22–26.

Murphy, J. T. (1988). The unheroic side of leadership: Notes from the swamp. *Phi Delta Kappan, 69*, 654–659.

Northouse, P. G. (2003). *Leadership: Theory and practice* (3rd ed.). Thousand Oaks, CA: Sage.

Paul, R. W. (1990). *Critical thinking: What every person needs to survive in a rapidly changing world*. Rohnert Park, CA: Center for Critical Thinking and Moral Critique at Sonoma State University.

Pellicer, L. O. (1999). *Caring enough to lead*. Thousand Oaks, CA: Corwin Press.

Perkins, D. (1995). *Outsmarting IQ: The emerging science of learnable intelligence*. New York: Free Press.

Perkins, D. (2000). *Archimedes' bathtub: The art and logic of breakthrough thinking*. New York: Norton.

Pert, C. B. (1997). *Molecules of emotion: Why you feel the way you feel*. New York: Scribner.

Piaget, J. (1990). *Child's conception of the world*. New York: Littlefield Adams. (Original work published 1923)

Pinker, S. (1997). *How the mind works*. New York: Norton.

Pinker, S. (2002). *The blank slate: The modern denial of human nature*. New York: Viking.

Pinker, S. (2007). *The stuff of thought: Language as a window into human nature*. New York: Viking.

Pleshette, L. (Executive Producer), & Weir, P. (Director). (1998). *The Truman show* [Film]. Hollywood, CA: Paramount Pictures.

Posner, M. I., & Rothbart, M. K. (2007). *Educating the human brain*. Washington, DC: American Psychological Association.

Prochaska, J. O., DiClemente, C. C., & Norcross, J. C. (1992). In search of how people change. *American Psychologist, 47*(9), 1102–1114.

Ratey, J. J., & Hagerman, E. (2008). *Spark: The revolutionary new science of exercise and the brain*. New York: Little, Brown.

Ray, P. H., & Anderson, S. R. (2000). *The cultural creatives: How 50 million people are changing the world*. New York: Harmony.

Restak, R. (2001). *The secret life of the brain*. Washington, DC: Joseph Henry Press.

Restak, R. (2006). *The naked brain: How the emerging neurosociety is changing how we live, work, and love*. New York: Three Rivers Press.

Ridley, M. (1996). *The origins of virtue: Human instincts and the evolution of cooperation*. New York: Penguin.

Rost, J. C. (1991). *Leadership for the twenty-first century*. Westport, CT: Praeger.

Runyon, K. E. (1977). *Consumer behavior and the practice of marketing*. Columbus, OH: Merrill.

Sagan, C. (1996). *The demon-haunted world: Science as a candle in the dark*. New York: Ballantine.

Schaie, K. W, & Willis, S. L. (1986). Can decline in adult intellectual functioning be reversed? *Developmental Psychology, 22*(2), 223.

Searle, J. R., Dennett, D. C., & Chalmers, D. J. (1997). *The mystery of consciousness.* New York: New York Review of Books.

Senge, P. M. (1990). *The fifth discipline: The art and practice of the learning organization.* New York: Doubleday.

Siegel, D. (1999). *The developing mind: Toward a neurobiology of interpersonal experience.* New York: Guilford.

Slavin, R. E. (1990). *Cooperative learning: Theory, research, and practice.* Englewood Cliffs, NJ: Prentice Hall.

Smith, F. (1990). *To think.* New York: Teachers College Press.

Snowdon, D. (2001). *Aging with grace: What the nun study teaches us about leading longer, healthier, and more meaningful lives.* New York: Bantam.

Sternberg, R. (1985). *Beyond IQ: A triarchic theory of intelligence.* New York: Cambridge University Press.

Sternberg, R. J. (1997). *Successful intelligence: How practical and creative intelligence determine success in life.* New York: Plume.

Stogdill, R. M. (1974). *Handbook of leadership: A survey of theory and research.* New York: Free Press.

Sylwester, R. (2000). *A biological brain in a cultural classroom: Applying biological research to classroom management.* Thousand Oaks, CA: Corwin Press.

Tishman, S. (2000). Why teach habits of mind? In A. L. Costa & B. Kallick (Eds.), *Discovering and exploring habits of mind* (pp. 41–52). Alexandria, VA: Association for Supervision and Curriculum Development.

Vygotsky, L. (1978). *Mind in society: The development of higher psychological processes.* Cambridge, MA: Harvard University Press.

Wells, W., Burnett, J., & Moriarty, S. (1995). *Advertising: Principles and practice.* Englewood Cliffs, NJ: Prentice Hall.

Wheatley, M. J. (1992). *Leadership and the new science: Learning about organization from an orderly universe.* San Francisco: Berrett-Koehler.

Wheatley, M. J. (2002). *Turning to one another: Simple conversations to restore hope to the future.* San Francisco: Berrett-Koehler.

Wheatley, M. J. (2005). *Finding our way: Leadership for an uncertain time.* San Francisco: Berrett-Koehler.

Wheatley, M. J., & Kellner-Rogers, M. (1996). *A simpler way.* San Francisco: Berrett-Koehler.

Wright, R. (2000). *Nonzero: The logic of human destiny.* New York: Pantheon.

Zohar, D. (1997). *Rewiring the corporate brain: Using the new science to rethink how we structure and lead organizations.* San Francisco: Berrett-Koehler.

Index